Collins

Cambridge IGCSE™

English as a Second Language

TEACHER'S GUIDE

Susan Anstey, Alison Burch, Lucy Cooper, Lucy Hobbs, Avril Kirkham, Shubha Koshy, Sioban Parker, Lorna Pepper, Celia Wigley

William Collins' dream of knowledge for all began with the publication of his first book in 1819.

A self-educated mill worker, he not only enriched millions of lives, but also founded a flourishing publishing house. Today, staying true to this spirit, Collins books are packed with inspiration, innovation and practical expertise. They place you at the centre of a world of possibility and give you exactly what you need to explore it.

Collins. Freedom to teach.

Published by Collins
An imprint of HarperCollins*Publishers*
The News Building, 1 London Bridge Street,
London, SE1 9GF, UK

HarperCollins Publishers Macken House,
39/40 Mayor Street Upper, Dublin 1,
DO1 C9W8, Ireland

Browse the complete Collins catalogue at
collins.co.uk

Authors: Susan Anstey, Alison Burch, Lucy Hobbs, Avril Kirkham, Shubha Koshy, Sioban Parker, Lorna Pepper

Additional content written by Celia Wigley and Lucy Cooper

Publisher: Elaine Higgleton

Product manager: Joanna Ramsay

Project manager/Series editor: Celia Wigley

Development editor: Lucy Cooper

Proofreader: Denise Cowle

Cover designer: Gordon MacGilp

Illustrator: Ann Paganuzzi

Typesetter: Hugh Hillyard-Parker

Production controller: Lyndsey Rogers

Printed and bound by Ashford Colour Ltd

Acknowledgements

The publishers gratefully acknowledge the permission granted to reproduce the copyright material in this book. While every effort has been made to trace and contact copyright holders, where this has not been possible the publishers will be pleased to make the necessary arrangements at the first opportunity.

Cambridge International copyright material in this publication is reproduced under licence and remains the intellectual property of Cambridge Assessment International Education.

Exam-style questions and sample answers have been written by the authors. In examinations, the way marks are awarded may be different. References to assessment and/or assessment preparation are the publisher's interpretation of the syllabus requirements and may not fully reflect the approach of Cambridge Assessment International Education.

Third-party websites and resources referred to in this publication have not been endorsed by Cambridge Assessment International Education

Text acknowledgements

Chapter 11: Student Book p. 216/Teacher Guide p. 115: Excerpt from SCORPIA RISING by Anthony Horowitz. Copyright © 2011 by Anthony Horowitz. Text copyright © 2011 Stormbreaker Productions Ltd. Boys with torch logo™ & © 2010 Stormbreaker Productions Ltd. Used by permission of Philomel Books, a division of Penguin Group (USA) Inc and Walker Books Ltd., London SE11 5HJ (UK)

Photograph acknowledgements

The publisher would like to thank the following for permission to reproduce pictures in these pages:

p. 159 Retro AdArchives / Alamy Stock Photo; p. 193 Vladmir Melnik/Shutterstock; p. 245 AS Food Studio/Shutterstock; p. 249 Ipatov/Shutterstock; p. 266 Africa Studio/Shutterstock

Contents

How to use this Teacher's Guide

The *Collins Cambridge IGCSE™ English as a Second Language Teacher's Guide* supports the Student's Book by providing comprehensive lesson plans and worksheets for every chapter to help teachers prepare, plan and deliver the course, as well as offering additional resources including advice on teaching speaking skills and a full exam-style assessment for student practice. While this resource is designed for teachers, it also contains student material which teachers can photocopy to use with their class. It is designed to offer comprehensive teacher support for the Cambridge IGCSE English as a Second Language syllabus (0510/0511/0991/0993) for examination from 2024.

Student's Book

The Student's Book is divided into two main sections. The first section (Chapters 1–12) comprises topic-based 'coursebook' chapters. Each chapter starts with a *Big picture* feature – stimulating images and questions that provide a way into the chapter topic. The *Thinking big* questions in this section provide an opportunity for students to start thinking about the new topic and about what they already know about it. Each chapter ends with a *Big task*, which allows students to showcase their skills and vocabulary in a real-world context. Both these *Big picture* and *Big task* elements are intended to provide work for one lesson, and both are supported in the Teacher's Guide by one-page lesson plans.

Between these two features, each one of Chapters 1–12 contains four sections (each four pages long), focusing on reading, writing, speaking and listening skills and the key sub-skills. Students build their skills following a step-by-step structure, ensuring progression and pace as well as opportunities for consolidation. The same structure with the same headings: *Getting started, Exploring the skills, Developing the skills* and *Going further* is used throughout the Student's Book, offering familiarity to students and teachers. Each of these four chapter sub-sections is intended to provide work for one or two lessons, and is supported in the Teacher's Guide by a two-page lesson plan, as well as photocopiable worksheets which can be found at the end of the book.

The second section of the Student's Book (Chapters 13–19) helps students to prepare for their examinations, providing them with practice in exam-style questions. Chapters 13–19 are organised around different exam-style question types for reading and writing, listening and speaking. The final section in the book contains sample answers and comments for each of the exam-style practice questions that have been specially written by the author.

Workbook

The Workbook supports the Student's Book by offering further practice of English language skills to consolidate and develop students' language learning. Intended to be used either in the classroom or at home, the Workbook is a write-in resource which provides additional opportunities to practise reading, writing, listening and speaking skills and to build vocabulary.

Online resources

Audio supports students in the listening and speaking activities. The **Audio tracks**, **Transcripts** of the Audio tracks and **Answers** can be found on collins.co.uk/internationalresources.

Digital resources

Collins offers teachers and students eBook versions of the Student's Book, Workbook and Teacher's Guide. These give teachers added flexibility in the way they can use the resources.

Using the Teacher's Guide

Planning

* A comprehensive **Contents map** provided at the start of both the Teacher's Guide and Student's Book gives teachers an overview of the content of each chapter.

* Detailed, ready-to-use **lesson plans** provide teachers with all they need to teach.

* The **Skills in focus** learning outcomes, together with the **Assessment objectives** that are covered in each lesson are listed in a box at the start of the section. These ensure that teachers cover the full Cambridge IGCSE English as a Second Language syllabus.

* A summary of the **question types** that are used in the lesson is provided at the start of each chapter.

* The **Resources** box provides cross references to the corresponding chapter in the Student's Book, as well as material in the Workbook and Worksheets which is also relevant to the lesson.

* Some lesson plans also contain suggestions of **online video clips** to complement the topic. These clips can be used as starter activities or to generate discussion during the lesson. Teachers are strongly advised to watch the clips in advance of the lesson to ensure they are appropriate for their class.

* The **Worksheets** supplement and extend the activities in the Student's Book. These are referred to at an appropriate stage in each lesson plan, meaning that time-consuming preparation is kept to a minimum.

Differentiation

* Each lesson plan begins with differentiated **Learning outcomes** so that teachers can monitor the level at which students are working and help them progress.

* Further differentiation opportunities are provided in the **Extra support** and **Extra challenge** boxes in the lesson plans, ensuring that all students are stimulated.

* **Worksheets** offer additional activities to suit a range of learning styles.

* **Further challenge** at the end of each lesson plan gives a specific tip or activity suggestion to ensure that all students are encouraged to work towards reaching their potential.

Assessment and exam preparation

* In the Student's Book each chapter also includes a 'Check your progress' table at the end, where students read can-do statements for the skills covered in the chapter and make a note of what they need to do to improve.

* An **assessment** feature in the lesson plans for Chapters 1–12 suggests opportunities to assess students' progress both during and at the end of topics, for example by using a particular question or activity.

* Lesson plans for Chapters 13–19 offer a step-by-step approach to prepare students for answering different exam-style questions. *The student as marker* section of these lesson plans contains:
    - an example answer to each of the practice questions
    - marking guidance for that example answer written by the authors
    - a marked and annotated version of that example answer written by the authors

Introduction

    – suggestions for how the example answer can be used in class.

- *The student as marker* section can be used in one of two ways:

  1 After the students have answered the practice question (in each of Chapters 13–19 of the Student's Book) themselves, as a means to understand the marking guidance and how it is implemented. Students can then understand how to produce a good answer when answering these types of questions.

  2 After the students have answered the practice question, and had it marked, the teacher can use the marking guidance to explain why marks were or were not awarded. The specimen responses can then be used to reinforce the lessons learned (i.e. what they should, or should not, be doing). Invite the students to make a list of 'Areas I should improve' after marking and returning work, using the marking guidance to help.

- At the end of the Teacher's Guide, there is an **Exam-style assessment** offering a complete practice test for students. The section is divided into three practice tests for Reading and Writing, Listening and Speaking, with mark schemes and sample responses, all specially written by the author.

Encouraging vocabulary and note-keeping

As students work through each chapter – especially Chapters 1 to 12, which focus on different subject areas – teachers may find it useful to create a word bank for each subject area, which can be added to at any point by students or teacher. This could be a large sheet of paper pinned up in a prominent position. This will help develop and reinforce students' vocabulary.

Teachers could also recommend that students maintain some form of notebook or journal to record their responses and developing vocabulary for the various chapters in the Student's Book. At some point students should add the words from the class word bank to their personal notebook or journal, along with any other words relating to this topic that they come across. Encourage students to take notes and to refer back to them constantly in order to reinforce what they have learned.

Speaking skills: Advice and guidance for teachers

At the end of the Teacher's Guide, there is a section offering advice and guidance for teachers on how to help students to improve their speaking skills in addition to guidance on giving exam-style speaking tests.

Delivering lessons online

There may be times when teachers need to deliver lessons online rather than face-to-face in the classroom, either because of circumstances outside one's control or in order to provide a blended learning approach to teaching. To support teachers with this, Collins offers teachers and students eBook versions of the Student's Book, Workbook and Teacher's Guide. These give teachers added flexibility in the way they can use the resources.

Teachers may choose to teach live online lessons, sharing their screen to show particular pages of the eBook, or teachers may record lessons to be viewed later. Students can also use the eBooks for directed self-study.

Preparing ahead

When planning to teach in the online classroom, remember to:

- Break it down
- Break it up
- Break out

Break it down: Keep everything short and simple. Remember that students are likely to find it more difficult to concentrate and focus online so teachers may have to break down activities into smaller chunks.

Break it up: Mix up the routine. Make the tasks less predictable by not following every activity in the Student's eBook so that the students are kept more engaged. Use the chat box or unmute students for quick written and verbal responses.

Break out: Build into lesson plans how to use the break-out rooms of the online platform. Consider the different groups of students placed in the break-out rooms. Consider the way in which the rooms will be used, for example, for a small group to plan a writing activity or for pair-work speaking activities. Depending on the platform, teachers may have the option to assign the break-out groups themselves, which will allow teachers to choose which students go with which other students. Other platforms may organise the groups itself, with students grouped together at random.

Before an online class, spend time looking at the lesson plans in the Teacher's Guide for each of the four sections as well as the *Thinking big* and *Big task* sections. Decide which parts are more appropriate for the live online lesson and which parts students can complete by themselves in their own study time. The online lesson is a chance for students to focus on key skills development, for students to produce language and for students to work in pairs or groups. It therefore makes sense to focus on productive language in the online lesson, such as speaking.

The eBook provides good opportunities for blended learning, using a flipped classroom approach. Consider setting research and thinking tasks as homework, including viewing videos and reading longer chunks of text. Once the students have been introduced to the content at home, the lesson can then be used to practise, develop and consolidate their learning.

The online lesson should also be used to check understanding of reading or listening tasks previously set. Asking students to read reading texts or listening to the audio files beforehand means that they will then be ready to participate productively in group activities or pair work. When students are back online, set them jigsaw tasks that encourage expressive and productive language.

Teaching online allows teachers to use the ever-increasing range of features and tools provided by the platform. Features that are particularly useful for online classes include screen sharing, participation tools, chat boxes, reaction tools, break-out rooms and whiteboards. Specific functionality will depend on the platform, but it is well worth getting familiar with all the functions and features available so that they can be used to the best of their advantage with students. It's also important for students to get used to the functionality and features of the platform – one way to do this is to spend ten minutes of the first lesson playing games to practise features.

Contents map

Section 3: Speaking	Section 4: Listening	Big task	
The importance of the internet • communicate your ideas clearly, accurately and effectively • keep a conversation going by developing ideas with details and examples.	**How technology is changing our lives** • identify relevant information • understand and select correct details and key question words • understand what is implied but not directly	Give a presentation on the best technological inventions.	
Polar exploration • research and organise ideas for giving a talk or presentation • plan an effective, individual opening for a talk or presentation.	**Underwater exploration** • recognise and understand facts when listening to short spoken texts • recognise and understand facts when listening to a longer and more difficult text • listen carefully and understand complicated	Prepare a presentation to win money for a chosen exploration project.	
Health around the world • use a variety of structures when you are speaking • link ideas using a range of conjunctions • speak using abstract nouns and noun phrases to give variety to your	**Better health** • understand and pick out specific details when listening • predict the kind of information you will hear, including units of measurement • recognise high numbers when listening.	Create a website about young people's health.	
How do we learn? • speak clearly using the most effective words to explain and describe • choose the correct vocabulary and level of formality for the listener.	**School and the real world** • select details from different kinds of spoken texts • use clues before you start listening to help you understand a text • understand what is implied but not directly	Research, plan and give a presentation on an ideal school.	
Competition and the arts • build a conversation by asking and answering questions • be an active listener and add new ideas.	**Competition in business** • understand and pick out facts in short spoken & written texts • recognise and understand opinions in short spoken and written texts • recognise and understand fact and opinion in	Write a talent show review.	
Job interviews • pronounce words and speak clearly to be understood in a conversation • speak up confidently and clearly.	**Unusual jobs** • predict to help you understand and select details • select details to make notes or fill in forms when listening to a range of texts.	Write a job application and act out a job interview.	
Pollution – slow poison? • express ideas clearly using the correct verb tenses • respond clearly, accurately and effectively to others, in conversation • communicate ideas clearly and	**Where has all the wildlife gone?** • use key words and context to help predict content • understand what is implied but not directly stated during an interview.	Plan and give a multimedia presentation on local environmental issues.	
Modern culture • use examples to support your opinions while speaking • include facts and expert opinions to support your point of view • use rhetorical questions to make your	**Disappearing ways of life** • understand and select relevant information in spoken texts • identify and understand opinions in a range of spoken texts • identify and understand conflicting opinions in	Write an article about a community whose culture and way of life are disappearing.	
Problems with transport • use a variety of grammatical structures accurately and effectively when you speak • vary the tense of verbs you use according to the situation.	**Where will we go and how will we get there?** • understand connections and differences between related ideas • understand what is implied but not directly stated in a formal spoken text.	Design a leaflet for a new transport system and deliver a presentation.	
Clothes and culture • use the right words when speaking about culture and clothing • use more specialised vocabulary appropriately.	**The price of fashion: who pays?** • listen effectively to fellow students • understand and select detailed information supplied by fellow students • understand what is implied but not directly stated in a conversation.	Organise a fashion show.	
Television • disagree politely in a conversation • keep a conversation going by rephrasing what the previous speaker has said.	**Film** • understand and select facts in both formal and informal spoken texts • recognise and understand opinions and attitudes in a more formal dialogue.	Debate on how good for you screen time is.	
Growing up • speak clearly and use the correct stress when speaking • vary your tone to interest your listener.	**Achievements of youth and old age** • recognise and understand ideas, opinions and attitudes • recognise connections between ideas.	Prepare a presentation about the different rights and responsibilities of young and old people.	

Contents map

Resources needed for this chapter

- **Student's Book**: Chapter 1
- **Worksheets**: 1.1–1.2
- **Workbook**: see suggestions in 'Resources' panel of individual sections
- **Audio tracks**: 1.1–1.2
- **Video clips**: see suggestions in sections 1.2, 1.3 and 1.4

The big picture

Give students about 10 minutes to absorb the various pictures in the collage of the Student's Book. Ask them to jot down the first thoughts, words or ideas that crop up as they look at the pictures.

Thinking big

Q3: To introduce the idea of technology, ask students to identify all their interactions with technology since they got out of bed this morning. This could include everything from their phone to a television, radio, laptop, etc.

Record students' ideas on a large piece of paper that you can refer to as you work through this chapter. Encourage students to add ideas on sticky notes as they go along for all the aspects of their lives that involve technology.

As your group works through this chapter, create a word bank for technology, which can be added to at any point by students or teacher. If you haven't done so already, suggest that students maintain some form of notebook or journal to record their responses and develop vocabulary for the various chapters in the Student's Book. Encourage them to take notes and to refer back constantly to these notes, in order to reinforce what they have learned.

Q1–2: If looking for a more structured activity, ask students to choose two pictures from the collage and explain why they have chosen them and what this says about technology. This activity encourages students to:

- think and make notes on their own when choosing their own pictures from the collage
- add to their vocabulary by speaking and listening to each other when justifying to their partner why they chose the pictures.

Students can then return to individual work to answer the key evaluative questions in **Q3**, in particular the final question, which asks students to write a definition of 'technology'.

The big task

'Techno Greats': the best technology invention

Students should do the *big task* once they have completed all four sections of the chapter.

This **big task** could carry on for several weeks as students prepare for the final presentations. Support your students by doing the following:

- Assign some class time to allow students to work collaboratively.
- Set up a 'Checklist for success' (suggestions below) that could be displayed in the classroom to monitor the progress of various groups.
- Set a manageable timeline and a final presentation date. Use a wall calendar as appropriate.
- Depending on the size of your class, you may set up qualifying rounds and a round of finals. Alternatively, all teams qualify for the final big task presentation.

Checklist for success

You could build up a checklist for success, perhaps using the following format.

Big task: 'Techno Greats'

In this final task you are required to combine your skills of:

reading, writing, speaking and listening

in order to communicate

clearly, accurately and appropriately

with your listeners and audience.

While the focus is on an oral presentation, make sure that you:

- use skimming and scanning while researching information
- organise your ideas clearly
- use details and examples to develop your ideas
- listen to ideas from other members of your group and help the group have a successful discussion
- and so on...

Audience

If you do decide to have qualifying rounds, teams that do not qualify should be allowed to vote. Encourage them to be a critical audience.

If possible, consider contacting the local marketing representatives of the inventions in the shortlist. If feasible, they might either attend the presentation or provide some free goods or accessories as prizes. Consider inviting a real audience from other classes and their teachers to vote and give their opinions.

Citing sources

This is also a good opportunity to mention that the work should be original and sources must be credited.

1.1 What is technology?

Assessment objectives

R3 Identify and select details for a specific purpose
R4 Demonstrate understanding of implied meaning

Reading skills in focus
* Skim and scan different kinds of texts for facts and details
* Understand what is implied but not directly stated in an online article

Question types
* Open response
* Multiple matching
* Reading headings, subheadings, captions

Differentiated learning outcomes

* All students should attempt to select a few facts and details from straightforward texts by skimming and scanning.
* Most students should select relevant facts and details from a range of texts by using skimming and scanning; they should also, with guidance, show some understanding of implied meaning.
* Some students should extract relevant facts and details from a wide range of texts by skimming and scanning effectively; they should also understand more complex texts where meaning is implied.

Resources
* **Student's Book**: Section 1.1
* **Worksheet**: 1.1
* **Workbook**: Section 1.1

Getting started

Use the photo of the old mobile phone on the page as a stimulus for discussion. Ask students to identify what the technology is and how it is different from modern mobile phones. Students can be in a large group or smaller groups.

Q1: Encourage students to use their notes and thoughts from the **Big picture** to help them. Allow discussion time and, as each group feeds back, others should take notes of key words or ideas. After each group feeds back, clarify any words or phrases that might be new or unusual to the class.

Encourage students to record in their personal notebook or journal interesting adjectives that might come up when discussing old technology, e.g. *ancient*, *obsolete*, *redundant*, *clunky*, *messy*, as opposed to *wireless*, *sleek*, and so on.

Create interest in the origin of the computer and build on students' prior knowledge about the technological inventions that have changed our world the most.

Exploring the skills

Remind students of the key skills of skimming and scanning when there is too much text to read. If possible, bring in advertisement offers for new technology either from a magazine or show a website on a device. Ask students to identify the most attractive text features of the advertisements. These will probably include:

* the price
* offers or promotions (what the offer is and how long it lasts)
* location of a sale, i.e. which website, etc.

Ask students why they jumped to this information. Was this by skimming or scanning? The answer might be that while students *skimmed* the text ignoring less relevant information, they were *scanning* for the information that was most relevant to their own questions. Remind students that:

* skimming = reading quickly for the gist and overall meaning
* scanning = looking for specific information in answer to a question.

Introduce students to the text in **Q2**, 'Computing then and now'. Clarify the vocabulary in the **Glossary** and any other words. Then ask students to work in pairs answering **Q2** to **Q4**.

Give extra support for **Q3** by clarifying that this question requires students to identify the type of text represented here. Encourage them to identify that the text is factual (so can't be **d**), is written in self-contained chunks (the separate paragraphs) (again can't be **d**) and is not trying to be persuasive or critical (which **a)** and **b)** require).

Give extra support for **Q4** by explaining that this requires scanning and looking at the question. Explain that it helps to highlight key question words, such as 'Who?', 'When?' or 'Which?'. Students should try to work out from the question word which answers are likely to be in words and which in numbers. See the **Top tip** to help them.

Give extra challenge by asking students to frame their own skimming or scanning questions for the passage at the top of the page or for the advertisements you might have used earlier. Students are more likely to be engaged if you use advertisements that are current, real and localised from English newspapers or flyers.

Developing the skills

Students should practise their skimming and scanning skills while reading the online article on the opposite page. Ask students to identify the purpose of each of the following features:

* the images
* captions that go with the pictures
* headings or subheadings, text in bold.

Q5: Ask students to work individually or in pairs, noting down their answers.

Give extra support by handing out **worksheet 1.1**, which offers students further practice in the skills of skimming and scanning.

Give extra support by asking students to bring in their own collection of advertisements and promotional information for the latest technology they enjoy. Ask them to point out why these advertisements caught their attention. Also, ask them how their advertisements differ from the one from the 1980s on **worksheet 1.1**. (The 1980s advertisement contains more text than today's advertisements.)

Give extra challenge by asking students to design questions for the advertisements of their choice. This could be done in pairs or groups to increase competition and enjoyment of skimming and scanning. As students become more proficient in these skills, you could add a time limit.

Going further

Q6: Make sure students understand the meaning of 'implied' and can correctly answer Q6ii).

Give extra challenge by asking students to find examples of implied meanings in the other advertisements they have been discussing. Examples might be: 'Don't miss out…act now!' or 'Look no further!' or 'This changes everything…again!'

Assessment for learning	Ask students to pin up their advertisements around the room or to create a collage from them on a large piece of paper. Use sticky notes or annotations to highlight where features such as titles, pictures, labels, headings, subheadings, coloured text, and so on are used.
Further challenge	Ask the more confident students to highlight words and phrases in the advertisements that have implied meaning. Ask them to explain why this is persuasive or convincing. Notice that 'an offer to die for' indicates the use of idioms. Draw students' attention to idioms and encourage their use, as these are an indicator of fluency when used correctly.

Chapter 1
Technology

1.2 Smartphones on the brain

Assessment objectives

W1 Communicate information, ideas and opinions

Writing skills in focus
* Collect and organise ideas before writing to explain or inform
* Communicate ideas clearly and effectively through writing

Question types
* Writing a report (formal)
* Presenting pros and cons

Differentiated learning outcomes
* All students collect a few ideas before writing; then they should be able to carry out simple writing tasks that give straightforward information or explanation, using a limited range of vocabulary.
* Most students organise some of their ideas before writing; then they should be able to give clear information and explanations, attempting to use some more subject-specific vocabulary.
* Some students organise their ideas clearly; then they should be able to write clear and detailed explanations, using a range of vocabulary, including subject-specific words, precisely.

Resources
* **Student's Book**: Section 1.2
* **Workbook**:
  Section 3.1
  Section 3.4

Getting started

Discuss the idiom 'Smartphones on the brain'. Explain that if you have something on the brain, you think about it all the time. To build on students' own knowledge for this activity, put them in groups of three or four.

* Group 1: Ask students to imagine a world without smartphones and with only landlines. What would be the advantages and disadvantages?
* Group 2: Ask students to imagine a world before telephones of any sort. What would be the advantages and disadvantages?

Get students to create a two-column table to record the advantages and disadvantages of each era – one table for each group. They should use the column headings 'Advantages' and 'Disadvantages'.

Q1: Ask students to share their ideas with a partner. They must take notes and ask clarifying questions as their partner speaks to them. Highlight the difference between 'cell phone' and 'mobile phone'.

Exploring the skills

Explain to students that all writing has a clear format, reader and purpose. As stated in the Student's Book, the purpose could be any of the following:

* to describe what something looks like
* to explain how something works
* to give information – facts and details about something.

Q2: Introduce the task and ask students to identify the format, reader and purpose of this task. If a school or community magazine is available, bring in the real material as an example, or for students to critique.

* Purpose: to present the advantages and disadvantages of smartphones, particularly in the context of the local school and community.
* Reader: school community – parents, teachers, students, support staff.
* Format: school magazine article – could include relevant photos/images.

Q3: Get groups to talk each other through their concept maps. Students should add any interesting words to their personal notebook or journal.

> **Give extra support** for **Q3** by first asking students to sort the list of points into advantages ('A') and disadvantages ('D') and then adding their own points from **Q1**.
>
> **Give extra challenge** by discussing the benefits of the concept map as an organiser. Explain how this allows us to group points in a more interesting way with one new idea per box, putting main ideas in larger boxes and related ideas in smaller boxes. Suggest colour coding using felt-tips or markers for visual ease.
>
> **Give extra support** by providing main idea boxes to students who might need this.

Developing the skills

Q4: Read the question and ask students to identify the *format*, *readers* and *purpose* of this task. Go through the bullet points and design a new concept map with appropriate boxes as suggested in the Student's Book.

Q5: Tell students that they are going to write a report using the writing plan on the next page. Highlight what kind of text a report is and what students should bear in mind.

> **Give extra support** by explaining to students that the report should describe and explain the current situation without giving an opinion of any sort; discuss what kinds of phrases they should *avoid*, e.g. 'I think', 'in my opinion'.
>
> **Give extra challenge** by asking students to be increasingly precise and formal in how they communicate the information.

Going further

Q6: Ask students to write their report. Explain to them that they should also check the spelling and punctuation at the end of their report. Remind them to use precise formal language. Explain why accurate, technically precise language is essential to reporting and explaining. Discuss the importance and value of maintaining their personal notebook or journal to include formal and less formal versions of vocabulary/phrases.

After students have written their reports, discuss strategies, e.g. use of vocabulary books, their journals and personal notebook or translation notes in their first language. Grouping similar ideas and concept mapping are useful for this task.
Some online programs offer 'visual' dictionaries and thesauruses, e.g. the 'How it works' section on the Visual Thesaurus website. (It is possible to subscribe to a 14-day trial of this program.)

> **Give extra challenge** by getting students to find synonyms for words that they tend to use repeatedly, e.g. *good, bad, dangerous, ugly, pretty, nice, sad, happy*.

Assessment for learning	Highlight the difference between informal and formal language. Provide students with short extracts of spoken text and ask them to turn these into more formal pieces of speaking/writing with a focus on increasingly precise vocabulary. • Student: 'My tummy hurts…I need to see the nurse for a pill.' • Nurse: 'I am giving you a painkiller for the pain in your stomach, which might help.' • Leave note: 'The student is excused from school as she has severe stomach pain.'
Further challenge	Give students three situations that enable them to become increasingly precise, moving from informal spoken text to more formal written text. For example, talking to a friend about too much homework, talking to a teacher to negotiate less homework and writing a letter to the principal about homework at your school. Encourage the use of resources such as visual thesauruses or students' own dictionaries to enable them to identify more precise language for more commonplace words.

1.3 The importance of the internet

Assessment objectives

S1 Communicate a range of ideas, facts and opinions

S3 Develop responses and maintain communication

Speaking skills in focus

- Communicate ideas clearly, accurately and effectively
- Keep a conversation going by developing ideas with details and examples

Question types

- Discussing in pairs
- Observing and analysing communication
- Role-play

Differentiated learning outcomes

- All students should be able to communicate simple ideas and attempt to respond to questions or comments made by others in a conversation.
- Most students should communicate their ideas clearly, responding relevantly and at some length to what is said in a conversation, offering some details and examples.
- Some students should communicate ideas clearly, accurately and confidently, interacting appropriately and actively developing the conversation with examples and details.

Resources

- **Student's Book**: Section 1.3
- **Video clip**: see 'Developing the skills'
- **Workbook**: Section 5.4

Getting started

Q1-2: Talk to students about the technology that is in their home. Encourage students to jot down their thoughts without worrying too much about accuracy at this stage. Then ask students to form pairs and ask each other the questions. Ask them to try to keep the conversation going by using their partner's responses.

Exploring the skills

Focus on the key speaking skill of communicating accurately and effectively. Stress the two-way nature of conversations, focusing on the list of bullet points at the bottom of the page.

Give extra support by setting a small group of students the task of deciding where they could go for a picnic at the end of the term. Other students observe, using the list of bullet points to assess whether it is a good conversation.

Q3: Ask students the question: Has the internet made our lives better? Get students to discuss this in pairs. Then ask students to read the notes from other students and discuss these. If there are any words they don't understand, they should try to work these out together by guessing from context. Draw attention to the Top tip.

Start a word bank to display terms relating to the internet and add to this throughout the session. (You could also allow time at the end of the session for students to add terms to their personal notebook or journal.)

Give extra challenge for **Q3** by asking students to evaluate whether the internet has made our lives better and where. If the class falls naturally into two groups – one that agrees the internet has improved our lives and another that thinks it has not – use them to jot down arguments and counter-arguments for the internet on a class flip chart. Display for the duration of the unit.

Developing the skills

Reinforce the importance of active involvement in all types of speaking, whether chatting or giving a formal talk. Both speaker and listener have a vital role in helping communication along. Body language is also a key feature of all conversations. Watch Visualz' YouTube video 'Communication basics – body language', (5:55 minutes). On the first viewing, ask students to watch the whole clip without taking notes. On the second viewing, ask students to jot down key words and phrases. Then ask students to feed back to each other so that they cover all the main ideas on communication and body language.

Q4: Ask students to look at the communication checklist together and discuss. Discuss the list as a class pointing out the four areas. Then ask students to have a conversation about whether the internet has made our lives better or worse in pairs.

Q5: When the students have finished, ask them to assess how they did using the checklist.

Q6: Next the students join another pair and peer review each other's conversations using the checklist. Their peers listen closely and observe the students and make notes and tick the relevant points in the checklist. The students then share their observations. Bring the class together and ask if they found the peer reviewing and observation useful.

Going further

Focus on guiding students into sustaining longer and more meaningful conversations and dialogue. Explain that this happens by asking questions, using examples and giving more details.

> **Give extra support** by preparing students for **Q7–9**. Before they tackle the role-play task, ask them to have a conversation, in pairs, about an IT difficulty that they have had recently. Place one student in the role of the interviewer/sympathiser and the other student as the person with the IT problem. Suggest that this could be any of the following situations: losing a mobile phone, losing files on the computer, suffering a computer virus attack, dropping the computer and breaking it, spilling coffee on the keyboard. Students are also free to choose a situation of their own.

Brainstorm with students the sort of questions that the interviewer might pose (all questions transferable to **Q9**):

* What happened – how and when?
* What were the consequences – from physical damage to the machine as well as damage to files and information?
* What were the complications? Respond to specific facts that the person with the problem is talking most about.
* How was the issue resolved? What support was used?
* What has the person learned from the process?

Assessment for learning	Ask the students who have performed well in task 4 to repeat their conversation and ask the class to look at the communication checklist again to observe why these students were identified as having the best dialogue.
Further challenge	Ask students to see how they might improve the structure and fluency of their conversations.

1.4 How technology is changing our lives

Assessment objectives

L1 Demonstrate understanding of specific information

L4 Demonstrate understanding of what is implied but not directly stated

Listening skills in focus
- Identify relevant information
- Understand and select correct details and key question words
- Understand what is being implied but not directly stated in a more formal conversation

Question types
- Informal conversations
- Formal conversations

Differentiated learning outcomes
- All students should recognise key question words, understand a straightforward text and answer some simple questions about it.
- Most students should use key question words, understand a range of texts and answer detailed questions about them.
- Some students should use key question words, understand a range of texts, including complex texts, and answer questions on a spoken text, including those that require some inference.

Resources
- **Student's Book**: Section 1.4
- **Audio tracks**: 1.1, 1.2
- **Video clips**: see 'Getting started'
- **Worksheet**: 1.2
- **Workbook**: Section 4.1

Getting started

Video clip: Watch Mohamm Q's YouTube video 'Communication from the past to the present', (4:22 minutes).

Q1: Play the video clip and ask students to think of some questions that their parents or grandparents might be able to answer about an earlier age of communication technology. On a second viewing, ask them to jot down key dates and pieces of technology from the past that intrigued or interested them, such as the cassettes or record player.

Q2a): The video clip will have built some prior understanding of some of the pictures in the Student's Book and summed up the evolution of technology from earlier sections. Students should now be better equipped to talk about the pictures.

Draw students' attention to the more complex questions in **Q2b) and Q2c)**. Now play the following **video clip**: maverick294's YouTube video 'Communication of yesterday, today and tomorrow', (5:00 minutes). This is a more challenging clip as the implications of new technology in the present and the future are considered.

Suggest some conditions under which older forms of communication might need to be revived, such as after natural disasters (earthquakes, typhoons, tornadoes or tsunamis), nuclear disasters, meteorites hitting satellites and disrupting internet communications, and so on. It might be interesting to talk here about how in recent years people had discussed how the national postal services of countries were being used less and less to send letters as people sent emails and messages via their phones. However, more recently there has been a change with people needing the national postal services once again as they buy things online and need these to be delivered.

Exploring the skills

Remind students that effective listening is as important as being a good speaker in order to make a conversation meaningful. Brainstorm with students the ways in which they could predict when important pieces of information are about to be heard on announcements, instructions and television or radio broadcasts. Examples include the following:

- 'The bus to Victoria will now leave at 10:45 am instead of 10:30. We apologise for the delay.'
- 'Here in the studio with me is...'
- 'Buy two and get one free at...supermarket. Hurry! While stocks last!'

Q3: Play **audio track 1.1**. To help students build the skill of listening for key information, you could pause recordings at points when you think important messages have been given.

Q4: Play **audio track 1.1** again for students to seek out implied meanings in this household conversation between Edmond and his parents. What assumptions are the parents making about Edmond's schoolwork? What does Edmond think his parents don't understand?

Developing the skills

Q5: Clarify to students that the next recording is a continuation of the situation, this time featuring the Chans (Edmond's parents) and his teacher, Ms Burroughs. However, this conversation is more detailed. Point out that Edmond is not actually present during the parent–teacher meeting. Brainstorm how this might affect the conversation and what is said.

> **Give extra challenge** in **Q5e)** by asking students whether they can identify what exactly Mr Chan's complaint is regarding the school's use of computers? What is being implied here? What is Mrs Chan's attitude or concern? Why does she move him on from this point quickly?
>
> **Give extra support** by giving students **worksheet 1.2** and asking them to note down the 'pros' and 'cons' of using computers for learning.

Going further

Q6: Remind students that they are continuing to look for implied meaning.

> **Give extra support** for **Q6** by inventing or quoting typical phrases that teachers might use on report cards or in parent–teacher conversations.
>
> **Give extra challenge** by asking students to identify other phrases that indicate implied meaning in the recording, e.g. 'I suspect it's not always schoolwork...', 'I'm afraid homework isn't always in on time', 'students like Edmond, who might get carried away online'. These words imply that the teacher is being a little protective of Edmond but feels obliged to tell his parents he is not working hard enough.

Q7: Remind students once again to highlight key words in the questions. Check that students understand exactly what information the questions are seeking.

Assessment for learning	**Q8**: Ask students to watch their peers' role-plays of the conversation at home between the Chans and their son, Edmond. Ask students what they think worked well and what did not work well in the role-plays. Students should give their reasons.

Further challenge	Ask students to record a telephone conversation between Mrs Chan and Ms Burroughs that takes place a few weeks later. Focus on implied meaning and listening between the lines. Students should first script this activity using scriptwriting conventions and perhaps using information about body language from the first **video clip**. For example: *Mrs Chan:* Hello – may I speak to... *Ms Burroughs:* ...

Resources needed for this chapter
- **Student's Book**: Chapter 2
- **Worksheets**: 2.1–2.2
- **Workbook**: see suggestions in 'Resources' panel of individual sections
- **Audio tracks**: 2.1–2.5
- **Video clips**: see suggestions in sections 2.1–2.4

The big picture

Write the title 'Exploration' on the board. Ask students what parts of the Earth and the universe beyond Earth are being explored at the moment (e.g. Mars, the bottom of the ocean).

Ask students if they know of any explorers past or present, and where the explorers travelled to. What is it that made these explorers famous? You may prefer to focus on the explorers shown in the collage. Use the information below as prompts, asking if any students have heard of these explorers or know what they are famous for.

You could set up an 'Explorers bank', listing on a large sheet of paper or on the board explorers whose names come up during work on this chapter.

Photo notes

The photos show the following (working clockwise):

- British explorer Ranulph Fiennes (1944–), the first person to cross the North and South Poles by surface means and the first to cross Antarctica on foot
- canyon country adventure
- astronaut Bruce McCandless making a space walk using a manned manoeuvering unit (MMU)
- a diver filming an Atlantis submarine off the coast of Maui, Hawaii
- a Chinese stamp issued in 2005 to mark the 600th anniversary of the first expedition by Zheng He, a Chinese explorer. Students will learn more about Zheng He in Section 2.1.

Thinking big

Give students a few minutes to work in pairs through **Q1–3** in section 2.1. The questions there focus on bravery, but encourage students to think of other qualities they associate with exploration and explorers. After students have finished their discussion, bring the group back together to create a word bank on the board of adjectives associated with exploration and explorers, e.g. *scary, frightening, exhilarating, brave, courageous, fearless.*

Exploration project presentation

Students should do the b*ig task* once they have completed all four sections of the chapter.

Remind students of the different stages of giving a presentation (see below). One of the major aims of this chapter and **big task** is to research and organise ideas. Therefore, make sure you give students time to do the research needed to prepare for the presentation.

Brainstorming

Remind students of the 'Wh?' question words (*What, Which, Where, Who ... * and *How*) and to think about why *their* country might want to invest in an exploration project. Demonstrate one question that students could ask about space exploration – for example: 'What are the benefits to India of having a space mission?'

Ask a confident student to give a question about underwater exploration – for example: 'What do explorers expect to find underwater off the coast of China?' Allow students time to discuss their questions in groups.

Research

If possible, set the research for homework, asking students to use the internet or the library to find answers to their questions.

Organising information and writing first draft

After students have done their research, remind them that they cannot use all the ideas – a two-minute presentation is not long. Go round checking students' notes to make sure that they have discarded any irrelevant arguments and have chosen only their most winning/persuasive arguments and organised them.

Editing

Remind more confident students that a persuasive presentation needs a good opening. Ask them how they will achieve this, e.g. using a photo, asking a question, telling a story.

Giving the presentation

Help decision makers to agree a list of criteria for how to judge the merit of a presentation, such as:

* clear ideas – only two or three main ideas
* clear organisation
* presentation (e.g. use of pictures)
* clear speaking.

Assessment objectives

R1 Demonstrate understanding of specific factual information

R2 Demonstrate understanding of the connections between ideas, opinions and attitudes

R3 Identify and select details for a specific purpose

Reading Skills in focus

• Select relevant details when reading in order to make notes

Question types

* Note-taking
* Reading headings, subheadings
* Open response questions

Differentiated learning outcomes

• All students should select a few relevant details, then attempt to write notes.

• Most students should select some relevant details and use them to write clear notes with a reasonable degree of accuracy.

• Some students should select nearly all the relevant material and write concise notes.

Resources

* **Student's Book**: Section 2.1
* **Video clip**: see 'Exploring the skills'
* **Worksheet**: 2.1
* **Workbook**: Section 1.1, 1.3
* **Other**: Atlases for the 'Going Further' section

Getting started

Q1: Go back to the list of explorers you started in **The big picture** and create a longer class list of explorers on the board. Using this list to prompt them, students should discuss the **Q1** questions in pairs. Remind students that notes are short phrases not sentences.

Q2: Ask students to discuss the questions in pairs and then feed back to the whole group. Add any new words or phrases to the exploration word bank you started in **The big picture**.

Exploring the skills

Introduce the theme of the text – the legendary Chinese explorer Zheng He – by watching Farland Chang's YouTube video 'Greatest naval explorer you never knew? China's Zheng He', (2:49 minutes).

Remind students of Zheng He from **The big picture**. Tell students or elicit from them that headings are a feature of a non-fiction text. Ask students for a definition of a heading (a title). Headings give us an idea about the section that we are going to read. Headings are useful because they help us to narrow down where to search for answers to questions.

Ask students where they think they will find the information to the pre-reading questions (**Q3**). Model the answer for the first question, explaining that the words in the main heading (e.g. 'fleet' = a large number of ships) indicate what will be found in the following paragraph. Students read and find out whether the information they want is contained in their identified paragraph.

Developing the skills

Q4: This exercise practises scanning a text for specific purposes.

Give extra support for **Q4** by making sure that students understand they only need refer to the second column of text, which gives details of Zheng He's voyages.

Q5: Encourage students to think what they themselves would find exciting, e.g. being a member of a crew of thousands, sailing with 300 ships, battling pirates, coming home to China with a giraffe on board the ship.

Make sure students understand the meaning of 'dynasty' (defined in the **Glossary** box) and 'ambitious'. Support them with any other unfamiliar words (e.g. porcelain, lacquerware, ivory, pearls, tankers, merchants, imperial, emperor, ostriches, officials). Ask students to discuss in pairs whether the journey shows the great power of the Chinese Ming dynasty, and elicit answers from pairs, ensuring that they explain their reasons – for example:

* The ships were enormous (giant).
* There were 300 ships in the fleet.
* There was a crew of 27 000 people.
* The ships were filled with expensive items such as silk, porcelain and lacquerware.

Give extra challenge by asking students to complete **worksheet 2.1** and think about the writer's underlying attitude to Zheng He.

Going further

Q6: Write a sentence on the board and a phrase with two or three words.
For example:

* sentence: I went to the North Pole by helicopter.
* note: North Pole – helicopter

Ask students to identify which is the note. Stress that notes are not sentences. A note can be just one word – notes are only there to jog the memory.

Introduce the reading passage as someone's account of their trip to the North Pole. Point out the **Glossary** box with definitions of some of the words and phrases. After reading the first time, check students' understanding of 'remote' and 'accessible'. Ask them what they understand by 'stir the hearts and minds'.

Check that students' notes only refer to the things that enabled the writer to make the trip to the North Pole. Students should not have notes about the last paragraph, which is all *opinion* about the North Pole.

Give extra challenge by asking students in pairs to give a short spoken summary of the information to their partner.

Assessment for learning	Ask students to research an explorer of their choice. They should choose a short reading passage about their explorer and write notes under their own choice of headings.
	In pairs, students should exchange texts and write notes under the headings they give one another.

Further challenge	Students should revise their answers to the above exercise, this time making sure they use their own words as far as possible.

Assessment objectives

W1 Communicate information, ideas and opinions
W2 Organise ideas into coherent text using a range of linking devices

Writing skills in focus

* Collect and organise ideas
* Write for or against a point of view
* Include your own ideas when writing
* Respond to ideas with a different opinion

Question types

* Note-taking
* Writing your opinion
* Presenting advantages and disadvantages

Differentiated learning outcomes

* All students collect and organise a few ideas in support of a point of view, using ideas they have gathered mainly from other sources.
* Most students collect and organise some ideas and develop these ideas a little, in support of a point of view; a few of these ideas may be their own.
* Some students organise and develop ideas, including their own, to support a point of view effectively.

Resources

* **Student's Book**: Section 2.2
* **Video clip**: see 'Getting started'
* **Worksheet**: 2.2
* **Workbook**: Section 3.5

Getting started

Q1: Brainstorm with students the names of the planets and stars. Also look at the photographs in the Student's Book: a Chinese satellite orbiting in space; the night sky; and the first African American woman in space, Dr Mae C. Jemison. Ask students to find out which countries have space programmes:

* Many countries have the capability to send satellites into space, e.g. Mexico.
* Some countries and organisations have the ability to launch rockets and satellites, e.g. the European Space Agency, India, Iran, Israel, Japan.
* Only a few have the capability to send crewed missions into space, e.g. China, Russia, the USA.
* Other countries are joining the space race, e.g. South Africa and a Pan-Arab Space Agency.

While discussing this, create a space word bank on the board, including words and phrases such as: *crewed missions, uncrewed/crewless missions, launch, satellites, astronauts, galaxy, the solar system, planet, star, rotate, spin, axis, revolve, orbit.*

You could introduce the theme of this section with a short video of a rocket launch, for example by searching 'Rockets 101 National Geographic' and playing the first 40 seconds.

Exploring the skills

Q2–3: This part of the lesson introduces students to KWL charts (standing for **KNOW – WANT** to know – have **LEARNED**). A chart is a good way of encouraging students to tackle non-fiction themes by accessing experience or information they already know. It also helps them to focus their reading when researching what they need to know in order to write or talk about a theme. Students should use their ideas from **Getting started** to copy and complete the first two columns of the KWL chart. As you elicit students' ideas and questions, add to your space word bank.

Give extra challenge by asking students to write example sentences using chosen words from the space word bank.

Q4: Each student should focus on two or three questions. Stress that their research will mean that they have to scan lots of information in order to find specific answers to their questions. The aim is *not* to copy vast amounts of information but to find specific short answers to their specific questions. The aim is for students to recognise which information is *relevant* as well as which information is *not relevant*. In the next lesson, elicit from several students both the questions they asked as well as the information/answers they have found.

Q5: This question helps students recognise points that may not be relevant to an argument. A personal statement about looking up at the moon and stars **(c)** is not directly relevant to the topic of space exploration.

Q6: Together with students, model the mind map for the *disadvantages* of space exploration, eliciting possible questions they could ask: How many people have lost their lives? What are the dangers of space exploration? How much does it cost to launch a rocket? What exactly have been the benefits? Why don't countries work together to explore space? What are the effects on the upper atmosphere of sending a rocket into space? What happens when sky junk (old satellites, etc.) comes down? Then ask students to work in groups to map the *advantages* of space exploration.

Developing the skills

Q7: Allow students time to read and discuss the advantages and disadvantages of space exploration mentioned in the article. Encourage them to take notes, following up on their practice in note-taking in Section 2.1.

Q8: The speech gives practice of presenting a *one-sided view of an issue*. Remind students that they need only give *either* the advantages *or* the disadvantages. Students will have to use their own ideas and refer to the phrases in **Q6** in order to create logical sentences. Encourage them to write sentences that express their own opinions. Suggest that students can slightly alter the quotes to make their points – for example, if they don't agree that space is the *most exciting* place left to discover, they could start: 'It is undeniably true that space is *an exciting* place to discover...'

Give extra support by asking students to complete **worksheet 2.2**, which can help them structure their ideas and give them the linking words between paragraphs. Remind students to add examples to each paragraph in support of each idea.

Give extra challenge by asking students to reread what they have written and check the following before writing a final draft of the speech:

- one idea only in each paragraph
- punctuation
- 100–150 words
- spelling.

Going further

Q10: This exercise gives practice in stating a different opinion. Students should refer back to the **Language booster** to choose phrases which introduce their opinion.

Q11: Ask students to look back at their research, the reading passages and their speech to complete the third column of their KWL table.

Assessment for learning	Ask students to research, organise and write a short (150-word) article for their student newspaper on the advantages of space tourism. Remind students they can use some of the phrases in **Q10** and the **Language booster**.

Further challenge	Students use the phrases in **Q10** confidently to introduce their own opinions and to integrate their supporting material effectively.

Chapter 2
Exploration

Assessment objectives

S1   Communicate a range of ideas, facts and opinions

Speaking skills in focus
* Research and organise ideas for giving a talk or presentation
* Plan an effective, individual opening to a talk or presentation

Question types

* Preparing and giving a talk or presentation
* Giving opinions with supporting arguments

Differentiated learning outcomes

All students should research and organise a few ideas, and give a short talk or presentation with a limited structure.

* Most students should research and organise some relevant ideas, and give a talk or presentation that is planned and has a clear opening.

* Some students should research and organise ideas thoroughly, and give a talk or presentation that is well planned, with an effective individual opening.

Resources

* **Student's Book**: Section 2.3
* **Workbook**: Section 5
* **Other**: A4 coloured paper (for **Q4**)

Getting started

Remind students of the exercise (**Q6**) in section 2.1 about the North Pole.

To elicit understanding of 'polar' ask them to look at the maps in **Q1** and to identify the North and South Poles. Talk to them about what they know about these regions. For example:

* North Pole: in the Arctic Ocean, the smallest of the world's oceans. Mostly covered by sea ice. In summer, whales, seals and other creatures go to the Arctic looking for food.
* South Pole: in Antarctica, the world's coldest, driest and windiest continent. Covered by a thick sheet of ice. Very few plants and animals.

Discuss the answers to **Q1** in the class, drawing on learning points from Sections 2.1 and 2.2 to talk about motivations for exploration as well as the challenges.

Q2: Students should choose one of the photos and write one or two notes per bullet point. It may not be obvious exactly where the photo is taken but they illustrate features of the polar regions.

* The first photo shows a mountain range in Antarctica, and was taken during an expedition to the Vernadsky Research Base.
* The second photo is a view of an Antarctic research station.
* The third photo shows a polar bear mother with two cubs on ice. The melting ice around them may prompt students to talk about global warming and threats to the ice cap.

Ask students to share their answers, either in small groups or to the whole class. To support them for the next task, confirm the subject matter of each photo.

Exploring the skills

Q3: This exercise gives students practice at organising their ideas for a very short talk – the aim is to give them confidence when speaking.
Q4 shows students that it's useful to find ways to organise their points, even for a very short talk. Support students with any unfamiliar words (eg. viruses, traders).

Ask students to use coloured paper to help organise the points into themes. If coloured pieces of paper are unavailable, students can use different coloured pens, or highlight the text in different colours on screen.

Developing the skills

Q5: This exercise asks students not only to organise their ideas but also to think of the organising structure as well. They need to read all three paragraphs and pick out the points for and against tourism to Antarctica. In pairs, they should discuss and decide how they're going to organise the points into two groups: they could use colour coding again, or they may decide to list them on two separate columns.

Give extra support by asking students what organising structures they can remember or have used, e.g. themes; advantages and disadvantages; only for or only against; past, present and future (organisation according to time); what you see/hear/touch/smell/feel.

Give extra challenge by asking students to add points of their own.

Q6 Students should now use the points from **Q5** to conduct a short role-play. Student A should use the list of points grouped under 'advantages' and Student B should use the list of points grouped under 'disadvantages'. Bear in mind that some of these points will be used again in the final task (**Q8**) so this role-play can be kept quite short.

Going further

Q7: Openings are important for both speaking and writing tasks, because if the opening is boring, then there is every chance that the reader/listener will turn the page or switch off.

As a class go through the items in the **'Did you remember to…?'** section. Elicit definitions and/or examples of each point before asking students to tackle **Q7**. Explain that rhetorical questions may seem to require a yes/no answer, but in fact, we do not expect an answer at all. Rhetorical questions are a way of expressing strong feelings or opinions. For example, instead of saying 'That's an ugly building', you might say 'Isn't that an ugly building?', but you do not expect an answer. Explain that an 'anecdote' is a story based on someone's own experience. Encourage students to discuss why they like the different features.

Q8: Remind students of the 'advantages' and 'disadvantages' they grouped in **Q5**, and the examples of openings in **Q7**. Explain that for this exercise they only need to give the opening of a presentation but that their opinion (advantages/disadvantages) should be made clear in this opening.

In groups, have students practise giving their openings to each other, and then give each other feedback on what was effective in grabbing listeners' attention.

Give extra challenge by asking students to think about 'register': for example, whether it is important to greet the audience formally or whether it can be less formal. Point out that a less formal opening may not be appropriate if you are making a presentation to people who are older than you or to people in authority, for example.

Assessment for learning	Ask students to record and replay their presentations. They should mark their own presentations against the items in the **'Did you remember to…?'** section, awarding one mark for each item.
Further challenge	Ask students to follow on from the opening paragraph by continuing with the rest of the presentation. Look back at the writing frame in Worksheet 2.2 as a reminder of a structure they could use.

Assessment objectives

L1   Demonstrate understanding of specific information

Listening skills in focus

- Recognise and understand facts when listening to short spoken texts
- Recognise and understand facts when listening to a longer and more difficult text
- Listen carefully and understand complicated instructions

Question types

- Short recordings
- Long recordings
- Gap-fill
- Listening for instructions

Differentiated learning outcomes

- All students should understand and pick out some required facts in shorter spoken texts and one or two facts in more difficult texts; they should attempt to follow complicated instructions but will make errors.
- Most students should understand and pick out most required facts in shorter spoken texts and some facts in more difficult texts; they should be able to follow complicated instructions with some hesitation.
- Some students should understand and pick out all required facts in shorter spoken texts and most facts in more difficult texts; they should follow complicated instructions accurately and confidently.

Resources

- **Student's Book**: Section 2.4
- **Audio tracks**: 2.1–2.5
- **Video clip**: see 'Developing the skills'
- **Workbook**: Section 4.4
- **Other**: Origami paper

Getting started

Q1: Write all the 'Wh' question words on the board to help students think of questions: *What? Who? Why? When? Which? Where? How?* Elicit a few questions from the class before asking students to begin working on their own.

Exploring the skills

Write the following three sentences on the board and ask which of them can be proved to be true and therefore count as facts:

- 'The sea was a beautiful blue colour.'
- 'The Atlantic Ocean is over 8000 m deep.'
- 'The Mariana Trench is in the Pacific Ocean.'

The last two can be proved to be true and are facts. Discuss how you could *prove* that the Atlantic Ocean is 8000 m deep (e.g. send down a line and measure it when it hits the bottom of the ocean floor). You could prove the location of the Mariana Trench by looking in an atlas. The first sentence is an opinion as you cannot measure beauty.

Q2: Students look at the advertisements. Elicit from students what they are advertising. Write the following on the board: 'Only $25 per hour'. Ask whether it is a fact or opinion. If it is a fact, ask how they would prove it. (It is a fact – they could prove it by looking at the company's price list.) Play **audio tracks 2.1** and **2.2** without stopping.

Q3: Play **audio track 2.3**, which includes pauses allowing time for students to note responses to the questions. Give students time at the end to check their answers. Afterwards discuss the answers, asking students why a sentence or phrase is a fact or not, and how it can be proved or how it is impossible to prove.

Q4: Repeat the process with **audio track 2.4** and phrases from the second advertisement.

Q5: Play **audio tracks 2.3** and **2.4** again if necessary. The aim of the question is to encourage student discussion while going through each sentence in the advertisements identifying facts. There is no correct answer. There are more facts in the second advertisement but it is still riddled with opinions and is much longer. The first advertisement has fewer facts but has a greater *percentage* of facts.

Developing the skills

To introduce the topic, search for the Youtube video 'The Alvin Submarine Part 2: Incredible Views On-Board the Deep-Sea Vessel'. Before playing it, write the term 'hydrothermal vent' on the board and explain what it is: an underwater volcano that lets off gases under the ocean.

Q6–8: Introduce the listening task by eliciting from students what they would like to discover if they went on a deep-sea dive. The video clip and **Glossary** in the Student's Book introduce some of the vocabulary in the listening task. Ask students to identify the photo of the remotely operated underwater vehicle and write the term 'ROV' on the board. Explain that it's an advanced submarine and ask students to listen out for the initials 'ROV' in the audio.

> **Give extra support** by checking through the listening passage to see if there is any other vocabulary that you think you need to pre-teach.

Q7: Play **audio track 2.5** all the way through without stopping. Play the track again, this time pausing at the end each section to give students time to write notes in answer to parts **a)–d)**.

Do not assume that students will read through the form for **Q8**. Tell them to do so and ask them if they can predict the type of words they need to listen for, or alternatively examples of possible words. Tell them they need to listen *carefully* for the exact details/words used. Play **audio track 2.5** again pausing if necessary (longer for less confident students) to give students time to complete the details in **Q8**.

> **Give extra challenge** by asking students to listen again to the interview and to put their hands up when they hear a fact.

Going further

Language booster: Teach students that we use the imperative to give instructions and demonstrate this by asking what the root form is of 'folded' (fold), 'went' (go), 'listened' (listen), 'made' (make), 'brought' (bring), etc. Ask students when they are likely to see or use instructions. Elicit and praise suitable answers, e.g. in a recipe book for making a dish, giving directions to people for how to get somewhere, giving directions to people to tell them how to do something.

Q10: Students should take turns to give the instructions and make the boat, and similarly for **Q11**. Before they start, ensure their understanding of 'crease' by demonstrate folding and creasing a piece of paper.

> **Give extra challenge** by asking students to make the boat without looking at the diagrams.

Assessment for learning	Ask students to choose a simple activity, e.g. how to put on shoes and tie laces, or how to make an omelette. They should think of six to ten instructions explaining how to do the activity. In pairs, they tell their partner what to do, and the listener should then mime the activity. They can only do what their partner tells them to do.
	Afterwards, pairs should discuss how easy it was to understand the instructions and how they could have been improved.
Further challenge	In pairs, students explain to one another how to play a game or sport, e.g. draughts or 'battleships'. Afterwards they discuss how clear the instructions were and how they could have been made clearer.

Resources needed for this chapter

- **Student's Book**: Chapter 3
- **Worksheets**: 3.1–3.6
- **Workbook**: see suggestions in 'Resources' panel of individual sections
- **Audio tracks**: 3.1–3.5
- **Video clips**: see suggestions given in each section

The big picture

Introduce the overall theme by pointing to one photo that shows someone who is healthy and one photo that shows someone who is sick or doing something unhealthy. Ask students what the problem is and how the person might feel. Ask students to make a word bank of health vocabulary on the board or on a flip chart, e.g. *do yoga, run a marathon, have a headache, have a fever, have a cough, to stay in bed.*

Thinking big

Q1: Demonstrate taking notes by asking one student the questions in the list of bullet points about one of the photos, e.g. the child being vaccinated, and making notes on the student's answers. Show students that notes are short phrases, not sentences, e.g. 'being vaccinated – healthy – TB vaccination prog in our country – advantage – prevents illnesses – disadvantage = cost'.

Q2: Get feedback by asking different students what each photo shows and which of the activities they do.

Q3: Possible answers for why it is important to be as healthy as possible or make good lifestyle choices could be to live longer, to live fuller lives while we are alive, to avoid being sick, to improve the amount of time we can work/earn money (if you are sick it is very difficult to do a job/earn money).

Photo notes

The photos show the following *(working clockwise):*

- a sick girl with a thermometer
- runners at the start of the Cursa de la Merce in Barcelona, Spain
- shelves with vitamin supplements in a health food shop
- a man doing yoga
- a burger and fries
- *(centre)* a doctor preparing an injection for a boy in a hospital clinic.

The big task	# A healthier lifestyle: creating a website for young people

Students should do the *big task* once they have completed all four sections of the chapter.

Make sure you give students time to do their research. One of the major aims of this chapter and **The big task** is to research and organise ideas.

Write the task on the board: 'Create a website for young people about how to have a healthier lifestyle.'

As an alternative, students could discuss another aspect of health that is important to them, such as a global issue like malaria, but they should retain the same aim of informing other young people.

As a class, work with students to break down the title of the task into sections:

* Format: website
* Readers: young people
* Content: information about ways to stay healthy and the importance of staying healthy
* Purpose: to encourage young people to lead a healthier lifestyle.

Format

Q2–3: Break down the *format*: a website. Note that it is not necessary to ask students to prepare a real website. Students can prepare a handwritten website with text on one sheet of paper being the equivalent of a page on a website. Ask students to read **Q2**, which talks about the structure of a website – separate pages with each page dealing with one subject or aspect.

Ask students to think about the headings for the navigation bar (the list of linked headings usually down the left side or along the top of a web page). You could ask students to research a website they use and write down all the titles on the navigation bar. It may prompt them to want to add a 'Search' box or a 'Join now' link, or to create a forum or social section where people can leave comments.

Style

Q4–6: Break down the *style*: websites are often written in short punchy phrases. Many of them use the command form, e.g. 'Watch the video now' or the question form 'Do you know these special techniques for playing basketball?' Text is often short (a short paragraph, e.g. 50–75 words) and photos are important, especially on the home page.

Audience

Analyse the *audience* (the people likely to be reading/watching and listening): the website is for young people. Ask students to think about what foods young people like to eat that are good and bad for them. Ask students to think about the types of exercise that young people are likely to do – even if they are not classified as a traditional sport, e.g. skateboarding.

Chapter 3
Health

3.1 Healthy eating

Assessment objectives

R1 Demonstrate understanding of specific factual information

Reading skills in focus
- Select facts and details accurately from a written text
- Understand the importance of units of measurement
- Understand phrases about time
- Use key question words to help find answers

Question types
- Open-response questions
- Multiple matching
- Reading diagrams
- Reading recipes

Differentiated learning outcomes
- All students should identify some facts, including units of measurement, in texts, and sometimes use key words to help them identify answers.
- Most students should understand and select relevant details, recognising the significance of units of measurement, and often using key question words to help answer questions.
- Some students should understand and select all relevant details, including appropriate and precise measurements, and consistently make successful use of key question words when finding answers

Resources
- **Student's Book:** Section 3.1
- **Video clip:** see 'Exploring the skills'
- **Worksheet:** 3.1
- **Workbook:** Section 1.1
- **Other:** items of fresh food, teaspoon, tablespoon, measuring jug, weighing scales, bag of pasta shapes

Getting started

Introduce the theme of this section – food and healthy eating – by bringing in items of food into the classroom, especially fruit and vegetables. Ask students to identify the food and, if they can, what food group each one belongs to. Write a list of associated vocabulary on the board as students speak, e.g. *carbohydrates, proteins, vitamins, minerals, fats and oils, recipe, ingredients*. Ensure you include vocabulary in the 'food pyramid' diagram shown in the Student's Book.

Q2: After studying the pyramid diagram, students should be given time to reflect on whether they have a healthy diet.

Exploring the skills

Introduce units of measurements by bringing in a teaspoon, tablespoon, electronic weighing scales (if you don't have any, maybe the science department does), and a measuring jug, plus some water and pasta shapes. Ask students to estimate and then weigh/measure out 100 g of pasta or 2 tablespoons of pasta, 150 ml of water, etc.

Check that students know how many grammes are in a kilogramme. Check that students read the **Language booster** for the written abbreviations of measurements.

> **Give extra challenge** by extending the list of abbreviations in the **Language booster** to distance, e.g. m = metre (or mile, as in '10 mph'); km = kilometre; ft = foot. Some of them are symbols, such as the use of the double prime mark, which looks similar to a double quote mark (") for inch and single prime mark, which looks similar to a single quote mark for foot (').

Play the **video clip**, 'Perfect Basmati rice How-to video' on the 'Show me the curry' website (2:17 minutes). This clip gives simple instructions for how to cook basmati rice. Discuss with students whether that is how they or their parents prepare rice.

Q3: This recipe is taken from a social media site and gives friends' opinions on the recipe. After reading the recipe, check that students understand the heading

'Ingredients' by asking them what you need to make the recipe. Check that students understand the word 'Method' by asking them how to cook the recipe.

Q4: Don't assume that students will understand the recipe even if they have strong language skills, as cooking vocabulary is specific and technical. Answers to the first four comprehension questions should be short – just the times or the amounts. The remaining three questions are multiple matching. Further practice of the language of recipes is covered in the Developing the skills section.

Q6: Students should check back and look at the food pyramid. The recipe is healthy and contains protein (chicken), vegetables (onion, garlic, tomatoes) as well as herbs and spices and dairy (yoghurt) and can be served with a carbohydrate (couscous).

> **Give extra challenge** by asking students to think about what they would add to their current diet to make it more healthy and balanced.

Developing the skills

Language booster: Demonstrate how to write the method of a recipe by giving the first instruction from a recipe. Make sure students understand they need to give *numbered* instructions. Introduce the term 'imperative form', which is always used for giving instructions, e.g. *boil, fry, cook.*

> **Give extra support** and check that students understand the technical terms by asking students to complete **worksheet 3.1**. Be prepared to explain any terms they do not understand. Add these words to the class word bank.
>
> **Give extra support** for **Q7** by asking students to identify and copy all the phrases of time used in the recipe: 'until soft', 'for about a minute', 'for 15 minutes', 'occasionally', 'until the chicken is soft', 'about 30 minutes'. Check they understand what they mean, e.g. does 'for about a minute' mean *more* or *less* than a minute or something else?

Going further

Remind students that a fact is something you can prove to be true. Write the following sentence on the board: 'Pizza is eaten all over the world.' This is a fact. Ask how they would prove this was true – e.g. by asking people in each continent if they eat pizza, or by checking on the internet to see whether pizzas are available in shops or cafés in different towns and cities throughout the world.

Q8–9: Students should give short, factual answers. Remind them that they can anticipate the answer from the question word. For example, 'Where were the large, flat breads first baked?' suggests the answer should be a place (answer = in Greece).

> **Give extra challenge** by asking students to find out and write down three facts about a national dish of their home country or the community where they live now.

Assessment for learning	Ask students to bring in a recipe for a dish they have made or could make to share with their fellow students. They should also: • *either* write the recipe for their dish using abbreviations – make sure students give a list of ingredients and numbered instructions • *or* write a paragraph about their dish ensuring that it includes five acts. Working in pairs, students should assess their partner's recipe checking for: • headings: 'Ingredients' and 'Method' • abbreviations for the list of ingredients • a list of ingredients • numbered instructions • use of imperative form to give instructions, e.g. 'boil', 'fry', 'turn down'.
Further challenge	Ask students to write a review of a meal. In pairs, discuss how the style here differs from the style of a recipe. Identify the phrases giving opinion compared to those giving facts.

Assessment objectives

W3 Use a range of appropriate grammatical structures and vocabulary

Writing skills in focus
* Use a range of different kinds of sentences when writing
* Use simple, compound and complex sentences accurately
* Include appropriate linking devices and noun phrases to add detail and variety

Question types
* Long writing questions
* Writing instructions
* Writing a magazine article
* Persuasive writing

Differentiated learning outcomes
* All students should use simple structures correctly and with few errors in punctuation; they may attempt compound sentences with limited success.
* Most students should use simple and compound sentences correctly, showing some variety in structures, including the use of straightforward noun phrases.
* Some students should use simple and compound sentences correctly and with confidence, demonstrating a variety of structures and incorporating more complex noun phrases.

Resources
* **Student's Book**: Section 3.2
* **Worksheets**: 3.2–3.4
* **Workbook**: Section 2.1

Getting started

Q1: Get feedback from students. Make a class list of the reasons why we should do exercise on the board, e.g. *strengthen muscles, get fit, lose weight, feel better, feel more relaxed, stay young, live longer.*

Q2: Write the comment from the article on the board. Ask students what the comment says: that exercise slows the effects of ageing. Ask if this benefit was on their list of reasons for doing exercise from **Q1**. Underline the important words or phrases in the comment before students discuss, e.g. 'running…reduce the effects of ageing…older people…new lease of life'. Ask students to think hard and be precise about each part, for example:

* What is running? When does jogging become running?
* What exactly are the effects of ageing? Is it just wrinkly skin?
* How old are 'older people'?
* What does 'new lease of life' mean? (This is a phrase emphasising that they are much more lively/successful than they have been in the past.)

Exploring the skills

Simple sentences: Write the following phrases and sentence on the board and ask students to identify the sentence, e.g. 'He walks to school every day.' – 'to school' – 'every day'. Ask students how they identified the sentence. Make sure students list: the capital letter at the beginning of a sentence, the full stop at the end, the subject and the verb in the sentence. Tell them that a phrase (e.g. 'to school') does not make complete sense on its own. Ensure students understand 'subject' and 'verb'.

> **Give extra support** by asking students to complete **worksheet 3.2**.
>
> **Give extra challenge** by asking students to identify the subjects and verbs in the extract about running. Ask students to write sentences of their own about running.

Language booster: Do this as a group or class brainstorming activity, asking students to think of as many different sports as they can.

Compound sentences: Write example compound sentences on the board. Underline the conjunctions 'and', 'but' and 'or.'

When looking at the other sentence from the same book, 'You may not break a world record but you can record a personal best.', point out to students that 'record' in the first instance is a noun and second is a verb. Remind students about the different pronunciation, i.e. that the noun has the stress on the first syllable and the verb on the second. Also, talk about how 'personal best' is now often abbreviated to 'PB'.

Q3: Get feedback asking students to underline the conjunction and explain why they think a sentence is simple or compound. For each sentence ask them to identify the subject and the verb.

> **Give extra support** to students by asking them to complete **worksheet 3.3**. This asks students to complete sentences using the conjunction 'so' in addition to the others. **Give extra challenge** by asking students to write four compound sentences of their own using 'and', 'but' and 'or'.

Q4: Remind students they need to use the imperative form of the verb (base/root) for instructions to explain how to do the sport.

Developing the skills

Q5: Read both texts aloud for students as this will help emphasise the point that short sentences can sound boring and can also sound a bit aggressive. Show them that the first text is repetitive – the words 'he', 'trains' and 'it' are all used two or more times.

Q6: Ask students to underline the words that are repeated e.g. 'football', 'lots of', 'there are'. Challenge them to rewrite the text without repeating any words. Remind students that joining sentences with the same conjunction can also be boring, e.g. 'Bring your socks and put on your running shoes and wear your running vest and don't forget your …' Good writing uses a *mix* of conjunctions.

> **Q7: Give extra challenge** by asking students to identify one simple and one compound sentence in their paragraphs, and to explain why they used simple or compound sentences when they did. Remind students that a paragraph has one main idea and is usually four to five lines in length.

Going further

Q9: Noun phrases help students to write or speak about things (nouns) precisely, e.g. 'I do *strength exercises*' tells the reader/listener the type of exercises you do. Noun phrases also allow more information to be conveyed more concisely, e.g. 'I bought the *lower-priced tickets*,' is more concise than 'I bought the tickets that cost less than the other tickets…'..

> **Give extra challenge** by asking students to change or supply adjectives different from those in the word box in Q8, e.g. 'I like going for short walks in the rugged country.

Q10: Set up this exercise by discussing with students who the audience for the magazine article is – i.e. young people. Ask students how they can make the article interesting for young people in terms of content and style. Discuss level of formality.

> **Give extra support** by using the writing frame in **worksheet 3.4**.

Assessment for learning	Ask students to write a 150-word article to persuade fellow students new to your year to join a particular after-school activity. Use at least one simple sentence, one compound sentence and one noun phrase. Teacher to mark using these criteria.
Further challenge	Ask students to draw up a list of criteria to be used for the activity above. How can you judge if a piece of persuasive writing is successful or not? Then ask them to apply the criteria to their own work, perhaps working in pairs.

Assessment objectives

S1   Communicate a range of ideas, facts and opinions

S2   Demonstrate control of a range of vocabulary and grammatical structures

Speaking skills in focus

- Use a variety of structures when speaking
- Link ideas using a range of conjunctions
- Speak using abstract nouns and noun phrases to give variety

Question types

- Giving opinions with supporting arguments
- Discussing in pairs and groups
- Recording and analysing
- Making a persuasive argument

Differentiated learning outcomes

- All students should use simple structures and a limited vocabulary, with little evidence of abstract nouns or noun phrases when speaking.
- Most students should use simple structures and a straightforward range of vocabulary securely, with occasional use of abstract nouns and noun phrases for some variety.
- Some students should use a variety of structures accurately and consistently, incorporating abstract nouns and noun phrases appropriately to convey shades of meaning.

Resources

- **Student's Book**: Section 3.3
- **Video clip**: see 'Exploring the skills'
- **Worksheets**: 3.5, 3.6
- **Workbook**: Section 5.2 Section 5.3

Getting started

Encourage students to think about how different diseases are associated with different countries. For example, heart disease and diabetes are often linked to Western countries – often caused by obesity. Students are likely to talk about how COVID-19 has affected the world. Approach this subject with care as there may be students who have been affected by COVID-19. Point out that many diseases are waterborne, e.g. typhoid and cholera. Ask students if they know of any diseases that have been eliminated. For example, polio and river blindness have almost been eradicated. As you talk with students, start a word bank of diseases on the board, including terms such as 'cancer', 'heart attack', and so on.

> **Give extra challenge** by talking about the second bullet point – disease prevention. Teach the phrase 'preventable disease'. Point out that many killer diseases are preventable, e.g. obesity can be prevented by eating a healthy, balanced diet and exercise, malaria can be prevented by the use of netting over the bed at night. Many other diseases (e.g. infections of the eye) can be prevented by something as simple as washing your hands, although this is often difficult in areas that have no running water. Other prevention measures include vaccination programmes and ensuring that there are trained midwives at childbirth.

Exploring the skills

Q3: Elicit and make a class list of words associated with the photo.

Reinforce the vocabulary by asking students to do **worksheet 3.5** (but ask them to leave the last line of the worksheet until they have finished **Q7**). Ask students to add any new words or phrases to their personal notebook or journal.

> **Give extra challenge** by asking students to research and set one another questions on malaria.

Q4–6: Prepare for the conversation in **Q6** by writing both the speech bubbles on the board and break them down into sections – for example:

* 'clean water – dirty water – cause illness'.

Q7: Ask students to prepare for this task by reading the newspaper extracts and also by researching either waterborne diseases or vaccines. Ask them to find out, for example, exactly what illnesses are caused by dirty water and how to improve sanitation. Some students might think the second extract is about COVID-19 as the text is relevant to that health emergency as well.

> **Video clip:** Play Unicef's YouTube video 'UNICEF and ECHO aim to prevent waterborne disease in Togo' (2:43 minutes), which looks at preventing waterborne diseases and diarrhoea, in order to stimulate discussion. **Give extra challenge** by asking students to complete the last line on **worksheet 3.5**.

Developing the skills

Q8: Before students answer the questions, make sure they understand what is meant by a 'vitamin supplement'. The photo on the page will help to make it clear. Also they came across this word in Section 3.1.

Q9–10: Put all student As and Bs together to prepare their arguments. Challenge pairs to have a conversation of at least three minutes. Ask several pairs to perform their role-play in front of the class. Challenge the rest of the class to listen and to put up their hands when they hear compound sentences using joining words such as 'and', 'but', 'so' and 'or'.

Going further

Remind students about noun phrases: words used to expand the idea of the noun. Write 'preventable disease' on the board. Ask students what it is. Do the same for the rest of the words in **Going further**.

Q11: Copy and complete the table with students for the first one or two noun phrases. There are many noun phrases for food – encourage students to think of how they could describe a particular food or drink, e.g. running/bottled/pure water.

Language booster: Write the word 'bread' on the board. Tell students this is a noun. Tell them you can touch it so it is called a *concrete noun*. But there are nouns that name things that cannot be touched. These nouns are called *abstract nouns*. Give examples of abstract nouns, e.g. *desire, strength, kindness, knowledge, perseverance*. Then ask students to do **Q12** and ask each pair to provide one example of a sentence. Support students with the pronunciation of 'fatigue'.

> **Give extra challenge** by asking students to complete **worksheet 3.6** on abstract nouns.

Assessment for learning	Ask students to work in pairs and to role-play going to the doctor with a cold or flu. Each person should aim to use an abstract noun while speaking: • The patient should describe the symptoms. These should be mild and not serious. • The doctor should prescribe and give advice about how to avoid the illness in the future. Assessment can be by teacher or self-assessment.
Further challenge	Get students to record the conversation with a partner. They should then listen and identify any abstract nouns and noun phrases. What improvements can students suggest? Can the vocabulary be more precise or subtle? Repeat this exercise.

3.4 Better health

Assessment objectives

L1 Demonstrate understanding of specific information

L2 Demonstrate understanding of speakers' ideas, opinions and attitudes

Listening skills in focus

* Understand and pick out specific details when listening
* Predict the kind of information you will hear including units of measurement
* Recognise high numbers when listening

Question types

* Short recordings
* Gap-fill
* Note-taking

Differentiated learning outcomes

* All students should identify and pick out some details, sometimes predicting the kind of answer to expect, including some numerical values, when listening.
* Most students should pick out most of the details as required, including complex high numbers, making occasional use of prediction from the questions.
* Some students should reliably pick out and understand all the required details, including complicated high numbers, utilising predictive skills appropriately.

Resources

* **Student's Book**: Section 3.4
* **Audio tracks**: 3.1–3.5
* **Video clip**: see 'Getting started'
* **Workbook**: Section 4.2* Section 4.3

*The audio for Workbook Section 4.2 contains some more complex vocabulary such as 'monstrosity', 'blob' and 'carving'. Please support students by pre-teaching this vocabulary before they listen to the recording.

Getting started

Better health is a combination of both moving (staying active) and eating well. Research tells us that when we stay active and eat well, we are not only healthier but also happier. Tell students that it is recommended that young people are active for 60 minutes a day and adults for 150 minutes a week. Being active is not necessarily doing sport – but it is doing something that raises your heart rate, and you can do this by going for a walk, going skateboarding, running, etc.

Q1: After students discuss the points, as a class make two lists with students: one of healthy habits (eating and leisure) and one of unhealthy habits (eating and leisure). For example: healthy = eating five portions of fruit and vegetables a day, eating regular meals, walking to school, cycling to school, running, kicking a ball, going for a walk in the park, washing the car, doing the gardening, dancing; unhealthy = eating junk food, watching TV, spending a lot of time on the computer, constantly playing videos.

Play the 'Teach every child about food' video clip of British chef Jamie Oliver discussing eating habits and the obesity crisis in America (21:53 minutes) on the TED talks website. This is a long video clip – watch it first to decide which parts to play.

Exploring the skills

Q2: Remind students about units of measurements learned in section 3.1 of this chapter and revise the relevant abbreviations, e.g. kilometre/km. Then ask students to think about scoring for sports – each one usually has a specific and predictable scoring system, e.g. football scores are usually given as 'xxx winning/losing 3–2'. Tell them that being able to predict the type of score helps you to hear the correct number, so a scoreline of 34–28 would be unusual in football. Remind students that if the score is zero in football, it's pronounced 'nil'. Note other examples:

* Platforms are usually measured in numbers 1 to (say) 15.
* Temperature is measured in degrees Celsius or Fahrenheit.

- Time on train timetables is usually measured using the 24-hour clock.

Q4: Remind students that this listening text is a report. Ask them if they expect there to be many facts or opinions. Tell them that reports often have lots of facts and that these facts are often expressed in numbers. Prepare students for the numbers by giving them a quick easy mental maths test, e.g. What is four times eight? What is half of 48? What is 50% of 96? What is 25% of 16?

Q5: Give extra challenge by asking students to draw two pie charts – one representing the percentage of adults in Britain who are obese and one representing the percentage of children in Britain who are obese. Students should draw and label the pie charts.

Developing the skills

Q6: Remind students that 'is important for…' is sometimes followed by the +ing (gerund) form of the verb, or a noun. Students do not need to know the term 'gerund' as long as they understand the concept of a verb being a noun. Talk about the fact that some people nowadays are vegetarian or vegan. Ask students what vegans might eat and drink (tofu, soya or oat milk, etc).

Q7: Before playing **audio track 3.3**, help students practise writing numbers where the words you say translate into symbols, e.g. 50%, ¼, 17:00, 30°C, 20–25, etc. Get feedback from students. Make sure their answers are numbers (only) and they have used the symbol – to represent the words, e.g. '1 to 2 servings' is written '1–2'.

Q8: Students read someone's reflection on what they eat.

Q9–10: Make sure students understand the meaning of the noun phrase 'junk food' by asking for examples. Encourage lots of discussion. Ask students to think about whether they would associate Britain with a poor diet or a diet low in nutritional value – something that is usually associated with poverty. Encourage students to think about their own diet – do they think they are at risk of low iron/calcium/Vitamin C?

Give extra support for the **Language booster** by providing students with copies of science textbooks for them to research the nutrition groups in their mother tongue.

Give extra challenge in **Q10** by asking students to write why they think teenagers are more affected than adults.

Q11: Ask students to make notes. Play **audio track 3.4** twice, pausing the second time after each person speaks to give students time to make notes.

Going further

Give extra challenge to **Q13** by writing non-round numbers, e.g. 3.25 million (spoken as 'three point two five million') and ask students to read them aloud.

Q14: Ask students to write the answers on the board.

Q15: Ask students to read their numbers aloud to check they know how to say them.

Assessment for learning	Ask students to research an issue to do with health and write a short (100-word) paragraph about it, including at least three numbers. Students should work in groups and read their text aloud while other members in their group write down the numbers they hear.
Further challenge	This exercise can be done either in pairs or as a class or for homework. Ask students to find an audio or video source online relating to eating habits among young people. They should listen to their audio file twice, pausing between the playings. They then make notes of the key points raised by the speaker(s). They should give a brief report to the rest of the class about what they have found from their research.

Resources needed for this chapter
* **Student's Book**: Chapter 4
* **Worksheets**: 4.1–4.6
* **Workbook**: see suggestions in 'Resources' panel of individual sections
* **Audio tracks**: 4.1–4.5
* **Video clips**: see suggestions given in sections 4.1–4.4

The big picture

Introduce the topic of education and learning by asking students how they learn and what exactly goes on in their brains when they learn. Clarify that this chapter is about learning in the past, present and future, and they should bring their own ideas to the material.

Encourage students to come up with comparisons that would help describe the brain. Some suggestions might be: a computer, a walnut, an orange with four segments, a set of flash bulbs, a calculator. Encourage students to justify why they have chosen a particular analogy.

Thinking big

Q1: Allow students to choose a photo from the collage that they think best describes learning. Encourage students to describe what aspect of learning the chosen photo is showing and why that appeals to them.

Q2: Ask students to write quickly using the prompt questions provided as a guide. Accuracy is not essential at this stage; instead, the focus is on engagement, clarity of ideas and new vocabulary. Encourage students to add their own ideas and anecdotes. It is helpful for teachers to model this exercise first so that students know what to expect. For example, you could talk about learning to ride a bicycle or learning to swim, perhaps using a series of related anecdotes.

Q3: Pair a more confident student with a student needing support and get them to share their experiences using the text they wrote quickly. Do not mark these texts and assure the students that this is for their eyes/use only.

Give extra challenge by asking students to identify the difference between learning a skill and learning information/content, using the differences between learning to ride a bike or learning to swim and learning their times tables.

Ask students to brainstorm why or how a teacher can influence their educational path.

<table>
<tr><td>

The big task

</td><td>

Creating and designing your ideal school

</td></tr>
</table>

Students should do the *big task* once they have completed all four sections of the chapter.

Student grouping: Decide how to divide the students into groups, based on mixed-ability groups.

The task

Explain that in this final task students are required to combine their skills of reading, writing, speaking and listening and their knowledge about education and learning.

Q1: Talk students through the prompts provided in the Student's Book. Remind students that the focus remains on the use of accurate vocabulary to inform, describe and explain.

Q2: Encourage students to discuss not only the format, but also audience and purpose of their presentation.

* **Format**: Presentation ideas could include: drama, role-play, a short film or audio recording with visuals, a photo story, PowerPoint/Google presentation, show and tell, speech with visual slides. Students choose how they would like to present this. Encourage them to discuss the advantages and disadvantages of each format – and above all to think about the impact they are trying to achieve.

* **Audience**: The presentation will be to classmates and to the teacher, but they should consider that this type of presentation would also be given to a board of governors, the principal and parent–teacher association, members of the press (as in **Q3**) or the local education department.

* **Purpose**: The students of today visualise the school of the future for tomorrow's students.

Q3: For this question, the students need to adopt the role of 'listener' – a newspaper journalist who has heard the presentation and is writing it up for an article. Hand out **worksheet 4.6** to help students structure this activity.

Assessment objectives

R1 Demonstrate understanding of specific factual information
R3 Identify and select details for a specific purpose

Reading skills in focus
* Select relevant details to answer questions
* Identify and select relevant information/details from more difficult texts

Question types

* Text comprehension
* Writing short notes
* Reading diagrams

Differentiated learning outcomes

* All students should pick out a few details, including those in charts and diagrams, sometimes making use of key words.
* Most students should pick out many relevant details, including those in charts and diagrams, making use of key words.
* Some students should usually pick out all relevant details, including those in diagrams and charts, making effective use of key words.

Resources

* **Student's Book**: Section 4.1
* **Worksheets**: 4.1, 4.2
* **Workbook**: Section 1.1

Getting started

Tell students that they are going to study how the brain works, and ask them to think about how young children learn. Ask students in pairs to think about the kinds of things they did when they were at kindergarten or nursery school. For example, they might have done some or all of the following: playing in the sand, listening to nursery rhymes, singing songs, colouring, building things, etc.

Ask students in the same pairs to think of a nursery rhyme or a song that they learned when they were young children. Many students may know 'Twinkle, Twinkle, Little Star' or 'Head, Shoulders, Knees and Toes'. This is also an opportunity for students who are not first language speakers to share a nursery rhyme or song in their mother tongue with their classmates and to explain what it is about.

As a class, talk about the characteristics that are associated with the nursery rhymes/songs (for example, they often rhyme, use a lot of repetition, sometimes they have actions associated with them). Explain to students that this is to engage young children and help learning and development.

Q1 and **Q2:** Now ask students what they know about the human brain. Reassure them that these are open questions which they may not have much knowledge of but that they're included to get them thinking about the brain.

Exploring the skills

Introduce to students the idea of reading for detail. This includes the following:
* Read questions carefully and take note of key words by underlining or highlighting them.
* Scan the text to find the relevant section to answer questions.
* Read the text in chunks. Effective 'chunking' enables students to read larger pieces or 'chunks' of texts and then relate them effectively to other parts of the text.
* Read around a key word to work out its context and what is being explained.
* Be prepared to look for another word or phrase that means the same thing as the key word: for example, 'ABC' is another term for 'alphabet'.

Read the passage on 'Brain facts' aloud and ask students to summarise the information for you in their own words.

Q3: Then encourage students to apply these skills to reading information in the article on 'Brain facts'. Remind students to read the questions first to know what they are looking for in a reading extract.

> **Give extra challenge** by giving students **worksheet 4.1**, which introduces some new facts about the brain. Students should add any new or unfamiliar terms to their personal notebook.

Developing the skills

Prepare students for the article on 'How your brain works with languages' by asking them which languages they speak. Celebrate the multilingualism of the classroom and encourage students to explain how and where they use their first languages to think and learn. Find out if any of the students are bilingual.

> **Give extra support** by introducing students to the words 'bilingual' and 'multilingual.' Split the word according to prefix and suffix, and explain how 'bi' and 'multi' work in this context (meaning 'two' and 'many'). You could bring in examples of similar words, such as 'mono' (meaning 'one', e.g. 'monotone') and 'tri' (meaning 'three', e.g. 'tricycle'). Also clarify the meaning of 'senile dementia'. You could mention Alzheimer's, which is a specific form of dementia, and talk about what this disease entails.
>
> **Give extra challenge** by asking students to write quickly about 'the languages I use to think in'. After reading the article, get students to return to their texts and add any new vocabulary items that might be relevant from those identified in the **Glossary**, e.g. 'intellectual', 'dementia', 'irrelevant', 'distracted'.

Q5: Get students to frame some questions of their own for this article. The questions must require reading for detail and focus on key words. Remind them of the key question words that they can use: What? Why? Who? When? How?, etc.

Going further

Remind students that looking for key words and important information in charts and diagrams is in fact more challenging than in straightforward texts because information is laid out in various chunks. Students would therefore need to look for the information in more than one place. Tell students that the exercises in **Q6** and **Q7** will allow them to test out Multiple Intelligences Theory for themselves.

Begin by asking students what their own language learning ambitions are. Ask them what prevents them from learning many more languages than they currently do. Brainstorm with students the main difficulties people around the world might have with learning a new language. This will lead nicely into **worksheet 4.2**. Analysing data in charts as in worksheet 4.2 is beyond the requirements of the syllabus for examination from 2024 but is useful for general English language practice.

> **Give extra challenge** by asking students to complete the sentences in **worksheet 4.2** (but not the final summary exercise for less confident students).
>
> **Give extra challenge** by asking students to summarise the information in the pie chart in a short paragraph. Encourage them to group the points. For example, some of the findings are to do with resources, while others are to do with the learners themselves.

Assessment for learning	Ask students to use the internet or magazines and find texts that include diagrams or charts. They should devise five questions on the graphic elements, exchange texts and questions with a partner and then mark one another's work and discuss the results.
Further challenge	Ask students to select texts that they find challenging, then repeat the activity above

Assessment objectives

W1 Communicate information, ideas and opinions
W2 Organise ideas into coherent text using a range of linking devices
W3 Use a range of appropriate grammatical structures and vocabulary

Writing skills in focus
- Use appropriate vocabulary effectively in writing to inform or explain
- Use a wide range of vocabulary for variety and clarity

Question types
- Writing an email
- Comprehension questions
- Writing a report

Differentiated learning outcomes

- All students should write to inform about or to explain a simple situation, using a limited range of simple vocabulary.
- Most students should write clearly to inform about or to explain a straightforward situation, using a suitable range of vocabulary.
- Some students should write effectively, to inform about, or to explain more complicated situations, using a range of subject-specific words.

Resources
- **Student's Book**: Section 4.2
- **Worksheet**: 4.3
- **Workbook**: Section 1.3; synonym section

Getting started

Q1: Begin by asking students to describe the sort of school they go to. There's no right or wrong answer to this so their descriptions may vary. For example: a secondary school, an international school, a school in the city, a day school, etc. Then ask them what they know of the history of the school. For example, when it was built, whether the number of students has increased since it was first opened, whether new parts have been added to the school over the years. If possible, get students to find photographs of their school in the past from either the school website or old year books.

Ask students how they think schools have changed over the past century. Focus on key descriptive vocabulary to describe education and buildings, e.g. desks in rows, traditional classroom, chalkboard/blackboard, metal desk, wooden floor/chair, clock tower, spiral stairway, arch, stone building, ceiling fan, inkwell.

Q2: Get students to name and identify features of an old-fashioned school in England from the photo provided. Students should talk in pairs about the prompts provided in the Student's Book.

Collate ideas and create a class word bank that can be easily displayed during all the sessions that make up this chapter topic.

Exploring the skills

Discuss the circular flow diagram which illustrates how to develop a vocabulary. Ask students to apply the diagram to a new word they have come across recently.

Q3: Ask students to work in groups and study the words in the box. Make sure they understand exactly what they mean; for example check that they understand the difference between a day school and a boarding school, and a term and a semester.

Q4: In preparation for the task of writing a welcome email, ask students to brainstorm terminology that is specific to your school and college and unfamiliar to newcomers. For example, 'USA' might mean 'Upper School Area' at your school; 'TCR' might mean 'The Common Room' (but it is only for senior students!). Get students to notice where words may be used differently in various countries, e.g. canteen/refectory/lunchroom/tuckshop/cafeteria. Refer to the bullet points provided in the Student's Book that suggest a structure for the email.

Developing the skills

Remind students that noticing and 'placing' new vocabulary items is a key skill to develop. Draw their attention to word and vocabulary clusters like those offered by the Visual Thesaurus.

Look up a trial version of a visual thesaurus. Ask students to type in the key word 'school' or 'education' to pull up clusters of related words.

Give extra support for **Q5** by asking students to predict the words they might encounter in a passage about ancient Egyptian schools. Clarify understanding of words such as 'papyrus', 'hieroglyphics', 'scribe', 'blacksmith', 'reed brush', 'rod'.

Give extra challenge for **Q5** by asking students to summarise the text on ancient Egyptian education for younger students at the school. All difficult words and new terminology must be explained in language appropriate for a younger audience.

Q7: Prepare students for the task of writing a magazine article on ancient schools and comparing them to present-day schools. Draw their attention to the format, readers and purpose of this text:

* format: magazine article
* readers: school community/local community
* purpose: to inform and explain with some comparison and contrast.

Students must make use of the prompts provided in the Student's Book to structure their article. Elicit class opinion on whether illustrations, photos or cartoons would be useful to illustrate the point. Focus on the use of accurate terminology around education, curriculum, discipline and so on. Remind students that difficult educational terms will have to be explained to a community audience of non-specialists.

Give extra support for **Q7** by handing out **worksheet 4.3**, which provides a writing frame with prompts for comparing and contrasting different types of schooling.

Going further

Q8: explain the importance of a varied vocabulary and how it's useful to learn synonyms to make texts more interesting.

Q9: In pairs, students discuss what changes they may have noticed in their own school over recent years. Prompt them to think about new ways technology has been used in the classroom and classes they may have had online. Ask them to think about ideas for schools in the future and what kind of a school they would like.

Ask students to feed back their ideas to the whole class for a wider discussion before the writing task of **Q10**. Students could take notes to help when writing their report.

Q10: Students write a short report about schools in the future, using ideas discussed in **Q9**. They should use vocabulary that they've learned during the lesson, including synonyms. Remind them they can use headings and subheadings to organise their points in the report.

Assessment for learning	Ask students, working as a class, to devise a list of subject-specific words relating to an appropriate topic with an educational focus, e.g. education in the past or in the future; technology in schools. In pairs, students should then test one another on the meanings of these words.
Further challenge	Ask students to take the list of subject-specific words and write a short piece (such as a short feature or article for the school prospectus) incorporating as many as possible. As teacher, you will need to feed back on how successful they have been.

4.3 How do we learn?

Getting started

Q1: Ask students to name the five senses. Ask them to think about these when describing their primary school. Discuss with students why using the senses is an effective way of describing memories or experiences.

Q2: Place students in pairs. Their task is to ask each other questions that will sharpen their writing and their memories. Encourage students to ask other questions as well as those in the Student's Book, for example:

* about your teacher – What kind of clothes did your teacher wear? Where was he/she from? Why was he/she your favourite teacher?
* about the school – What did the classroom smell like? What did the seats feel like?

Exploring the skills

Q3: Read the text describing the author's memory of their primary school teacher. Draw students' attention to underlined key words and which of the five senses these words reflect. Refer to the **Language booster** on nouns, verbs, adjectives and adverbs and get students to identify which parts of speech the key words represent.

Q4: Ask students to refer to their notes and plan a descriptive talk about their primary school/teacher using their initial thoughts and the best descriptive words they can think of. Students should then share this with their partners. Listeners judge how well these words create a 'word picture' or 'mental photo' of the teacher or the school.

Developing the skills

Remind students that in order to communicate well, their vocabulary needs to be very precise and descriptive. However, the vocabulary choices they make must depend on who their audience or listeners are.

Q5–6: Explain that **audio track 4.1**, which they are about to listen to, explains how the brain learns. Brainstorm the words and phrases that students predict will be part of the extract. Collect these on the board or flip chart. Go through the **Glossary** with the students to check their understanding of neurons, neural pathways, dehydrated and curious.

Students will hear/view the audio track twice. The first time they should listen for the overall gist and should only jot down key words.

Q7: Students discuss these questions in pairs. Make sure that they don't feel pressurised into sharing particular emotions if they don't want to.

> **Give extra support** by showing the **video clip** 'How the brain learns' (3:38 minutes) by searching 'How the brain learns eednycc' on YouTube. This contains lots of visual clues to words and phrases used in the audio track.
>
> **Give extra challenge** by asking students to complete **worksheet 4.4** in which they need to answer comprehension questions about the video clip.

Q8–9: In groups of three or four, students should now select those aspects of brain learning that they think are essential for younger students to know. Draw their attention to the key words that youngsters might find challenging and need to have explained. Once the content words are agreed, students work in pairs to construct their talk for younger students at their school. You could set up a real audience for this activity to maintain student motivation to do this well. Draw their attention to the **Top tip**, which encourages a combination of key information as well as advice.

> **Give extra support** by pairing reluctant speakers with more confident students. Get students to build on their prior learning by recounting when they last explained something to a youngster.
>
> **Give extra challenge** by asking students to vote for the talk that used the largest number of technical key words and explained them most effectively to younger students.

Going further

Q10: Audio track 4.2 encourages students to consider the level of formality of the speaker and to identify the target audience and purpose. Ask students to read through the questions before playing the track so that they know what they need to listen out for. After students have discussed the answers in pairs, go through the responses as a class.

- The speaker is most likely addressing older students. She mentions how useful Mind Maps are for written assignments. The language level and register of speech is not too formal but suggests an adult/teacher speaking to a group of students.
- It wouldn't be suitable for a younger audience because of some high-level vocabulary and concepts. A business presentation would be more formal.
- Example sentences/phrases that could be made less formal: 'When creating a Mind Map you need to consider a number of elements'; 'You can add pictures and images because these can often convey much more information than a written word and help to recall information'; 'if you are communicating with people from any other language group'.

Q11–12: Rather than have each pair prepare two separate talks, put students in two groups: A and B. Pairs of As prepare a short talk to *students* on 'How the brain learns', while the Bs prepare a talk aimed at *teachers*.

Q11 and **Q12** offer more sustained support for preparing talks on key learning areas for teachers and students. After listening to the talks, the Bs could comment on how well the As shaped their language for their target audience, while the As do the same for the talks given by the Bs.

Assessment for learning	Collect examples of where students are actively tailoring vocabulary and sentence structure to suit their audience. Relay these back to students asking them to point out where slang or casual language might be inappropriate. Ask students to suggest how slang might be formalised in context.

Further challenge	Students could be encouraged to give a talk about a specified topic to the teacher and class, making sure their information is highly accurate, using technical language. Give students a time limit within which to communicate all the important facts.

Chapter 4
Education

4.4 School and the real world

Assessment objectives

L1 Demonstrate understanding of specific information
L4 Demonstrate understanding of what is implied but not directly stated

Listening skills in focus
- Select details from different kinds of spoken texts
- Use clues before listening to help understand a text
- Understand what is implied but not actually stated in a conversation

Question types
- Informal conversations
- Short recordings
- Gap-fill

Differentiated learning outcomes

- All students should select a few required details from straightforward spoken texts, sometimes using pre-listening clues to help them. They understand simple spoken texts at a literal level.
- Most students should select some relevant details from a range of spoken texts, using pre-listening clues with some accuracy. They sometimes understand what is implied but not actually stated.
- Some students should select relevant details accurately from a wide range of spoken texts, including more complex ones, using pre-listening clues effectively. They can usually understand what is implied but not actually stated.

Resources
- **Student's Book**: Section 4.4
- **Audio tracks**: 4.3-4.4
- **Worksheet**: 4.5
- **Workbook**:
  Section 4.1
  Section 4.4

Getting started

Q1: Students should have prepared for this task as homework set at the end of the previous session. Ask students to share what they learned from speaking to their parents or another adult. Discuss the aspects of the school curriculum that students think are most transferable to the real world and which they feel are most practical for themselves and their future goals.

Q2: Students will need the outcomes of their homework task to create a table like the example in the Student's Book. Draw their attention to the difference between information/knowledge and a skill.

Exploring the skills

Ask students to think about a conversation they can only hear rather than also being able to see the speakers. This might be in the changing rooms, people talking in the corridor or parents discussing their children. Brainstorm with students how they know what is being talked about and who is saying what. What hints do they use as clues to piece together the conversation? Answers might include: voices, accent, attitude/tone (e.g. of irritation, interest, surprise, exclamation, admiration).

Ask students to give examples of words or phrases that might indicate admiration (e.g.'Fantastic!'), surprise/exclamation ('Really?'), irritation ('Not again!'), or admiration ('Wow!').

Direct students to the clues provided in the Student's Book: 'Who', 'Role', 'Context', 'Point of view or opinion'. Point out that the latter is the hardest to listen for as you have to 'read between the lines' or 'listen between the lines' for emotions or ideas that might not be directly stated.

Q3: Before playing **audio track 4.3** check awareness of Adora Svitak, a child prodigy. Ask: 'What is a prodigy'? (Answer: a person, particularly a very young person, who shows extraordinary talent or ability in one or several areas.) Play the track.

Give extra support by showing a video clip of Adora Svitak talking. You can find a good ten-minute talk by searching for 'Adora Svitak: What adults can learn from kids'.

Chapter 4
Education

Developing the skills

Q4: Remind students to focus on pre-listening skills. Ask them to prepare mentally for the ideas and language they might hear from a much older person called Alvin Toffler, author of *Future Shock*. Although he died in 2016, the discussion relates to comments he made when he was 70 years old. Toffler was deeply concerned about public education in the USA and spoke his mind. The students in the discussion in **audio track 4.4** reflect Toffler's use of terminology, e.g. 'the current school system is based on an old industrial revolution model'. Prepare students for the likelihood that they will not grasp every phrase on the first, or even second, hearing.

Ask students to review the questions before listening to the extract. Clarify the words in the **Glossary** as well as key ideas in the questions, such as: *public education, old factory/current school, new education system, 24-hour school*.

Play the track. Then ask students what they think Jeremy means by being a *night owl* and why this is used to describe someone who stays up late and is active at night.

Q5: Review the **Top tip** from the Student's Book on checking and clarifying questions to ensure understanding in a discussion.

> **Give extra support** by discussing aspects of education that resemble a factory: batches, students graduate by years and dates, fixed school timings, examinations to qualify, students of the same age schooled together, etc. Draw attention to where these are referred to in the text. For example, Toffler says the industrial model requires people to be on time as this affects the assembly line.
>
> **Give extra challenge** by asking students to summarise the ideas of Alvin Toffler and Adora Svitak in a short speech. What do the two have in common? (For example, they both feel education needs to be changed to meet 21st-century needs.)

Going further

Demonstrate to students what is meant by implied meaning ('reading between the lines') by using an example, such as when a friend asks you what you think of their terrible haircut. You say, 'Well, it's certainly different and you have definitely got everyone's attention!'

Q6: Tell students that they are going to hear **audio track 4.4** again, but this time they will be looking for examples of implied meaning. You may find it useful to do the first two questions as a class so that you can check that students have a clear understanding of what is required of them before they do the rest on their own.

Assessment for learning	For this task you will need to play the video clip of educationalist Sir Ken Robinson talking about creativity. Search 'Do schools kill creativity?' starting at 6.20 minutes.
	Ask students to pick out three examples of implied meaning. For each example, they should explain what the speaker really means in this context. One example is given in **worksheet 4.5** to start students off.
	Give extra support by suggesting places where there might be implied meaning, e.g.
	• Telling an imaginary story about an English teacher having Shakespeare in his class, saying '*... how annoying would that be...*'. This uses understatement as it would be very difficult for the teacher.
	• The teacher telling Shakespeare he must try harder. This uses irony as Shakespeare is probably the most famous playwright in the English-speaking world.
Further challenge	Encourage students to spot when and how the speakers in the audio tracks use irony and sarcasm and other types of humour to reveal their thoughts and opinions without being obvious or rude. Students could be encouraged to find and record internet audio files for this purpose, too, and then present them to the class with a brief oral explanation.

Resources needed for this chapter

- **Student's Book**: Chapter 5
- **Worksheets**: 5.1–5.6
- **Workbook**: see suggestions in 'Resources' panel of individual sections
- **Audio tracks**: 5.1–5.3
- **Video clips**: see suggestions in each section

The big picture

Introduce the theme of competition by asking students what competitions take place in school. This could be at a literal level, for example in schools that have a house system, with team points or sports days. There may be class prizes awarded at the end of the year. There may be competitions in sports and games, e.g. chess, badminton. There may be competition on a less explicit level – for example, there may be competition between students as to who gets the best grades or marks in an exam or who gets selected to represent the school in sports or other areas.

Ask for examples of competition outside school; alternatively, ask students if they can think of times when there is no competition.

Thinking big

Ask one or two students which competitions they would like to enter before the class attempts **Q1**. After completing **Q1**, ask students for their words or phrases associated with competition and start to create a class word bank on the board, e.g. *win/lose a competition, prize, pressure, performance, grade, mark.*

Q2: The emphasis here should be on lots of discussion. There is no correct answer – people enter competitions for all sorts of reasons, as the list shows.

Q3: Encourage students to come up with suggestions as to when competition can be unhealthy. This could include situations such as:

- when someone cheats in order to win in a competition
- when someone becomes so obsessed with winning they stop enjoying the activity concerned
- when someone's striving for success results in other people feeling ignored or put down
- when it affects someone's mental health
- when competition promotes individualism and stifles teamwork.

Writing a talent show review

Make sure students understand the basics of the task:

* _what_ – an article
* _who for_ – for the school magazine, which gets distributed, for example, to students, parents and teachers
* _what about_ – a school talent show _and_ the local TV channel that recorded the event.

Show students a few articles about rock/pop concerts (if possible) or any articles in newspapers. Ask them to identify common features in articles such as:

* headline (usually three or four words)
* subheadings
* photos and captions
* the byline (this is the name of the reporter/journalist)
* factual style (e.g. what happened, when, where, how, and so on, with opinion coming in the last paragraph).

Students should try to emulate the style of a magazine article.

This task is intended to be done by students working individually, although you may decide to bring in an element of group work, e.g. for **Q1**, the brainstorm could be done in small groups or pairs. Encourage students to use their imagination in this task – they can invent all kinds of likely and unlikely acts – within reason! They can also decide who wins and what happens on the night (**Q2**).

By now students should be proficient at distinguishing facts and opinions, but encourage them to check that they have both in their review (**Q4**).

For **Q6**, think carefully about how the competition will be judged, i.e. who will be involved in marking the reviews and how marks will be awarded.

Chapter 5
Competition

Assessment objectives

R1 Demonstrate understanding of specific factual information

R2 Demonstrate understanding of the connections between the ideas, opinions and attitudes

R3 Identify and select details for a specific purpose

Reading skills in focus

* Use text features to understand and pick out key points, facts and details
* Take notes on related details in a text

Question types

* Note-taking
* Finding information in headings, photos, fact boxes
* Identifying features of non-fiction texts

Differentiated learning outcomes

* All students should recognise some obvious text features, and then pick out a few of the required details from texts.
* Most students should use some text features to pick out many of the required relevant details from texts.
* Some students should use text features confidently to understand and select nearly all required important and related details in texts.

Resources

* **Student's Book**: Section 5.1
* **Workbook**:
  Section 1.1
  Section 1.3

Getting started

Q1: Focus on the photo showing two hippos fighting. Ask students what the hippos are competing for (e.g. to be the main or most important and powerful male and/or to make sure they have access to the most females for mating). Tell students that all animals (including humans) compete for *resources*. Resources are things you need to live but of which there may be a limited supply. The other photos show competition for food and competition for light.

Q2: Other resources that animals compete for are water, territory, shelter, attention from parents and even attention from humans. Nature is often portrayed as working on the principle of 'survival of the fittest'. However, nature permits coexistence – that is, species live side by side with other species, and each one feeds on a slightly different type of food and finds different kinds of shelter in slightly different places.

Exploring the skills

Ask or remind students of the purpose of headings, which were introduced in Chapter 2: headings are used to organise information and to give you an idea of what a paragraph contains. Ask students how the text features in the list are achieved:

* Photos and illustrations show you what something looks like.
* Fact boxes give summaries of basic information.

Explain to students that text features are used to make the text easier and quicker to read. Students need to scan a text to find all the features as this will help them find information fast.

Give extra support for **Q4** by ensuring that students understand that they need to identify the features, not the information.

Give extra support for **Q5** by giving a definition of 'apex predator': explain that 'apex' means the top or summit, such as the top of a mountain, and 'predator' is an animal that hunts and kills other animals for food. Therefore, an 'apex predator' is an animal that is so powerful/fast, etc., that there are no other animals that can kill it.

Q5: Brainstorm adjectives to describe a shark before attempting part **f)**.

> **Give extra challenge** by asking students to find out about the conservation status of sharks. (They are classified as endangered and numbers are 'decreasing very fast'. Overfishing and getting accidentally caught in fishing nets are the biggest threats to sharks.)

Developing the skills

To demonstrate the features listed in **Developing the skills**, bring into class several non-fiction titles and ask students to identify pages that use each feature and the purpose of each feature (see below):

- Captions explain what a photo shows.
- Bold or capital letters are often used to highlight important or key words in a text.
- Bulleted lists are used because they make the list easier to read.
- Maps give information about where places are, as well as features of locations, such as roads and railways, forests, rainfall, etc.
- Quotations show what people think about an idea.
- A navigation bar is found on websites (often along the top or down the side of the page) and works in a similar way to a table of contents.

> **Give extra challenge** by asking students to find other text features, such as an index, glossary, table of contents, footnote, and symbols such as flags or links to social media.
>
> **Give extra support** for **Q7** by eliciting answers from students and identifying what text features were used.
>
> **Give extra support** for **Q8** by encouraging students to consider the location of Iceland (where the expedition takes place), the 'expedition contribution' (or price) as well as their own interests (e.g. a passion for conservation) when answering the question.

Going further

Take the theme of competition further by referring students back to **Q5e)**. Then provide some information on sharks and killer whales. The biggest threat to both species is humans.

> **Give extra challenge** to **Q10** by asking students to compare a great white shark to a killer whale.

Assessment for learning	Ask students to go to the library or search on the internet to find a text which uses at least five text features. Students write down the title of the book or the webpage link, identify the text features and the purpose of each feature. The results can either be fed back to class or used as a written assessment.

Further challenge	Build on the previous task by asking students to give a presentation to the class to share their findings and discuss with one another and the teacher.

5.2 Competition in sport

Assessment objectives

W2 Organise ideas into coherent text using a range of linking devices

Writing skills in focus
* Use paragraphs correctly
* Link ideas to write a smooth-flowing paragraph
* Use a variety of connectives to join ideas within writing

Question types

* Summary writing
* Long writing questions
* Writing a short report

Differentiated learning outcomes

* All students should attempt to write in paragraphs, although there may be errors in punctuation, spelling and grammar even when using simple structures.
* Most students should organise ideas into paragraphs, attempting to link the ideas within them, although there may be some errors in punctuation, spelling and grammar when more complex structures are attempted.
* Some students should write well-constructed and coherent paragraphs, with very few errors in punctuation, spelling and grammar, even when using more complex structures.

Resources

* **Student's Book**: Section 5.2
* **Video clip**: see 'Getting started'
* **Worksheets**: 5.1–5.3
* **Workbook**:
  Section 2.2
  Section 3.3
  Section 3.5

Getting started

Q1: After pairs talk, get feedback from several students for each bullet. Ensure students explain their classifications (the way they have ordered their lists of sports). As students speak, start a word bank on the board with words associated with sport (the phrases will help and can be used for **Q3**). Include the following: *to be a swimmer, runner, gymnast, footballer, table-tennis player, to win/lose a competition, to play for the school team/a local club, to score a goal, to enter a tournament, to beat (another team), to play on a pitch, to kick a ball, to score a goal, to be a beginner/an expert at the sport.*

Q2: Ask students for the names of important sporting events while adding to your vocabulary list of words associated with the competition.

Video clip: for the spectacular lighting of the Olympic Games flame for the 2012 London Olympic Games, watch the Olympics YouTube video: 'Olympic Cauldron is lit for London 2012'. This video is 9:29 minutes long, so you may prefer to fast forward to around 5:00 for a shorter clip.

Q3: Encourage students to write complex sentences that are linked using connectives (e.g. *although, if, because, unless, until, after, before*) as this will be a theme of this section.

Exploring the skills

Ask how students know when a new paragraph begins. Remind them that the paragraph is often indented or there is one line space between one paragraph and the next. Then move on the conversation to the content of the paragraph. Ask students how many main ideas a paragraph contains (one). If possible, write the Haile Gebrselassie paragraph on the whiteboard and ask students to identify/underline the topic sentence and the supporting facts.

Q5: Get feedback from students asking for the topic sentence, main idea and supporting details for each paragraph.

Give extra challenge by asking students to complete **worksheet 5.1**.

Developing the skills

Q6: Write the sentences on the board and ask students to join them: 'Women's football is relatively new. A lot of people watched the 2019 Women's World Cup on TV.'

Encourage students to join them in several ways (see below) and identify the conjunctions/connectives. Tell students that conjunctions/connectives allow you to express the same information in many different ways with slightly different meanings. For example, the sentences joined by 'but' puts the emphasis on the newness of the women's game, whereas the sentences joined by 'despite' puts the emphasis on how many people watched the 2011 Cup.

* Although women's football is relatively new, a lot of people watched the 2019 Women's World Cup on TV.
* Women's football is relatively new, but a lot of people watched the 2019 Women's World Cup on TV.
* Despite how relatively new women's football is, a lot of people watched the 2019 Women's World Cup.

> **Give extra challenge** by asking students to add a last paragraph to the article 'The Highs and Lows of Women's Football' expressing their own opinion about the difference in what the women's and men's team earn. They could use any of the following ideas: suggesting why there is a difference, predicting whether it will change, their own ideas and reactions. Remind students to check their paragraphs for the features listed in **Exploring the Skills** on the previous page.

Q7: Encourage students to look at other pieces of writing to identify connectives.

> **Give extra support** by asking students to complete **worksheet 5.2** on connectives.
> **Give extra challenge** by asking students to write example sentences of their own using connectives.

Going further

Summarising a text is a useful skill for students to master, particularly when writing an essay. Remind students that if they go on to further education, they will need to be able to research, take notes and summarise texts. After reading the **Going further** text, ask students to give an oral summary of what happened last weekend. Remind them about logical order; for example, they should start with a topic sentence and should describe events in a logical order – starting with Friday evening or Saturday morning and working through to Sunday evening.

> **Give extra challenge** by asking students to think of different ways of ordering the information, rather than chronologically (i.e. by time). For example, they could order it by types of events, e.g. when they did school work, other work or leisure activities.

Q9: Ensure students know that this is a short report. That means that it should be only one paragraph and it should only contain the main idea(s). They should only include the most important details or facts, using a topic sentence and connectives to link their ideas. Students should use the summary-writing skills they have learned.

> **Give extra challenge** by asking students to expand their short report for **Q9** into an article describing a recent sports competition for the school magazine. See **worksheet 5.3** for extra support.

Assessment for learning	Ask students to re-read the text about the great white shark in 5.1. They should write a summary of the article using the notes they made in the table for **Q10** in 5.1.
Further challenge	Ask students, working in pairs, to check that their paragraphs include a *variety* of sentence structures and a *variety* of connectives.

Assessment objectives

S1   Communicate a range of ideas, facts and opinions

S3   Develop responses and maintain communication

Speaking skills in focus

- Build a conversation by asking and answering questions
- Be an active listener and add new ideas

Question types

- Asking and answering questions
- Active listening
- Rephrasing
- Turn taking

Differentiated learning outcomes

- All students should attempt to take part in conversations by offering short, straightforward responses to questions.
- Most students should take part in conversations, offering responses freely and sometimes asking questions themselves.
- Some students should sustain a conversation at some length, responding with confidence and sometimes adding new ideas.

Resources

- **Student's Book**: Section 5.3
- **Video clip**: see 'Getting started'
- **Worksheets**: 5.4, 5.5
- **Workbook**:
  Section 5.4
  Section 6

Getting started

Introduce the theme of the conversation and this section with Yehia Tang's YouTube video 'China's Got Talent 2011–2012 (The Phase III) Visual Arts', (4:05 minutes), which shows an unusual act from *China's Got Talent*.

Get feedback from students after discussing the questions in pairs. As they speak, create a word bank on the board with words and phrases associated with performing: e.g. *play an instrument, give a performance, play in a band/orchestra, perform in a dance group, go on stage, go for an audition, have a (dress) rehearsal, get stage fright, use a microphone, bow, the audience, the stage, backstage, clap, applause.*

> **Give extra challenge** by introducing one of skills in focus of this section (e.g. asking questions) by asking students to make up as many questions as they can think of about *China's/Vietnam's/Nigeria's/USA's/Arabs Got Talent.*

Exploring the skills

Emphasise that when engaging in a conversation, the people involved should try to contribute effectively to help move the conversation forward. Asking questions and expanding on answers are ways to do this. For example: 'Did you go away on holiday this year?' Model various answers:

- a short answer: *'Yes.'*
- a slightly longer answer: *'Yes, we went to visit my aunt, who lives on the coast.'*
- a full and expanded answer: *'Yes, we went to visit my aunt, who lives on the coast. While we were there, we went to…and we enjoyed playing…She has written that I should visit next year and I will definitely go because…What about you?'*

If needed, model this first in the students' mother tongue (if they share a common language) using an accessible topic.

Q2: The transcript is a conversation between friends and includes informal language and idioms: e.g. 'I'm addicted, 'got knocked out', 'anyway', 'wow', 'well', 'Not sure' ('I am' is omitted).

> **Give extra challenge** by asking students to underline words and phrases in the transcript that are idiomatic or informal.

Q5: Point out to students that although Bao dominates the second half of the conversation, it is Li who asks most of the questions, which largely determines the direction of the conversation. However, Bao also helps the conversation to develop by asking the question 'Who do you think is going to win?'

Developing the skills

Q8: Work towards this question by challenging students to have a conversation of two or three minutes for less confident students, or up to five minutes for more confident students, using some/one of the questions that they identified in **Q2–4**. They should also give an example, introducing it with one of the phrases listed in **Developing the skills**.

> **Give extra support** by asking students to do **worksheet 5.4**.

Going further

Q9: Model this first with a student. Ask them to ask you for your opinion on the latest film. They should ask an open question such as: 'What do you think about the latest film?'
Encourage students to *expand the conversation*, for example, say: 'Oh yes, the latest film is…and I went to see it with…at…last weekend. It was very scary, but it was too long and that made it boring – it lasted over three hours. That's too long!'

If students want to say they like a film, then they should say what part of it they liked – for example: 'The martial arts scenes were fast and exciting.' Go round listening to students to ensure they are introducing examples with the relevant phrases.

Q10: This is similar to **Q9** but this time with the focus on listening and responding. Again, model a conversation with another student, but this time you – the teacher – model the agreement and then rephrase the student's words. Be prepared to spend time on these tasks, as this is a challenging skill involving listening as well as the ability to produce synonyms. See **Workbook: Section 6** for more work on synonyms.

> **Give extra support** by asking students to do **worksheet 5.5**.

Q11: Remind students to use open questions like those they saw in **Exploring the skills** conversation, such as 'What do you think about…?', 'What happened?'.

Assessment for learning	Give students a new topic each, assigning one student the role of 'Speaker 1', and one the role of 'Speaker 2'. In pairs, they take part in the conversation and then feed back to one another on how well 'Speaker 2' and 'Speaker 1' did.

Further challenge	As above, but ask pairs to conduct their role-play in front of the class. The class can then feed back on the positive aspects of the conversation and make one suggestion for improvement. The teacher should use the opportunity to highlight what the students have done well.

Assessment objectives

L1 Demonstrate understanding of specific information
L2 Demonstrate understanding of speaker's ideas, opinions and attitudes
L3 Demonstrate understanding of the connections between ideas, opinions and attitudes

Listening skills in focus

*   Recognise and understand facts and opinions in short spoken and written texts
*   Recognise and understand facts and opinions in longer, more formal dialogues

Question types

*   Note-taking
*   Discerning between fact and opinion
*   Discussion

Differentiated learning outcomes

*   All students should be able to understand and select a few facts and a few simple opinions in shorter or more informal listening texts.
*   Most students should be able to understand and select much of the information required, and also recognise and understand straightforward opinions expressed in a range of listening texts.
*   Some students should be able to understand and select information precisely and also recognise and understand opinions expressed in a wide range of listening texts.

Resources

*   **Student's Book**: Section 5.4
*   **Audio tracks**: 5.1–5.3
*   **Video clip**: see 'Going further'
*   **Worksheet**: 5.6
*   **Workbook**:
    Section 4.3
    Section 4.4

Getting started

Q1–2: Show students logos of supermarket chains in your country. Ask students who they are, what they sell and what their relationship to each other is. Elicit from students that the companies are *in competition* with each other. Then ask who the market leader is (i.e. the company that sells more than most of its competitors). Make sure students understand that the market leader for trainers is unlikely to be the market leader for soft drinks.

Q3: Encourage discussion. In fact, all the scenarios show competition for your time and money, but in different ways. Get feedback from students on the different scenarios; encourage them to explain how each one shows competition. You can broaden the last two scenarios to discussions about needs (e.g. the need to earn money for food) and wants (the desire to relax). Some of the scenarios may not be relevant to your students so ask them to discuss those that are. **Q4**: Ask students to write their different definitions on the board.

Exploring the skills

Remind students about facts (see Chapter 2) – that they are things you can prove. Tell students that advertisements often include a lot of opinions rather than facts; they use opinions to make us want to buy a product. Write the example in **Exploring the skills** on the board and ask students to identify the facts and opinions. Ask them to identify the adjectives and then show them that adjectives often change facts to opinions. Tell them that words like 'great', 'best', 'wonderful', 'stunning', etc., are often used in advertisements to make us buy something and if we see these adjectives, they should act as a warning because they do not usually represent fact.

Q5: Encourage discussion. Go through each line of the advertisement with students asking them whether it is a fact or an opinion. Discuss why they think the phone is/is not free. Point out the asterisk (*), which tells you that you have to commit to a two-year contract and tell students that the small print/the text at the bottom is important.

Developing the skills

Introduce the listening text by asking students if they know what an influencer on social media does. According to collinsdictionary.com, an **influencer** is someone who is able to persuade a lot of other people, for example their followers on social media, to do, buy, or use the same things that they do. They are often paid or given free products in exchange for doing this. Explain to students that they are going to listen to an influencer talk about some products.

Ask students to read through **Q6** before you play the listening track. Then play **audio track 5.1** all the way through – this first time the students should only listen. Ask if there were any words they did not understand.

Then play the track again. Students should discuss answers to the questions. Then play the track again all the way through, asking students to check their answers.

Q7: Write the following sentences on the board: 'My phone is black.'/'My phone is beautiful.' Ask students to identify the fact and the opinion. Remind students of the difference between a fact (you can check it) and an opinion (you cannot prove that something is beautiful). Model sentence **a)** (using **audio track 5.1**) with one of your students and ask them to give the reason why it is a fact/opinion.

Students should write answers to **Q7** and check them with a partner. Get feedback, making sure students tell you the reason why they think each phrase is a fact or an opinion. Play the whole conversation again (using **audio track 5.1**) as a final reinforcement of vocabulary.

Going further

The listening text is based on: the c0y0tes YouTube video 'The evolution of mobile phones' (3:06 minutes). If possible, play the video clip before playing the listening text (**audio clip 5.2**) as the pictures may make some of the technical vocabulary easier to understand. This video was made in 2008 and things have moved on substantially since then; the listening text brings the history of the mobile phone up to date.

Q8: Get feedback after students have discussed the points. Ensure that students know that a 'history of…' is likely to contain more facts than opinions, as you are likely (but not always) to get a list of what happens when – things that can be proved.

Q9–13: This listening (**audio track 5.2**) has some technical vocabulary so start by helping students to complete **Q9** and then play the audio track allowing students to listen for the first time. Ask students if there are any words they still do not know or recognise. Ask students to answer the gist question ('What has happened to the popularity of mobile phones?'). Play the track again, this time asking students to copy and complete the table for **Q11**. Play **audio track 5.3**, asking students to copy and complete the table for **Q12**.

Q14–16: Encourage discussion. For example, **Q16**, what it says about society might be that advertisements make you feel like you always need 'the latest thing' when in fact you don't *need* it – you just *want* it!

> **Give extra support** by completing the rows of the tables in **Q11** and **Q12** together as a class. **Give extra challenge** by asking students to listen to the **Going Further** listening text (**audio track 5.2**) and put their hand up each time they hear an opinion.

Assessment for learning	Ask students to complete **worksheet 5.6**: Ask them to give/write three facts and three opinions about a product they know or have seen advertised.
Further challenge	Ask students to write the text for an advertisement for a household object. They should include three facts and three opinions. In pairs, discuss which statements are facts, and which are opinions.

Resources needed for this chapter

- **Student's Book**: Chapter 6
- **Worksheets**: 6.1–6.8
- **Workbook**: see suggestions in 'Resources' panel of individual sections
- **Audio tracks**: 6.1–6.8
- **Video clips**: see suggestions in sections 6.1, 6.3 and 6.4

The big picture

Many students will be at a stage in life when they are thinking carefully about the types of jobs they would like to do. Take advantage of their interest by encouraging them to find out further information about any jobs discussed in the chapter. Discuss and challenge stereotypes if they arise. For example, girls should be encouraged to enter the fields of science and engineering, e.g. becoming an oil technician, if that appeals to them; similarly, men should be encouraged to work in the caring professions, e.g. nursery teacher or nurse, if that is their ambition.

Introduce the overall theme by asking students what their job is. Ask several students what job they would like to do in the future using different key words and questions such as:

- What job do you do?
- What work would you like to do?
- What career are you thinking of? Teaching is a rewarding profession.

Write these key vocabulary items and questions on the board.

Thinking big

Q1–Q2. Before students look at the photos, ask them to brainstorm as a class all the jobs that they can think of and create a list on the board. Choose one of the jobs and ask students:

- what *skills* you need for that job (e.g. measuring skills)
- what *qualities* you need for the job (e.g. being accurate)
- *where* you do the job (indoors/outdoors)
- what the *rewards/drawbacks* of that job are.

Q3: All students should try to concentrate on giving reasons for their answer, for example: 'I prefer to work in a group'. Reason: 'I really enjoyed it when the class all went and helped at the community clean-up day.'

The ideal job

Q1–2: Remind students of the jobs they talked about in the *Big picture* and the language they've learned in sections 6.1–6.4 to help them talk about jobs. They can discuss their ideal job in pairs and then do some individual research to find out more about the job they're interested in. Once they've prepared a short fact sheet, they can share the main points in groups or to the whole class.

Q3: Look at the advertisement for the post of architect as a class. Break down the text into chunks, e.g. point out the text is not written in sentences – it is written in short phrases:

* 'young architect' – this phrase shows the company is looking for someone who has the qualifications but doesn't necessarily have a lot of experience
* 'busy city-centre company' – this phrase shows that the company is in the town and is busy/has a lot of work
* 'relevant degree and training' – this phrase shows that you must have gone to university to get a degree and also hold architectural qualifications.

Q4–Q5: Refer students to **worksheet 6.5** as a model application letter for both content and layout. They should start by writing notes in the form of bullet points, and then use their notes to write the full letter of application.

Q4–5: In pairs, students take it in turns to interview each other for the job: one takes the role of the interviewer, the other takes the role of the candidate. The interviewer should prepare by thinking of five questions to ask the candidate. Students then swap roles.

Assessment objectives

R2 Demonstrate understanding of the connections between ideas, opinions and attitudes

R3 Identify and select details for a specific purpose

Reading skills in focus

* Select facts from a range of texts which also contain personal opinions
* Recognise the language used to introduce facts and straightforward personal opinions

Question types

* Multiple matching
* Reading diagrams
* Note-taking

Differentiated learning outcomes

* All students should identify some simple facts and opinions in straightforward texts and show some awareness of the language used to introduce facts and opinions.
* Most students should identify and pick out facts and opinions in a range of texts; they should recognise and understand some of the language used to introduce facts and opinions.
* Some students should identify and pick out relevant facts and opinions in a wide range of texts; they should understand and respond to the language used to express facts and opinions.

Resources

* **Student's Book**: Section 6.1
* **Video clip**: see 'Further challenge'
* **Worksheets**: 6.1–6.3
* **Workbook**: Section 1.1; Section 6 Synonyms

Getting started

Before students do **Q1**, as a class brainstorm a list of skills on the board. Skills are often introduced with '–ing' words, e.g. communicating, being accurate, being good with numbers, drawing, mending, measuring, persuading, speaking, cooking.

Q1: When getting feedback from pairs, encourage them to use phrases such as 'I am good at…+ ing'. Concentrate on what they *can* do, not what they can't!

Exploring the skills

Q2: Introduce this section by writing the paragraph about Leila on the board. Remind students that a fact is something that you can prove to be true. Ask students to underline all the facts in the paragraph in blue and then circle all the opinions. Each time a fact/opinion is identified, ask the student how they knew it was a fact or opinion.

Q2: After students have read and matched each person to the correct work personality, get feedback from students. Help them to match the words or phrases that enable them to find their answers. For example, managerial work types are good at *organising* people and processes; Rashid is excellent at *organising* meetings and projects. Here, it is the word 'organising' that helps to match the person to the work personality.

Give extra support by breaking down the work personalities with students first to ensure they understand the vocabulary. Ask students to underline the important words, e.g. **Creative**: lots of <u>ideas</u>…<u>new</u> products.

Give extra support and challenge by asking students to complete **worksheet 6.1**. This worksheet should extend students' vocabulary of skills as well as giving extra support for **Q3**.

Developing the skills

Draw two people with speech bubbles on the board. In one write: 'For me, running my own business would be perfect.' And in the other bubble, write: 'In a survey, 600 girls said they wanted to run their own business.' Ask students which is the fact ('in a survey…') and which the opinion ('For me, running my…'). Underline the phrase 'For me' and explain it is a phrase used to introduce an opinion. Ask students to suggest other phrases used in the same way (e.g. 'In my opinion', 'I think').

Q4: Introduce the survey. Explain that it asks students for their views on work – whether they would like to work in an indoor or outdoor environment, whether they want to go straight into work or to college or university first, etc. Ask your students what they think the most popular responses might be. Ask students to identify only opinions. Get feedback. Each time ask them to write the phrase on the board that introduces the opinions. Afterwards, take time to reflect on the list created on the board. For example, you could reflect that opinions are often introduced with 'I' or use verbs such as 'like', 'want', 'feel', 'believe'.

Q5: Point out that information displayed in pie charts (with numbers, percentages, etc.) is likely to be factual.

Q7: Encourage discussion.

> **Give extra support** on identifying facts and opinions by asking students to complete **worksheet 6.2**.
>
> **Give extra challenge** by asking students to draw pie charts for your own class for questions 1, 3 and 4 of the survey.

Going further

Introduce the text by asking students what they want to do after leaving school. Elicit the three different options open to young people after leaving school as discussed in the first paragraph of the reading:

- going on to further education (training college or university)
- training for a specific job (on-the-job training or apprenticeship)
- starting work.

Tell students that sometimes opinions are not always introduced with 'I think' or 'I like'. Often these words are left unsaid. For example: '(I think) It's an excellent way to achieve your goals.'

> **Give extra challenge** by asking students if they agree with the opinions expressed in the reading text. For example, do they agree that you can only get the job you want with extra training and qualifications?

Assessment for learning	Ask students to work in pairs. They should each choose and research a job area and write a short paragraph about it with one fact and one opinion. They give their paragraph to their partner, who has to identify the fact and the opinion.

| Further challenge | Ask students to find an article from a newspaper or the internet where someone reviews their job, or search the YouTube video 'Event planning careers: creative jobs for organized people' (2:01 minutes), where a young person describes what is involved in the job of event management. Students should identify phrases where opinion is implicit – i.e. the opinion or attitude of the writer is implied without their actually stating it. |
| | **Give extra challenge** by asking students to complete **worksheet 6.3**. |

Chapter 6 Work

Assessment objectives

W4   Use appropriate register and style for the given purpose and audience

Writing skills in focus

* Use the appropriate tone and style when you are writing a letter or a magazine article

Question types

* Writing a letter
* Writing a magazine article

Differentiated learning outcomes

* All students should sometimes attempt an appropriate tone or style, with occasional awareness of the reader or purpose.
* Most students should attempt to use an appropriate tone and style according to reader and purpose.
* Some students should consistently use an appropriate tone and style, adapting them confidently for different readers and purposes.

Resources

* **Student's Book**: Section 6.2
* **Worksheets**: 6.4–6.6
* **Workbook**: Section 3.1; Section 6: Synonyms

Getting started

Before tackling **Q1**, ask students how they would usually tell friends about what they did at the weekend, if they could not see them. Their answers might include using social networking sites such as Facebook, WhatsApp, text, email or another method if those are not available. Then ask students to discuss the rest of the situations with a partner.

Q1: Get feedback to check answers. Note that sometimes more than one answer is possible and exact etiquette about written communication will differ from one country to another. For example, some organisations prefer job applications via email, while others prefer formal letters. However, the most important thing is to discuss the *tone* (attitude and formality) of each communication. Discuss why you shouldn't send job application letters via text (they are too long and complicated) or social network sites (they are too informal and you want to create a professional impression when applying for a job).

Exploring the skills

Q2: The letter shown is an example of how someone might write to a friend. Students should quickly work out that it is an informal letter – the fact that it is written on notepaper is a clue but they should also recognise the informal tone of the language. Ask students to underline the informal phrases, such as:

* contracted forms ('I've been')
* 'Hi' instead of 'Dear…'
* slang ('How are things?', 'What have you been up to?')
* idioms ('rushed off my feet', 'haven't looked back')
* exclamation marks ('rushed off my feet!')
* P.S. – this is usually only used in informal letters
* talking about family and friends – you usually only do this when you know the person well.

Q3: Note that the letter uses idioms, which often appear in informal English. Explain what is meant by an 'idiom': a group of words that have a different meaning when used together from the one they would have if you took the meaning of each word separately, used by first-language speakers. Idioms often make use of 'word pictures' – for example, 'every cloud has a silver lining' means 'every bad event usually has a positive side to it'. So the phrase has another meaning – it is not a literal description of a real cloud.

Encourage students to write down idioms when they read or hear them.

Developing the skills

Tell students that in English there is usually both a polite or formal as well as an informal way of saying the same thing. Demonstrate this by writing two different ways of ending a letter on the board, e.g.

* 'Can't wait to hear from you!'
* 'I look forward to your prompt response.'

Q4–Q5: Stress that a job application letter is a particular type of formal letter. Show or write the example letter from Lissa on the board and discuss with students why the tone would be unsuitable for that purpose. Then show the example letter from Mia and discuss the differences. Elicit from students that Mia's letter is more formal than Lissa's and is therefore more suitable for an application letter.

Make sure students identify the informal tone of Lissa's letter. Also discuss the content of the letter. For example:

* Is telling the store manager that you have got 'loads of friends' who would come to the store relevant? (No – applicants should highlight their own qualities/skills.)
* Do they think it is a persuasive thing to write? (No – the store manager may not want to encourage lots of young people into the shop.)
* What should the person write about instead? (Their work experience, skills, etc.)

Get feedback, giving time for discussion of formal vocabulary (e.g. 'Dear…', 'position', 'candidate'), content (e.g. Mia states her previous experience), clear structure, accurate punctuation and formal letter layout. All of this gives the overall impression of a *formal and professional* tone.

Give extra support for Q7 by asking students to complete worksheet 6.5 or use the letter of application in Q6 as a model for their writing.

Going further

Q9: Introduce this exercise by discussing the audience and tone with students:

* who is going to read the text: parents and students – tone likely to be formal
* what it is: an account of your experiences – attitude likely to be personal
* who it is for: the school magazine – tone likely to be formal.

Discuss with students if readers of the school magazine are likely to know anything about work placement schemes. Discuss with students how specific and detailed information makes the account more interesting (eg. 'a three-week placement', 'local hospital'). Discuss the use of the question at the beginning of introduction C: it introduces the theme; it draws the reader in; it doesn't assume prior knowledge.

Give extra challenge by asking if students can think of a more formal way of saying 'that's it for now...' and 'I'd give it 10 out of 10'.

Give extra support for Q10 by asking students to complete worksheet 6.6 to help them plan their magazine article.

Assessment for learning	Ask students to write a letter of application for a work placement scheme, e.g. with a local radio station. They should then also write a blog or diary entry about their first day at work at this place. They should aim to show the different levels of formality suitable for the different pieces of writing.
Further challenge	In the less formal task, students should aim to incorporate a few idioms appropriate to the reader and purpose of the writing.

Chapter 6
Work

6.3 Job interviews

Assessment objectives

S3 Develop responses and maintain communication
S4 Demonstrate control of pronunciation and intonation

Speaking skills in focus

* Pronounce words and speak clearly to be understood in a conversation
* Speak up confidently and clearly

Question types

* Role-play
* Asking and answering questions
* Discussing in pairs
* Recording and analysing

Differentiated learning outcomes

* All students should communicate straightforward ideas with some errors in pronunciation and intonation.
* Most students should communicate ideas clearly using pronunciation and intonation that are generally clear.
* Some students should communicate complex ideas confidently and fluently using pronunciation and intonation to help make ideas clear.

Resources

* **Student's Book**: Section 6.2
* **Audio tracks**: 6.1–6.4
* **Worksheet**: 6.7
* **Video clip**: see 'Developing the skills'
* **Workbook**: Section 5.2

Getting started

Q1: Encourage students to give reasons why an interview makes people nervous or why it is pressurising. Responses might include:

* It is important to give a good impression.
* It is a competitive situation as other people are applying for the same post.
* You really want the job, especially if it is a highly desirable job.

Tell students that the interview is also a chance for the candidate to find out if they want the job and they can usually ask questions – usually at the end of the interview.

Exploring the skills

Q2–4: Brainstorm with the class the reasons why it can be hard to understand what others are saying – whether it is in a first or second language. Discuss the issues raised by the problems in **audio track 6.1**. For example, there may be external issues – background noise, distractions, poor phone lines, etc. – but it is important, wherever you are, to be able to communicate ideas clearly to one another. This is not just down to knowing the words to use; you also have to speak up clearly and as confidently as possible. You also have to make sure you say the words clearly, especially when there may be other words that sound similar. **Q5**: Discuss occasions when mishearing can cause problems. Encourage students to provide examples from their own experience.

Q6–Q8: Students make notes and then work in pairs to give information, each student giving feedback on how easy it was to understand what they said.

Give extra challenge by asking pairs of students to practise telling a joke to their partner. If their partner laughs, groans, etc., then they have told the joke clearly.

Give extra challenge by asking students to work in pairs and role-play a telephone conversation. Student A pretends that their brother or sister is very sick. Student B is the doctor. Ask what temperature the sick person has and for other symptoms. Ask where they live so you can come and see the patient. Can pairs understand each other, including numbers?

Developing the skills

Video clip: Watch atlanticcanuck's amusing YouTube video 'Job interviews: good and bad' (7:10 minutes) about how not to behave in a job interview.

Chapter 6
Work

Q9a): Encourage students to talk about different feelings, not only negative (e.g. nervous, anxious, worried, pressurised, flustered, frustrated) but also positive (e.g. excited at the opportunity, keen to impress). Write the words on the board.

b) Students can prepare well by practising and rehearsing answers to likely questions such as 'Why are you interested in this job?' and 'What can you bring to this job?' They can also prepare well by:

* researching the company – finding out what they do and who their customers are
* arriving in good time
* dressing smartly and planning ahead what they will wear
* using relaxation techniques, such as deep breathing.

Q10–11: Stress that even if you are nervous, or shy (usually), you can do a lot to overcome this by planning, practising and also by using relaxation techniques.

Q13–14: Ask pairs to put the answers in order – good, okay, poor – and then give feedback. Ask for reasons why an answer is good, okay or poor.

* Good/better – for example, 'I've got a lot of relevant experience' is a good start, but then going on to say 'I've worked in an office for six months' is a positive answer and gives a concrete example.
* Okay – for example, 'I'm good at most things' is a positive answer, but being good at *most* things is very vague; you need to specify *what* you are good at.
* Poor– for example, 'I don't know really but it sounds fun' shows that you have not thought about the job and what it involves, nor why you could be good at it; 'sounds fun' implies that you are not serious about the job.

> **Give extra challenge** by asking students to improve the answers given to **Q13**, including the better answers. They can usually do this by giving concrete examples.

Q15: Discuss with students why they think the person will get the job, e.g. by speaking clearly, having a positive attitude, giving well thought-out answers to standard questions such as 'What skills do you have?' using formal language (e.g. 'achieve').

Q16 and **Top tip:** Discuss with students why adding an example makes a good answer a better answer – it gives the person listening a concrete example and reassures them that you are not making up skills you don't really have.

Going further

Q17–19: After recording and listening to the role-plays, ask all pairs to perform their role-plays, preferably in front of the class. Ask them to concentrate on speaking clearly so you can hear and understand them. Tell them you will mark them on their:

* clarity – how easily they/you can understand what their partner says
* expressiveness – how well they each express their feelings and attitudes.

> **Give extra support** by asking students to do task 1 on **worksheet 6.7**.
> **Give extra challenge** by asking students to do task 2 on **worksheet 6.7**.

Assessment for learning	For peer formative assessment, ask students to read aloud a short passage taken from a book. Students assess one another's readings, giving a mark out of five for clarity and a mark out of five for expressiveness.
Further challenge	Students practise reading a piece of writing of their own choice, perhaps from a novel, but remind students they should be using tone and expression to show subtle shades of meaning in their reading.

6.4   Unusual jobs

Assessment objectives

L1   Demonstrate understanding of specific information

L2   Demonstrate understanding of speakers' ideas, opinions and attitudes

Listening skills in focus

* Predict to help you understand and select details
* Select details to make notes or fill in forms when listening to texts

Question types

* Informal conversations
* Gap-fill
* Multiple matching

Differentiated learning outcomes

* All students pick out some simple details and attempt to complete notes or forms, sometimes using prediction to help.
* Most students select some relevant details and complete notes or forms, using prediction to help.
* Some students select nearly all required relevant details to complete forms, or to write notes, using prediction to help.

Resources

* **Student's Book**: Section 6.4
* **Audio tracks**: 6.5–6.8
* **Video clip**: see 'Assessment for learning'
* **Worksheet**: 6.8
* **Workbook**: Section 4.2*; Section 6: Synonyms

The audio for Workbook Section 4.2 contains some more complex vocabulary such as 'monstrosity', 'blob' and 'carving'. Please support students by pre-teaching this vocabulary before they listen to the recording.

Getting started

Q1: Challenge students to think of the *most* unusual jobs they can, e.g. chocolate engineer, horse whisperer, feng shui consultant. The photos show two reasonably common jobs – building work and office work alongside more unusual jobs in stunt performing and marine biology.

Exploring the skills

Q2: Write the following sentence from the dialogue on the board: 'my job is to put tags on them to <u>see how they behave, how often they feed, and where they go</u> – that sort of thing.' Ask students to think about what type of skill you need to see how something behaves – you can refer them back to **worksheet 6.1** with the list of skills. Prompt students to answer 'watching', 'observing', 'recording', etc.

Q3: Ask questions to encourage students to predict the vocabulary they are likely to hear in the listening passage. For example, ask students if they can think of a question they would like to ask the shark personality profiler. Remind students of usual questions asked in interviews, as well as thinking about where she works, e.g. she works in water with sharks so maybe she swims and need to wear a protective wetsuit. How does she feel about her work, e.g. maybe she is scared. Then ask students why it is useful to be able to predict. Prompt students to say that predicting helps you to think about the vocabulary that you might hear – it prepares you for the subject or theme of the conversation.

Q3–4: Play **audio track 6.5** pausing after each of Mandy's responses for 2–3 minutes – this gives students time to compare notes and check if what they predicted is what is discussed in the interview. Get feedback from students identifying those words and questions they predicted that do appear in the interview – this should help them to see the power of predicting. Play the track again and ask students to answer the specific questions in **Q5**.

Give extra support by reminding students of the questions they listened to and used in the speaking section of this chapter.

Developing the skills

Q6: Get students to describe what they see in each photo. Play **audio track 6.6**.

Q7: Model/write one form on the board. Go through each line. Ask students what type of information or words/numbers they expect to hear for each line of the form. For example, you would expect a number of years and/or months in answer to the question 'How long...'; you would expect the answer 'indoors/outdoors' to the starting question 'Where...' and so on.

Q8: Play the audio track again. Pause for 30 seconds while students check their answers. Then play the track again all the way through. Then get feedback from students. Make sure their answers are short and the exact details that are required on the form. Students should not give extra information or include sentences that are unnecessary.

Q9: Encourage discussion. These are very unusual jobs and should stimulate plenty of discussion. Encourage students to give their own views and opinions.

Give extra challenge by asking students to research an unusual job and write a short paragraph pretending to be someone who does that job. They must include all the information needed to complete one of the forms in **Q7**. They should then read aloud their description of their unusual job to their partner. Their partner listens carefully to their job and completes the form.

Q10–12: Students complete these tasks to prepare for the audio and check their understanding of vocabulary related to the topic.

Q13: Give students time to read the questions first; then play **audio track 6.7**. Play the track again, pausing between the paragraphs to allow students to write notes for their answers to **Q14**. Play the track again and then check the answers with students.

Going further

Q16: Write two or three of the questions on the board. Give pairs time to read and discuss the questions. Get feedback, asking students to predict the *type* of information they can expect to give for each question. For example, an answer to question **a)** could be the name of a place/town or the type of a place (e.g. in an office). Question **b)** implies that Edith did a different job before. Maybe the answer to question **g)** will be types of skill (see the list of skills in **worksheet 6.1**) or an attitude or personal quality (e.g. strong, focused, determined), or maybe it is a thing. The words 'voluntary work' and 'conservation project' might give you hints about the work she does now.

Q18-Q19: Play **audio track 6.8** without stopping. Then play it again pausing after paragraphs to allow students time to write their answers. Afterwards, give students one minute to check the answers. Get feedback from students.

Language booster: This is useful and necessary vocabulary for all jobs. Get feedback from students, asking for examples of the different types of work listed. Ask students to use each word in a sentence of their own. Tell students to add this vocabulary to their personal notebooks or journals.

Assessment for learning	**Video clip:** Visit the Careers Out There website and search for their video 'Becoming a biomedical engineer' (3:08 minutes). The language in the video clip is challenging, and so is the task in **worksheet 6.8**. They are suitable only with a strong group; they might be demotivating for less confident students. Prepare students by downloading the interactive transcript and discussing difficult vocabulary with them first. Then remove the transcript so students can concentrate on listening. Ask students to complete **worksheet 6.8**.
Further challenge	Select another video from the Careers Out There website and prepare a worksheet similar to **worksheets 6.3** and **6.8**. Play the recording twice with time for pre-reading (using the interactive transcript) and predicting. Pause in between playings to give students time to write and check answers. Pause also after the second playing to check answers.

Resources needed for this chapter

- **Student's Book**: Chapter 7
- **Worksheets**: 7.1–7.4
- **Workbook**: see suggestions in 'The Resources' panel of individual sections
- **Audio tracks**: 7.1–7.4
- **Video clips**: see suggestions in sections 7.1, 7.3 and 7.4 and 'The big task'

The big picture

Brainstorm with students the top environmental issues facing your town, your country, the wider region (e.g. Asia Pacific, the Middle East, the South China Sea) and the world. Take notes on a flip chart or display board that could remain in use for the duration of this topic and beyond. Explain that this area is a 'joint issues' board for all students to contribute to.

Get students to articulate as best they can what the wider issues are. These could include waste disposal, non-renewable energy, water, soil or air pollution, nuclear waste, food contamination and so on. Approach this topic with sensitivity and care as it is a topic that many young people feel very passionately about. Some feel angry/hopeless because we have not yet made significant changes to our lifestyle.

Once you have collected some thoughts, introduce Carl Sagan. Tell students they don't need to understand every single word, but instead need to understand the thoughts.

> **Carl Sagan** (1934–96) was a famous American astronomer, astrophysicist and cosmologist. He was born to Ukranian immigrant parents and grew up in a modest Brooklyn neighbourhood. Sagan's inquisitiveness and passion for the stars led him to degrees and doctorates in astrophysics from the University of Chicago, UC Berkeley, Cornell University and Harvard. Carl Sagan cared deeply about our place in the universe and famously made a short film called *The Pale Blue Dot*, a phrase he uses to describe the fragility and wonder of our planet Earth.

Thinking big

Working clockwise, the photos on these pages illustrate the following:

- the Earth seen from space – Carl Sagan's 'pale blue dot'
- deforestation of the rainforest in Borneo, Malaysia, to make way for planting palm oil (linked to destruction of habitat for wildlife)
- gridlock at rush hour, exhaust fumes being emitted from cars contributing to air pollution
- a mountain gorilla, an endangered species from the Virunga mountains, Rwanda
- a hummingbird feeding from a beautiful tropical flower in Costa Rica (Costa Rica is often held up as an environmental model that the rest of the world can learn from as it reversed deforestation that took place in the 1970s and 80s)
- flooding in Ukraine, possibly due to climate change.

Q1: Allow students to look at the photographs carefully. Check whether students can describe the picture or identify the key environmental issue(s) they represent. Students should then prioritise the pictures as suggested in the Student's Book.

Q2: Encourage students, working in pairs, to justify their choice and order of images and compare their most important to least important issues. Encourage students to explain their choices with at least **one** key justification.

Q3: Regroup as a class and count up most important votes to least important votes to nominate the top three issues for this class.

<table>
<tr><td>

The big task

</td><td>

Saving the planet: giving a multimedia presentation

</td></tr>
</table>

Resources

Students should do the *big task* once they have completed all four sections of the chapter.

* **Video clip**: see below

This is an additional clip to get students thinking about all the environmental and wildlife issues they have encountered so far. It also combines the skills of reading, writing, speaking and listening. Issues are well summarised in this clip. The young Severn Suzuki makes a passionate plea to adults worldwide to solve environmental issues urgently. Students might have watched this video if they did the 'Further challenge' task in Section 7.4. **Video clip:** be2212's YouTube video 'The best speech: Severn Suzuki' (6:49 mins).

Q1: The video clip should set the scene nicely to introduce **The big task** to students. Explain that they will be planning and giving a multimedia presentation of the most urgent environmental or wildlife concerns in their city or region. Offer students a wide choice in this section and encourage them to work in interest groups.

Explain that a multimedia presentation entails a mixture of reading, viewing, listening and presentations. Skits or a short play could also be part of the presentation.

Encourage students to include visuals to grab attention, but point out that they should be prepared to explain the science and the geography behind these. They could, for example, include real photographs or objects to make their point – for example, shells corroded by acid rain, photos of dead birds or marine life tangled in nets.

Ask students to consider interviewing local experts, activists or other teachers and classmates on their opinions regarding the chosen issue.

Q2: Suggestion for students: the guests for multimedia presentation could be junior students at your school or primary students from a school nearby. Talk students through areas that must be covered according to the list of bullet points provided in the Student's Book and encourage them to add their own ideas to these.

The presentation could include, for instance:

* accurate facts, statistics and graphs to back up concerns about the issue chosen. Students could research how their local government or community keeps environmental data (e.g. agriculture and fisheries, environmental protection), or they could contact local environmental groups or the local newspaper office
* relating the global issues to local issues, saying what is happening locally
* suggesting actions students can take as individuals or as a school to help tackle the issue locally
* inviting suggestions from the audience to act on local issues while thinking globally.

Checklist for success

Stress the importance of using all the skills covered in this chapter:

* *reading* graphs, statistics, diagrams and other visual information aids; explain that they appear frequently in newspapers and magazines and are widely used in school subjects, such as geography. In the world of work and further study, they are often used in presentations; pie charts are a useful way to summarise information about two or more groups
* *writing* effectively using key facts and details and appealing to the readers' senses
* *speaking* about ideas to others and responding to their questions and concerns
* *listening* to experts and activists and understanding the big ideas that they are communicating.

Chapter 7
Environment and wildlife

7.1 Our carbon footprint

Assessment objectives

R1   Demonstrate understanding of specific factual information

R2   Demonstrate understanding of the connections between ideas, opinions and attitudes

R4   Demonstrate understanding of implied meaning

Reading skills in focus

* Find and select facts and details in factual information
* Understand what is implied but not directly stated in a text

Question types

* Text reading
* Reading factual information
* Note-taking

Differentiated learning outcomes

* All students should show a basic understanding of factual informational texts, and use them to find a little of the information they need. They should understand literal, straightforward texts.

* Most students should show some understanding of factual informational texts and use them to find some of the information they need. With some guidance, they should understand some of what is implied but not directly stated.

* Some students should show a confident understanding of factual informational texts, and use them successfully to find information. They should confidently and securely understand what is implied but not directly stated.

Resources

* **Student's Book**: Section 7.1
* **Video clip**: see 'Getting started'
* **Workbook**: Section 1.1

Getting started

Please note: The information on pie charts and bar charts in this chapter is beyond the requirements of the syllabus for examination from 2024 but is useful for general English language practice.

Q1: You could start by watching a cartoon about global warming – there are plenty available on YouTube (search for 'Global warming cartoon'). The first time, students should just watch and listen. The second time, get students to jot down words or phrases that describe the key environmental issues shown in the cartoon. This should provide an accessible way of getting into the topic of our carbon footprint. Regroup as a class and feed back on the names of issues that have been shown. This should link to the prompts in **Q1**.

Exploring the skills

Q1-3: Brainstorm with students where they might read factual informational texts. Bring in a local newspaper, PTA magazine, school population report or government publication that includes factual information.

Understanding factual informational texts is a useful life skill. They appear frequently in newspapers and magazines and are a common feature in school subjects such as geography and in the world of work and further study. They sometimes includes charts or digrams. Explain to students that pie charts are a useful way to summarise certain kinds of information, and bar charts are useful when comparing information about two or more groups. Emphasise that pie charts show percentages or proportions, so to create a pie chart you first have to work out the correct percentage for each category being displayed.

Students read about a typical person's carbon footprint and discuss the questions.

Q4: Refer students to *The Greenhouse Effect* text and the related questions. Ask the following warm-up questions to check prior understanding:

- Where does Earth get its heat and energy from?
- What happens to the heat of the sun once it hits Earth?
- Why are cloudy days sometimes warmer than sunny days?

Refer to the **Top tip** and the importance of mentioning units or percentages.

Developing the skills

Explain that some informational texts include bar charts. Examine examples of simple bar charts from real information around you at school. Encourage them to follow the steps , looking at the title, information on the x axis and y axis, the key or legend, units and gradations on both axes.

Now refer students to the bar chart showing carbon emissions by country in 2010 and 2013.

Q5: After students have examined this chart carefully, ask them to read the information about reading texts online. Once this is done, students do some online research and answer the questions..

> **Give extra support** by drawing attention to the **Did you remember to …?** box.
>
> **Give extra challenge** by asking students to identify trends in bar charts, e.g. 'GHG emissions rose substantially between 2010 and 2013 in rapidly developing economies such as China and India, but in already developed countries …'.
>
> **Give extra challenge** by asking students to compare countries.

Going further

Explain to students that writers give us many clues about their attitudes, thoughts and actions through their language. Good readers are able to 'read between the lines' and spot these easily. This is called understanding what is implied but not directly stated.

Together, read the text, *A Waste of My Time?*, which outlines a journalist's dilemma with regard to recycling newspapers. During the second reading, ask students to spot words and phrases that convey inner thoughts, attitudes and actions.

Q6–7: Ask students to justify their choices. For example, they could contrast the changes in attitude/actions from, 'I shrugged my shoulders…' to 'I sighed. I was responsible…' Ask students to name these thoughts, attitudes and feelings, e.g. laziness, feeling helpless, awareness, guilt, shame. Some of these are difficult concepts and high-level vocabulary so support students as necessary.

Now ask students to examine the pie chart included as part of the article. Why do they think this chart grabbed the journalist's attention? What would have happened if there had been only text on the page?

End the session by discussing the key question: 'So what are the benefits and effects of using pie charts and bar graphs in complex pieces of text?'

Assessment for learning	Ask students to write their own 'Green guilt' diary entry of about 150 words. This could be about a time when they couldn't be bothered to recycle; or when they dropped rubbish/trash into the school bin without separating it; or when they printed something unnecessarily and wasted lots of paper; or an idea of their own. Remind them to make use of the vocabulary learned in this section.
	Assess their writing for range of vocabulary or other qualities.

Further challenge	In their 'Green guilt' entries, students should be urged to use a range of language that uses implied meaning to express their inner thoughts, attitudes and actions.
	Alternatively, ask students to write about their own 'Green discovery' experience mimicking that of the journalist

Water – the most precious resource

Assessment objectives

W1 Communicate information, ideas and opinions

W3 Use a range of appropriate grammatical structures and vocabulary

Writing skills in focus

* Use details to develop ideas when writing descriptions
* Make descriptive writing convincing using the five senses

Question types

* Long writing questions
* Descriptive text
* 'Zooming in' technique

Differentiated learning outcomes

* All students should attempt to develop descriptions with one or two details, including references to the senses.
* Most students should develop descriptions satisfactorily, using details and some reference to sense impressions.
* Some students should develop their descriptions well, incorporating relevant details and some sense impressions appropriately.

Resources

* **Student's Book**: Section 7.2
* **Workbook**:
  Section 2.3
  Section 3.6

Getting started

Remind students that poets and writers of fiction have always relied on descriptions using all five senses to make their writing come alive. The environment and wildlife can be looked at through a factual, non-fictional lens or through a deeply emotional lens. Mike Gould does this through his short poem. Read the poem and ask students to suggest which environmental issue Gould is concerned about and what leads them to this conclusion.

Build students' knowledge by asking what concerns they themselves might have about fresh water and its importance to human survival in their part of the world. Brainstorm any issues around water that are specific to their region/town/country. Display through the word bank any interesting issues or vocabulary that might build the topic of water and its conservation.

Q1: Read the poem together and ask students to point out where Gould uses the five senses to make the poem more vivid. Focus on phrases like 'liquid silver', 'sultan's jewels', 'king's palaces' and 'treading dust.' Ask students to describe further the images that these words evoke. Some of the language in the poem is high level, such as 'dazzling' (a synonym of 'brilliant'), 'sultan' (a ruler in some Muslim countries) and 'tread' (set one's foot on something, or walk through) so students may need support.

Exploring the skills

Remind students that although we cannot always use literature or poetry to make our point, it is very effective to use the following:

personal experience, examples, facts and images.

Direct students to the annotated text on our problems with water. Recap the effectiveness of using the five senses for description and the importance of adjectives and adverbs in adding detail to a description.

Q2: Introduce the idea of a topic sentence in any paragraph. It is the main sentence that tells you what the rest of the paragraph will be about. (Students have learned about topic sentences in earlier chapters.) Talk students through the sentence in the Student's Book, building it slowly with factual detail and vivid imagery or descriptive words.

Developing the skills

Go through the sample paragraph on a childhood swimming lesson. Remind students that good descriptions must 'show' rather than 'tell' what is happening. The best way to do this is by including five-sense descriptions and accurate vocabulary.

Q3: The table in the Student's Book gives a good framework for including ideas about all the senses. Encourage students to include two ideas for each of the senses. Then ask students to share these in pairs and give each other suggestions that allow the reader to experience the situation in a vivid way.

Q4: Students rewrite the text of the boy's first swimming lesson in their own words.

Q5: Preparation: Ask students to imagine a world where water is so scarce that swimming pools would be an unimaginable luxury. Ask students to brainstorm some of the problems we would have as water ran out.

Now go through the annotated example in the Student's Book and draw students' attention to facts, examples, vivid imagery and powerful verbs that work well in this description from 2065.

> **Give extra support** by writing your own account of your first swimming lesson and annotating it for students.
>
> **Give extra challenge** by asking students to add details of people involved in the swimming lesson, for example 'the fierce, red-eyed, hairy swimming coach' or 'the strange little boy who cried all the time'.
>
> Ask students to write a short description of their own 2065 scenario using the five senses.

Going further

Q6: This activity asks students to notice the technique of 'zooming' in from the general to the specific or close-up looking at details and the five senses.

Q7: Students imagine they are the writer in **Q5** and they have stepped out of their home and they describe how the shortage of fresh water has affected the village in 2065. Students can include sense impressions here, using the five senses and noun phrases, e.g. 'the *dry grass* at the edge of the highway…', 'the *muddy lake* is now too shallow for fish and remains unusable', 'the *machine-gun sound* of rain on the *tin roof* is too rare these days…'

Q8: Prepare students for a more objective, modern piece of writing, i.e. a newspaper article. This uses factual detail and description. Remind students to have one clear topic sentence per paragraph and to use the rest of the paragraph to support, supplement or back it up with details, such as facts or examples.

Make sure that students jot their growing vocabulary on water and water shortages in their personal notebook or journal. This may range from literary to factual. Encourage the use of real data where available.

Assessment for learning	Pair up students to peer-mark **Q7** and identify where their partners have used sense impressions. Ask students to provide a mark or a smiley face for each well used detail. If appropriate, more confident students could be paired with those needing more guidance and support.
Further challenge	Ask students to write a 200-word description on a set topic: 'My favourite room'. Encourage them to spend five minutes thinking and planning. Pair up students to peer-mark their descriptions and note where they have alternated effectively between sense impressions and facts, showing independence of thought and use of idiom.

Assessment objectives

S1 Communicate a range of ideas, facts and opinions
S2 Demonstrate control of a range of vocabulary and grammatical structures

Speaking skills in focus

* Express ideas clearly using the correct verb tenses
* Respond clearly, accurately and effectively to others, in conversation
* Communicate ideas clearly and confidently in a more formal talk

Question types

* Discussing in pairs and groups
* Preparing a more formal talk
* Giving a more formal talk

Differentiated learning outcomes

* All students should express a few straightforward ideas using very simple verb forms; respond to others briefly when encouraged; and will attempt to communicate one or two ideas in a more formal speaking situation.
* Most students should express straightforward ideas clearly, attempting a range of different tenses; respond appropriately to others in conversation; and communicate some ideas relevantly in a more formal speaking situation.
* Some students should demonstrate the ability to use a variety of tenses accurately when expressing quite complex ideas; respond confidently and securely in a conversation; and communicate some complex ideas clearly in a more formal speaking situation.

Resources

* **Student's Book**: Section 7.3
* **Video clip**: see 'Getting started'
* **Workbook**: Section 5.2

Getting started

Show Arnanto Akbar's YouTube **video clip**, 'Pollution is a global killer' (3:30 mins). Prepare students for the vocabulary in the video by putting some of the key words used in it on a classroom word bank. Some of these words and phrases could include:

acid rain – oil spills – pollution – nuclear meltdown – evacuation – radiation – disease – women and children at risk – climate change – global killer – solvable problem.

View the clip once in its entirety and then again with pauses for each of the environmental accidents and disasters depicted, all created by humans. Get students to add words to the word bank at each stage based on what they see.

Q1: Ask students to use the video to stimulate a discussion in pairs around the questions in the Student's Book. Most of the questions bring the issues surrounding pollution down to a personal level.

Q2: Students should quickly note down their own ideas about pollution in their own city or region.

Exploring the skills

Explain to students that tenses are important when communicating clearly. Tenses allow a listener or reader to know *when* something happened and *how immediate* its effects are. This is extremely important when talking about issues, such as the environment. Go through the differences between the simple present tense and the present continuous tense. Make sure students can spot these in a range of sentences.

Draw students' attention to the subject–verb agreement table in the **Language booster**. Encourage students to develop an easy way of remembering which subjects agree with which verbs. As a rule:

* If the subject is *I/you/we/they*   = verb without 's', e.g. 'play'
* If the subject is *he/she/it*   = verb with 's' ending, e.g. 'plays'.

Q3: Ask students to tell each other three facts they have learned recently in science or geography. The listener writes these down. Both students examine the verb tenses of the sentences. Some facts, especially historical facts, will be in the past tense – for example: 'Marie Curie discovered two elements: radium and polonium.' However, students will discover that many scientific facts are in the simple present tense – for example: water boils at 100 degrees centigrade; water is a liquid that forms ice in its solid form and forms steam in its gaseous form.

Q4: To contrast with the simple present tense, students write down three sentences about what is going on immediately in their classroom or the room next door; they will mostly use the present continuous tense, for example: 'Ms Milner is teaching. She is using a music video with 7M. She is singing along.'

Q5 gives students more practice in using different verb forms and practising vocabulary related to the topic.

Developing the skills

Review with students the importance of listening carefully to partners and responding clearly, accurately and appropriately to them.

Q6: In pairs, students read the extracts about pollution and do the following:

* Pick out any new or difficult words.
* Guess words from context.
* Look for topic sentences that tell them what the paragraph is about.

Use this opportunity to get students to revise what they know about facts, examples and statistics in a text. Remind students that they read about carbon dioxide (CO_2) in Section 7.1 and the article here, 'A silent killer', is about carbon monoxide (CO).

Q7: Students now relate the information they have read to air pollution in their part of the world.

> **Give extra support** by allowing students to consult their journals to support their discussion on pollution.
>
> **Give extra challenge** by encouraging students to find words related to the ones they already know. Ask them to cluster related words in webs as suggested by the visual thesaurus (**www.visualthesaurus.com**).

Going further

Q8: Get students to prepare for a more formal talk on air pollution. This could include individual, pair and group research. Try to encourage the use of book and magazine sources as well as the internet. Students will deliver this talk in groups or pairs. Encourage students to plan ideas under the following headings:

* What is air pollution?
* The dangers air pollution causes to our health and happiness
* What can be done about air pollution?

Remind students that the talk must be formal, using accurate terminology. Students will bring in facts, examples and description as appropriate.

Assessment for learning	In the above task, assess how students organise their information. Students should aim to have at least three examples or details for each prompt. Offer graphic organiser options like: a brainstorm, spider diagrams, concept map, fishbone diagram, cause-and-effect table. Demonstrate and offer credit where this is being done.
Further challenge	In the same task, students should aim to include at least five examples or details for each prompt. Students should check that they have a highly structured talk that flows naturally using linking words and phrases and appropriate connectives. Brainstorm a list of possible connectives with the group, e.g. 'although', 'on the other hand', 'therefore', 'as a result of'. Your feedback should focus on organisation and fluency.

Where has all our wildlife gone?

Assessment objectives

L1 Demonstrate understanding of specific information

L2 Demonstrate understanding of speaker's ideas, opinions and attitudes

L4 Demonstrate understanding of what is implied but not directly stated

Listening skills in focus

* Use key words and context to predict content
* Understand what is implied but not directly stated during an interview

Question types

* Short extracts/short answers
* Multiple choice
* Listening to an interview

Differentiated learning outcomes

* All students should use key words to pick out a few details in a basic spoken text; they should be able to answer straightforward multiple-choice questions with limited success.

* Most students should use key words to understand a spoken text and pick out some details, showing occasional ability to infer meaning; they should answer multiple-choice questions with some success.

* Some students should use key words successfully and securely to select required details, even in complex spoken texts; they should consistently show inferential understanding, and answer complex multiple-choice questions successfully.

Resources

* **Student's Book**: Section 7.2
* **Video clip**: see 'Further challenge'
* **Worksheets**: 7.1–7.4
* **Workbook**: Section 4.1; Section 4.5*

Audio track 4.9 in Workbook Section 4.5 contains one item of more complex vocabulary: 'strike a note of caution', so please support students by pre-teaching this vocabulary before they listen to the recording.

Getting started

Draw student attention to the photo of the bee.

Q1: Remind students that humans are not the only victims of environmental pollution. Humans, in fact, have ways of escaping the worst effects of pollution we create as we do not live in the oceans like marine life; nor do we have to rely on trees and forests for homes like birds or small animals. Ask students to consider the effects of pollution on animal habitats and the plant and animal species on our planet.

Q2: In pairs, students should identify an animal or plant species that is endangered in their region. Encourage students to undertake authentic research on this issue by contacting the appropriate authority on this in government or the local community. Students also consider which animals and birds are no longer easily seen and why this might be so.

If students struggle understanding the words 'habitat' or 'endangered', point them to the **Glossary** box on the next page.

Exploring the skills

Remind students of the skills covered in Chapter 4, which suggested that students use the clues they have to predict what words, phrases and information might be included in a spoken text before listening to a spoken text and answering questions.

Q3–4: Direct students to focus on identifying key words in the questions before hearing the extracts and making some basic predictions about what they are likely to hear. Check that they understand each bullet point in the Student's Book. Play **audio track 7.1** for Q3 and play **audio track 7.2** for Q4.

Q3: Give extra support to students by giving them **worksheet 7.1**, which will help them practise the skill of spotting key words from questions and the extract. The transcript of **audio track 7.1** is also included on the worksheet so students can read while listening.

Developing the skills

As a pre-listening exercise, explain to students that they must predict key words and phrases that they are likely to hear in a recording. This is easier to do once they have identified the key words in the questions and know what they are listening for.

Q5: Direct students to the checklist table in the Student's Book. They work individually to complete the first two columns and then in pairs they try to define as many words as possible.

Q6: Introduce the interview (**audio track 7.3**) and clarify the meanings of the words 'journalist' and 'wildlife conservationist'. Students might be interested to know that the word 'bungalow' originated in India. Play the audio track.

Give extra support by discussing with students the birds and animals they associate with India. Ask students to guess what a wildlife conservationist does.

Going further

Q7: Prepare students for the second part of the interview with Prerna Bindra (**audio track 7.4**). Clarify that *implied* meaning is where the speaker hints at or gives clues about what they mean, without actually stating it outright.

Ask students the following questions to prepare them for the audio track.

* What might be some of the problems that tigers face in India?
* What could be the problems that conservationists like Prerna Bindra face?
* What could young people do to help the cause of preserving tigers in India?

Before the first listen-through, get students to read through the multiple-choice questions and identify key words. Remind students that they will hear every recording twice. Play the track.

Students must decide which of the questions might expect them to use clues to work out what is implied but not directly stated (e.g. part **vii**, where the listener can use Prerna's attitude, tone of voice, etc. to decide which adjective is most suitable).

Give extra support by handing out **worksheet 7.2**, which is a glossary of some of the more difficult vocabulary in **audio tracks 7.3** and **7.4** before students listen to the tracks.

Give extra challenge by asking students to write a letter to the editor of their local newspaper outlining their concerns about one of the following:

* areas of conflict between their neighbourhood and wildlife in the vicinity
* effects of pollution on animal and plant life in their area.

Assessment for learning	Using **audio tracks 7.3** and/or **7.4**, ask students to identify tones in a speaker's voice. In discussion, offer useful vocabulary, e.g. *enthusiastic, depressed, disgusted, surprised, happy* or *unhappy*. On a second listening, ask students to raise their hand at a change in tone – you can then pause the recording for discussion.
Further challenge	**Video clip**, be2212's YouTube video 'The best speech – Severn Suzuki' (6:49 minutes) Ask students to listen to the speech by Severn Suzuki. Ask them to make notes and identify exactly how Suzuki plays on a listener's emotions while she is open about her own emotions. Play the recording a second time so students can identify words or phrases to use as examples in their written critique of the speech. **Worksheets 7.3** and **7.4** can be distributed to support this task. You can assess the written responses for understanding of inferred meaning as well as rhetorical devices and persuasive techniques.

Resources needed for this chapter
- **Student's Book**: Chapter 8
- **Worksheets**: 8.1–8.6
- **Workbook**: see suggestions in 'Resources' panel of individual sections
- **Audio tracks**: 8.1–8.4
- **Video clips**: see suggestions in sections 8.1–8.4

The big picture

Find out what students know about **Culture and society** by writing the words on the board and asking for definitions. Prompt ideas by asking: 'What activities does culture include?' and 'How would you define your society?' It does not matter whether their definitions are correct – the main idea is to get students thinking.

Thinking big

Remind students that notes are one word or short phrases, not sentences. For each photo ask students to discuss whether it shows the religion, art or culture of the community or country. In many cases it can be all three, for example the Rio carnival is linked to religion (it is linked to the beginning of Lent), lifestyle (it is synonymous with Brazil) and is also an expression of art (in music and costume).

Give extra support by explaining to all students what each photo shows and underlining that culture is their *way of life* (see notes below).

Give extra challenge by asking students to find five pictures that best represent their culture – either that of their country or that of the place where they live now. Students may have different cultures – parents from different countries as well as coming from and living in different cultures. Students then explain to their partner why they chose their pictures. Together they should choose the three photos that best represent their culture.

Notes on photos

- Wall painting from the tomb of Tutankhamun showing the Egyptian opening of the mouth ceremony, performed so that the dead person would be able to breathe, see, hear and speak in the afterlife.
- Portrait of a woman with traditional hand painting from Rajasthan in India.
- The Rio carnival is a famous festival held in February in Rio de Janeiro, Brazil, in the week before Lent; it is renowned for its outrageous and beautiful costumes.
- Chinese tea ceremony during a wedding. In China, tea is often offered to say thank you to your elders on your wedding day.
- Thanksgiving Day Parade in New York, USA.
- A football supporter blows a vuvuzela at a football game in South Africa, 2010. Football is an integral part of modern culture in Africa and football matches are noisy and exuberant.

Disappearing ways of life

Remind students of the disappearing Bahasa Indonesian culture that the girl talked about in **audio track 8.4.** Ask what was lost (the language, the knowledge of trees and plants and what you could use them for, e.g. as medicines for different illnesses). Tell them that a dying or endangered language is a big indicator of whether a lifestyle is disappearing. A language is not only a vocabulary and grammar but also holds the knowledge of that culture. Explain to them that a language is:

* **safe** when it is spoken by all generations
* **vulnerable** when most children speak it but only in certain places, e.g. at home
* **endangered** when the children no longer learn the language and it is only spoken by grandparents
* **extinct** when there are no speakers left. (source: Unesco)

Ask students if they know of any other disappearing languages or cultures, particularly if the culture is geographically close to your country. Ask if they can think of other reasons why a community might die out (e.g. a language or culture is banned by the most powerful group in a country), although be aware that this might be a politically sensitive question. Give them the example of how, at different times in history, Irish, Welsh, Scottish and Cornish languages were banned by the English for political reasons and that these languages almost died out. Or of how the Roma people want to keep their travelling lifestyle which makes it difficult for them to have permanent jobs or go to school (both of which require them to stay in one place) and therefore get schooling or jobs inside their own community.

Q1: Students work in groups. They will definitely need to do research for this **big task** and it should take the majority of the time. Before students start, draw up a list of endangered languages or cultures relevant to your community so that if groups are stuck, you can ask them to research a pre-chosen community. If necessary, have a few websites showing photos of the relevant cultures to inspire students.

Direct students to 'Atlas of the World's Languages in Danger' on the Unesco website or the information on the Enduring Voices project on the National Geographic website. These explain further how languages die out.

Copy the KWL table onto the board and then, together with the class, complete the first two columns for one of the less confident groups. Encourage students to think of difficult questions – for example:

* Where does the community that speaks this language live?
* Why is this language dying out?
* What is special about their culture?
* How many people still speak it?
* When do people speak it?
* How can we make sure that this culture and lifestyle stay alive?

Set the research questions for homework and challenge students not only to find out information but also to come with relevant photos, videos and audio recordings. Make sure that students listen attentively to what each person in their group has to say, making notes at the same time. Check how well each person has listened by going round checking the quality of notes in the third column of the KWL table and allocating marks for the quality of the notes.

Q2–3: Students should use the notes they made in their KWL table to plan and write their article for their school magazine.

Chapter 8
Culture and society

8.1 Art and culture

Assessment objectives

R1 Demonstrate understanding of specific factual information

R2 Demonstrate understanding of the connections between ideas, opinions and attitudes

Reading skills in focus

* Understand and select information
* Identify the overall viewpoint and understand the main points in a text
* Make notes to summarise a text

Question types

* Note-taking
* Summary writing
* Open-response questions
* Presenting pros and cons

Differentiated learning outcomes

* All students should be able to pick out a few of the required points from straightforward texts, sometimes identify the overall viewpoint and make a few notes of related ideas for a summary.
* Most students should understand and pick out some relevant details from texts, identify an overall viewpoint and make some relevant notes of related ideas for a summary.
* Some students should understand and pick out relevant details confidently from complex texts, identify an overall complex viewpoint and make concise notes of related ideas for a summary.

Resources

* **Student's Book**: Section 8.1
* **Video clips**: see 'Exploring the skills'
* **Worksheets**: 8.1–8.3
* **Workbook**: Section 1.2 Section 1.3

Getting started

Q1–3: Go through the list of art forms with the students making sure that they know what each one is. If possible show pictures of them, as well as pictures of art forms in their society. Encourage students to engage with the idea that different art forms are an important part of a society's culture. Emphasise that different cultures have different art forms. For example, carpet weaving is an art form that is highly valued in many countries, e.g. Iran. Tell students there often can be disagreement or different opinions about what counts as art – especially 'new' art forms, for example hip hop.

Exploring the skills

Write the words 'positive' and 'negative' on the board. Explain to the students that often the *main* point of view is either going to be *in favour of/for* an idea or *against* an idea. Having a main point of view that is positive does not mean that you cannot say or see any negatives, and vice versa.

Q4: For an example of hip hop dance, and a hip hop dancer explaining how to do basic dance moves, use the Fit For A Feast YouTube video, 'Hip Hop Dance Tutorial - Hip Hop Combo Lesson Part 1 (7:36 minutes) Part 2 (7:32 minutes).

Q5: Explain that the different texts are online comments by people giving their views about hip hop – a modern dance form linked to African American urban culture. Hip hop is both a music and dance form. Students should *first* complete *only* columns one and two (the 'positive' and 'negative' columns). The 'Overall point of view' should become obvious by the number of points that they note in the positive or negative columns, e.g. if there is a lot of text in the negative column, then the overall point of view is likely to be negative. Ask students to copy and complete the table for both texts. Check answers as a class.

Give extra support by allowing less confident students to complete the table for one text only. You can also give students more practice in note-taking with **worksheet 8.1**.

Give extra challenge by asking students to make notes for **Q5** and to change what is said in the text into their own words. Students need to show the ability to write notes in

Developing the skills

Q6: This section of questions encourages students to explore further the opinions given in the text using their reactions to the text as a springboard for discussion. Make sure students understand the meaning of the following words to answer the last two questions:

* *persuasive* – likely to make people agree to what you say or believe what you believe
* *inspirational* – giving you new ideas and a strong feeling of enthusiasm

For questions **c)** and **d)**, students should look back at the list of notes they made for the table in **Q5** and state either 'I agree with this opinion because…' or 'I disagree with this opinion because…' Tell them that they need to give reasons why they agree or disagree.

For question **g)**, students might find one speech more persuasive because it is nearer their own view, or perhaps they find the more formal speech more trustworthy.

Going further

Remind students that notes:

* are short
* are not sentences
* use their own words
* encapsulate the full meaning (and therefore summarise a text).

Q7–8: Introduce the dialogue by telling students that it is about calligraphy. If possible, show the students some examples of Chinese calligraphy. Tell students that the dialogue they are going to read is basically a disagreement between father and daughter. Each has a different *point of view*. In pairs, students should practise reading aloud the dialogue. After reading aloud, students should make notes on their own about the main points of view expressed by father and daughter.

Students should then compare notes in pairs. Encourage each pair to comment on the usefulness of their partner's notes using the list (e.g. that notes are short, not sentences, use their own words, convey the meaning accurately). Get feedback as a class.

Give extra challenge by asking students to complete **worksheet 8.2**. This activity takes the Student's Book exercise a step further by challenging students to create a summary from their notes. Stress to students that whenever they have to write a summary, it is usually a good idea to make some notes first.

Assessment for learning	Students need to know – and be able to use – a variety of phrases to introduce ideas and opinions. Ask students to write phrases used in the dialogue (e.g. to *revere* something, to give *status to* something, to *approve of* something) in their notebook journal.
	Ask students to complete **worksheet 8.3** to practise using the phrases and give their own ideas and opinions. Make sure students understand that 'one thing…' means that there is more than one and that their opinion is only one of many!

Further challenge	Select a news item from a local newspaper and ask students to produce a summary of it as a script for a 'News in brief' radio item. Set a word limit of 150 words. Instruct students to make notes first.

Chapter 8
Culture and society

Celebrations and culture

Assessment objectives

W1 Communicate information, ideas and opinions

W3 Use a range of appropriate grammatical structures and vocabulary

Writing skills in focus

* Use examples to support your point of view when writing
* Use powerful language to make your opinions persuasive
* Include opposite points of view to develop your own

Question types

* Long writing questions
* Writing a blog
* Presenting pros and cons
* Persuasive writing

Differentiated learning outcomes

* All students should express a straightforward point of view using one or two examples to support it; they will try to use language and opposite points of view to make their writing persuasive, but have limited success.

* Most students should express a clear point of view with some relevant examples to support it; they will occasionally use powerful language and include an opposite point of view to try to make their argument persuasive.

* Some students should confidently express a clear point of view with highly relevant examples to support it; they should deliberately select powerful language and make effective use of opposite points of view to develop their own argument persuasively.

Resources

* **Student's Book**: Section 8.2
* **Video clip**: see 'Exploring the skills'
* **Worksheet**: 8.4
* **Workbook**:
  Section 3.2
  Section 3.5
  Synonym section
* **Other**: photos of celebrations in your community

Getting started

Introduce the theme of this section by showing students photos of celebrations in a range of cultures or communities.

Q2–3: As students give their talks, write words they use on the board to create a word bank associated with celebrations, for example:

> *put on a pageant – take part in a parade – festival – family dinner – new clothes – march past – flags waving – cheering – dancing – drumming – dress up – costumes – celebrate the past/our heritage.*

Exploring the skills

As an introduction to the Cau Ngu – Whale Festival – which is a celebration in the south of Vietnam, play the first couple of minutes of mi to's YouTube video `Khai mạc lễ hội Cầu Ngư năm 2016 tại xã có mật độ dân cư đông nhất Việt Nam', which shows the parade at the Whale Temple.

Q4: Show the video. If necessary, write the 'Wh' questions words on the board as prompts to students writing questions, e.g. *What? Where? When? Why? Who? How?*

Q5: Tell students that the text is from a travel brochure and is therefore trying to persuade you to visit Vietnam.

Q6: Students should try first to complete the table on their own as most of the details can be lifted from the text. Then get feedback from students as a class exercise.

Developing the skills

Students should be supported in developing and using a wide range of vocabulary to help them develop their language skills, and **Q7** and **Q8** focus on building vocabulary. Encourage students to create their own 'synonym banks' to encourage them to take responsibility for enlarging their own vocabulary. They can use their personal notebook or journal to do this.

Using strong positive vocabulary is mainly about finding synonyms for basic words. You can have synonyms for adjectives (e.g. *good – spectacular*), verbs (e.g. *drink – sip – glug – drain*), nouns (e.g. *celebration – festivity – pageant*). Make sure students know that synonyms don't always mean exactly the same thing (e.g. 'sip' means 'drink by taking just a small amount at a time').

Q8: When students have completed the table with positive phrases, ask them to underline the adjectives as these are often the strong positive words in phrases selected from the passage.

Give extra support by asking students to complete **worksheet 8.4** on using strong positive vocabulary/synonyms.

Q9: Do the first bullets with students by asking how they would describe their countryside. For example, is it peaceful? Lush? Brilliant green? Deserted? Parched? Enchanting? Dangerous?

Q10–11: The diagram in the Student's Book is an example for students to model their own thinking for their own celebration. Remind students of the celebrations they talked about in the **Getting started** section.

Going further

After students have read the **Going further** section, tell them that by acknowledging another viewpoint, they show that they have taken the time to think about someone else's perspective.

Q12: Introduce the text by asking students to think of a reason why someone might want to cancel a celebration. For example, it costs too much money, it is only the military on parade, too many people end up with injuries, hours and hours are wasted while practising for the parade, people have lost interest in the celebration, and so on.

Q12–13: Ask students to note down phrases used to acknowledge another viewpoint.

Q13–14: Ensure students understand that in order to oppose a viewpoint, you have to have a *specific* counter-argument. You cannot simply rubbish someone else's argument, however incorrect you think it is. Show this by asking which is the better counter-argument to 'We waste time practising for the parade'. Give two alternatives: 'But that is a stupid argument' and 'But during this time we learn how to work together and cooperate on a project that builds hope for the future of the nation.' (The second argument specifically states what you learn from spending the time practising for a march past.)

Give extra challenge by asking students to identify the other following persuasive techniques also used in the text:

- stating a viewpoint firmly
- using numbers and facts to support an argument.

Q15: Remind students of ways to plan their writing to argue for a point – you can refer back to the structure and suggestions given in Chapter 2.2.

Give extra support by as a class asking students for reasons for holding a celebration in your country. Write the reasons on the board as students think of them. Students who need extra support can refer to the list as they write their blog.

Assessment for learning	Ask students to find out about a celebration in another country and write the text for a TV advertisement that describes that celebration and aims to persuade someone to go and visit.
Further challenge	As above, but ask students in pairs to review one another's work. Instruct them to find opportunities to improve vocabulary choices and to utilise alternative opinions to support their own arguments, if appropriate.

8.3   Modern culture

Assessment objectives

S1   Communicate a range of ideas, facts and opinions

Speaking skills in focus
- Use examples to support your opinions while speaking
- Include facts and expert opinions to support your point of view
- Use rhetorical questions to make your speaking effective

- Giving opinions with supporting arguments
- Discussing in pairs and groups
- Making a persuasive argument
- Interviewing and responding

Differentiated learning outcomes

- All students should be able to express a simple point of view, using one or two examples, facts or other evidence to support it; they should identify the use of rhetorical questions.
- Most students should express an opinion clearly, using some relevant examples, facts or other evidence to support it; they should make use of rhetorical questions with guidance.
- Some students should express an opinion effectively, incorporating relevant examples, facts or other evidence to support it; they should use the occasional rhetorical technique successfully.

Resources

- **Student Book's**: Section 8.3
- **Workbook**: Section 5.3
- **Video clip**: see 'Exploring the skills'
- **Other**: clips from video games

Getting started

Q1: Get feedback from students after discussing the questions in pairs. As they speak, create a word bank on the board with words associated with gaming, for example:

to play online – to be an online user of XX game – to play on the DS/Xbox/Wii – to download a game – to be part of the online community – to use the console.

Give extra support by asking students to make notes and add words/phrases to their personal notebook or journal.

Exploring the skills

Watch 'Jane McGonigal: Gaming can make a better world' (19.47) on the TED Talk website on how gaming can make a better world. This video is useful for showing the thought process behind a positive attitude to gaming and you may find it useful to share part of the video with the class.

Write the example on the board 'Gaming is an important part of young people's culture.' Ask students to supply reasons why you might think that, e.g. 'Many young people spend many hours playing online games', or 'Many young people socialise with people they meet online'. Make sure students understand that giving an example to support an opinion is giving the reason why you think in a certain way. After students have supplied possible examples/reasons, write the example reason that is given in the Student's Book. Stress to students that all the suggestions given (as long as they are sensible) are examples or reasons to support the opinion. There is no single correct reason.

Q3: Before they attempt the question, check that students understand that Opinion 1 is against or negative about gaming, and Opinion 2 is in favour of or positive towards gaming.

Q4: Ensure you leave enough time for pairs to think of good reasons why you might think video games are – or are not – an important part of modern life. However, the main focus of the question is the interview. Ask a few pairs to come to the front to show their interviews.

Developing the skills

Write the three example facts on the board. Encourage students to explain that saying 'many young people' is weak and imprecise, whereas stating exactly how many people, of what age and where ('five million people under the age of 20') is far more precise, as it gives the reader/listener a better idea of why you hold an opinion. This makes it a stronger fact.

Q5: All the words in the box are techniques that are used to persuade the reader/listener. Remind students that they have been introduced to many of the techniques in previous sessions (for example acknowledging another point of view was introduced in section 8.2 on 'Writing').

Give extra support by asking students to give you phrases that introduce the different techniques before they do **Q5**. For example:

- personal introduction – e.g. 'Good morning... My name is... I am...'
- acknowledging the other point of view – introduced by phrases such as 'while it is true that...', 'to some extent...'.
- speaker's point of view – introduced by phrases such as 'In my opinion', 'I believe...'
- repetition x 3 – repeating a word or phrase three times, e.g. 'I can...', 'you can...', 'we all can...'
- use of examples – introduced by phrases such as 'for example...', 'for instance...'
- numbers/facts to support opinion – e.g. '25% of people...', '2 million young people...'
- use of expert opinion – introduced by phrases such as 'Evidence shows that...' or 'Research carried out in... demonstrates that...'

Give extra challenge by asking students in groups to think about the following statement/opinion: '*Video games are too expensive for young people.*' In groups, and then as a class, make a list of:

- the type of evidence or facts that would support this opinion
- who you would ask for an expert opinion
- who you would go to find out prices/profits of different video games.

Going further

Give extra support for **Q6** by suggesting students insert a question at the very start.

Q7: Ask students to underline the important words in each of the opinions and discuss what they mean, e.g. what is the meaning of 'addictive'.

Giving a presentation is a daunting task for most people. To make it less daunting, encourage students to rehearse in front of a partner or the mirror before giving their presentation to their group. Praise all students for their efforts, picking out when students use any of the techniques listed in **Did you remember to..?**

Give extra support by focusing attention on the most important technique (use of examples) or limiting the techniques for less confident students, e.g. include two examples instead of three, no need for rhetorical questions/repetition.

Give extra challenge by asking the more confident students to identify the techniques used by other students in their presentations.

Assessment for learning	Ask students to give their presentations (**Q7**) in front of the class. Other students should record their use of supportive evidence.
Further challenge	Remind students of the possibilities of other stylistic techniques for their presentations, such as rhetorical questions, use of 'we' to include the audience, use of repetition. Students should assess one another's presentations with particular focus on rhetorical techniques and their effectiveness.

Assessment objectives

L1   Demonstrate understanding of specific information

L2   Demonstrate understanding of speakers' ideas, opinions and attitudes

L3   Demonstrate understanding of the connections between ideas, opinions and attitudes

Listening skills in focus

* Understand and select relevant details in spoken texts
* Identify and understand opinions in a range of spoken texts
* Identify and understand conflicting opinions in an informal spoken text

Question types

* Gap-fill
* Multiple matching
* Multiple choice
* Note completion

Differentiated learning outcomes

* All students should identify a few relevant details and understand straightforward opinions in simple spoken texts.
* Most students should understand and pick out relevant details in a range of spoken texts. They should recognise and understand some conflicting opinions.
* Some students should understand and pick out nearly all the relevant details in a wide range of spoken texts, including the more complex ones. They should consistently and confidently understand more sophisticated, conflicting opinions.

Resources

* **Student's Book**: Section 8.4
* **Audio tracks**: 8.1–8.4
* **Video clips**: see 'Going further'
* **Worksheets**: 8.5–8.6
* **Workbook**:
  Section 1.1
  Section 4.4
* **Other:** photos of rural and urban cultures/groups in your country

Getting started

Q1: Show students photos of houses in the countryside and the city in your country. The photos in the book show a rural/traditional (country) lifestyle with Bedouins in the desert and modern living in flats and apartments in Riyadh in Saudi Arabia.

Q2: The main aim is to encourage discussion – there will be many things that are associated with both country and town life. For example, commuting to work.

Give extra support by brainstorming with students a list of things that people do in the country and the town.

Give extra challenge by asking students which of the things offered in the town/country offer the most benefits and drawbacks.

Exploring the skills

Q3: Remind students about facts (see Chapters 2 and 5) – that they are things you can prove. Write the examples in **Exploring the skills** on the board and ask students to identify the facts and opinions. Ask students to underline the phrase that shows which sentence is an opinion. Tell students that some phrases are 'indicators' that something is an opinion, e.g. 'It is normal/wonderful/strange/bad that...' Ask students to supply one sentence for each of the phrases in the **Did you remember...?**, all of which are used to introduce or signal opinions.

Give extra support by asking students to complete **worksheet 8.5**, which allows students to tick boxes rather than relying on listening and copying out the sentences. When you go through the answers with students, discuss the reasons for each sentence being a fact or opinion. For the facts, ask students to say how they can be proved.

Give extra challenge by asking students to change the opinions to facts in **Q3**.

Q4: Check students' understanding of 'rural' (meaning 'far away from large towns or cities') and 'urban' (meaning 'belonging to, or relating to, a town or city'), as well as any difficult words from the listening text: e.g. *club together, keep in touch, virtually impossible, residence permits, inner courtyard*. Play **audio track 8.2.**

Q5: Ask students to read through the questions before you play the audio track again. Ask them to discuss what they think the answers will be and whether the answer to each question will be a fact or an opinion. For example, the answer to the question 'How does she feel about …?' is likely to be an opinion as feelings are always opinions (you cannot prove what someone feels). Play **audio track 8.2** *in two parts* with a pause between the two people. Give students time to make notes after each part. Go through the answers, asking students to explain whether each answer is a fact or an opinion.

Q6: Play **audio track 8.3** (the person 2 section of the listening) again. Leave students enough time to write notes.

Give extra support by pausing the audio track after each sentence.

Give extra challenge by splitting the class in two. One part puts up their hands when they hear a fact; the other part puts up their hands when they hear an opinion.

Developing the skills

Give extra support for the speaking and listening exercise by asking students how they would describe their town, e.g. the market is dirty/full of rubbish; the town square is modern; the school is well-regarded; the countryside is peaceful; the traffic is appalling.

Students can complete **worksheet 8.6**. This will help them prepare their ideas and opinions about the advantages of their home town.

Q7: Although the aim of the exercise is to write an article, emphasise the listening aspect – that you should listen to the opinions of each member of the group carefully and make notes.

Going further

Q8: Show students a map of Indonesia. Elicit that it is made up of many islands. Tell students that people from the various islands speak different languages but that there are official and more common languages – Bahasa Indonesia and Malay. Ask students what people from a remote Indonesian island might know that they do not, e.g. how to fish, how to navigate in a boat.

Give extra support by asking less confident students to complete only parts **a)** to **c)**.

Give extra challenge by asking students to listen to **audio track 8.4** and put their hand up each time they hear an opinion.

Q10–12: According to UNESCO, 43% of the world's languages are endangered – at risk of dying out. The main reason for this is that children no longer learn the language at school or in the home. Students can use their answers to the listening comprehension to answer **Q11** and **Q12**.

Show the National Geographic YouTube video 'Dying Languages' (2:43 minutes).

Read more about disappearing languages using the UNESCO website's Atlas of the World's Languages in Danger.

Assessment for learning	Ask students in pairs to read aloud their facts and opinions about their home town from **worksheet 8.6**. Their partner has to listen and make notes. In pairs, ask them to discuss whether each point is a fact or an opinion.
Further challenge	Play a more sophisticated listening/video text, e.g. a recorded news item on a contemporary event or a propaganda film from the past, and ask students to discuss in pairs how much is fact and how much is opinion. In class feedback, consider occasions when opinions can be presented as if they are facts, and what problems this may cause.

Resources needed for this chapter

- **Student's Book**: Chapter 9
- **Worksheets**: 9.1–9.7
- **Workbook**: see suggestions in 'Resources' panel of individual sections
- **Audio tracks**: 9.1–9.4
- **Video clips**: see suggestion in section 9.3

The big picture

Ask students how they get to school each day. Elicit different modes of transport such as on foot, by bike, by car, by train, by bus. Start to build a vocabulary list on the board of words associated with transport. Ask students why transport is important – because it makes us mobile. Ask students how this helps us and add their ideas to the board: e.g. it helps us get to work, to school, for leisure, for sport, for exploration.

Thinking big

Q1: Make sure students write notes, not paragraphs or sentences.

Give extra support for **Q3** by reminding students to write notes, not paragraphs or sentences. Model the answers to the first two questions with students first (see below).

For changes in transport systems, ask students how people used to travel in their country 200 years ago (probably on foot or by horse). What things have changed since then? For example:

- Invention of electricity allows for development of subways.
- Invention of the engine allows for development of cars and buses.
- Invention of tarmac allows for development of roads.
- Being able to tunnel very deep allows for development of network of subways.

Model thinking of one advantage and one disadvantage of one form of transport. For example, with regard to walking:

- Advantages include that it is healthy and fun; it gives you time to think.
- Disadvantages are it is slow and can be tiring, depending on how long you have to walk; it is also often dependent on the weather (e.g. rain, snow, rain, very hot sun).

Notes on photos

Working clockwise from top left:

- Mongolian nomads, who roam the vast plains with their horses, yaks, sheep, goats and camels
- a busy road in Bangkok, Thailand – buses and taxis compete with cars and motorcycles on heavily congested streets of Bangkok
- the Nozomi Shinkansen Bullet Train at Tokyo Station, Japan
- an airliner carrying passengers large distances – part of a network that criss-crosses the globe
- Tuk Tuk taxis, motorcycles and cars at an intersection in Siem Reap, Cambodia.

New transport system leaflet

This **big task** has two elements:

* the leaflet (written)
* the presentation (spoken).

The leaflet

Help students think about features of leaflets. Show them an A4 sheet of paper folded into three to make a classic simple leaflet. Ask them to think about the different kinds of information that might appear on different panels, e.g. eye-catching title/image on the front page/panel; contact details on the back page/panel.

Emphasise that there is not much space so leaflets need to give information in short concise sentences. Features of leaflets are:

* not too much text
* clear, easy-to-understand information
* important details only
* big title and picture on the front page
* clear headings
* bullet points to list advantages
* photos or illustrations
* information such as telephone numbers and websites for further information.

The presentation

This is where students can try to be persuasive. Remind students that they can be persuasive by using the following:

* using strong positive language
* giving examples to back their opinion
* using 'we' to connect with the audience
* using rhetorical questions
* using facts and statistics
* using pictures instead of words (students should try to make sure they have a visual to attract the audience's attention).

Tell students that they should practise 'speaking the words' by trying out the presentation either in front of someone else or in front of the mirror.

They should know the first sentence or paragraph off by heart so that the opening of the presentation can make a more direct, and hence stronger, impact.

Chapter 9
Transport

9.1 Development of transport

Assessment objectives

R1 Demonstrate understanding of specific factual information
R2 Demonstrate understanding of the connections between ideas, opinions and attitudes
R4 Demonstrate understanding of implied meaning

Reading skills in focus

* Identify and understand opinions in a range of texts
* Recognise the language used to express opinion
* Recognise and understand opinions which are implied but not directly stated

Question types

* Text reading
* Note-taking
* Distinguishing facts from opinions

Differentiated learning outcomes

* All students should understand some simple opinions in straightforward texts, recognising some of the language used to express opinions.
* Most students often understand opinions, recognising most of the language used to express them, and sometimes understanding implicit meaning in different types of text.
* Some students should understand sophisticated opinions, consistently recognising the language used to express them; they should confidently understand implicit meaning in a wide range of texts, including more complex ones.

Resources

* **Student's Book**: Section 9.1
* **Worksheets**: 9.1, 9.2
* **Workbook**:
  Section 1.1
  Section 1.2
* **Other**: atlas page showing Russia and China; photos of bullet trains from China and Japan

Getting started

Q1: Get feedback for each bullet/discussion point from several students. Together with students build a word bank on the board of words associated with transport including basic travel vocabulary, e.g. *by car – by train – by plane – on foot – flexible means of transport – become mobile – travelling for work.*

Also, as this chapter includes much about rail travel, build up a list of associated vocabulary for trains, e.g. *change trains – buy a ticket – sit in the waiting room – reserve a seat – track – rails – railway network – train timetable – commuter train – high-speed rail – bullet train.*

If trains are not a familiar form of transport in your area, this may be adapted, although a working knowledge of this range of vocabulary will always be helpful.

Exploring the skills

Introduce the teaching focus of this unit by asking students whether the **Exploring the skills** example is a fact or opinion. ('The development of new forms of transport is …') Highlight that the first part of the sentence is opinion, but the second part is fact. You could prove it by finding out how long it takes to send items around the world now and 100 years ago.

Q2: Ensure students identify and write down the phrases used to introduce opinions. For part **d)**, brainstorm with students synonyms for 'I think' and 'In my opinion…' For part **e)**, the way students answer this might be affected by recent changes in travel and transport.

Give extra support by asking students to identify opinions and phrases that signal opinions in **worksheet 9.1**.

Developing the skills

Q3–4: Before students read the text in **Q3**, ask them to read through the 'Key facts about the railways in China' in **Q4** and to anticipate the type of answers required for each blank line. For example, 'Length of China's rail network now _____ km' is likely to have number.

Q5: Write the opinions on the board: 'Lives have been transformed as a result of the increase in railways' and 'Many people believe the railways are the most important development of the last 200 years'. Check that students understand why these are opinions.

Q6: Ask students whether they agree with the opinions on the board; alternatively, model what you think about the writer's opinion using one of the phrases that signal opinions. For example:

* 'In my opinion/view, the railways are *not* the most important development of the last 200 years; I think that the car/plane/electric car is because…'
* 'I disagree that the railways are the most important development because I think the car/plane/electric car is…'

Give extra support and focus by asking students to think about the effect of the train and car/plane/electric car on one area in their community, e.g. work or family. Then they can discuss whether the railway is the most important development of the last 200 years *in their community*. If your country or community does not have a train network, then ask students to compare the bus with the bicycle, or the car with the plane.

Going further

Q7–8: Introduce the theme of the reading by asking students what they know about the Trans-Siberian Railway and asking them to look at the photo. Show them the route of the railway in an atlas, pointing out Moscow and Vladivostock/Beijing. Encourage students to say it is the longest train journey in the world and for this reason it is famous. Ensure students understand any difficult vocabulary such as 'time zones' (show students an atlas page with time zones), 'feature' (most interesting part) and 'legendary' (very famous/so famous that people tell stories about it). Together with students identify the facts in the text.

Give extra support for **Q8** by limiting the question to evaluating only whether the writer is positive or negative towards the railway. Students should find one or two words that are positive/negative to prove their evaluation.

Give extra challenge by asking students to complete **worksheet 9.2** to come to a greater understanding of the writer's underlying attitude.

Q10: Ask students whether there are any phrases such as 'In my opinion… ' (there are none). Tell students that they can *infer* the opinion by paying attention to the positive verbs, adjectives and phrases.

Assessment for learning	Ask students to find a non-fiction text where the writer states their opinion using one of the phrases studied in this chapter (e.g. 'In my view'). Discuss with students where they are likely to find such a text, e.g. a newspaper article or editorial. Students should note down the opinion. Make a class collection on the board of the texts and the opinions. Ask students to discuss whether they agree that all the statements are opinions.
Further challenge	Ask students, working in pairs, to find an editorial from a newspaper. They should annotate it together, highlighting words and phrases that *imply* an opinion, either positive or negative, without actually stating it explicitly. Students can share or compare their annotated newspaper with those of other pairs.

Chapter 9
Transport

9.2 The impact of transport

Assessment objectives

W2   Organise ideas into coherent text using a range of linking devices
W3   Use a range of appropriate grammatical structures and vocabulary

Writing skills in focus

* Use relative pronouns to join sentences and add information
* Use a variety of structures when writing descriptions
* Join ideas and sentences using connectives

Question types

* Note-taking
* Informal emails
* More formal articles

Differentiated learning outcomes

* All students should occasionally attempt complex sentence structures including relative pronouns and connectives.
* Most students should write with some variety of structures, using relative pronouns and connectives to form complex sentences.
* Some students should write with a reasonable range of sentence structures, incorporating relative pronouns and a variety of connectives securely.

Resources

* **Student's Book**: Section 9.2
* **Worksheets**: 9.3–9.5
* **Workbook**:
  Section 2.1
  Section 2.2

Getting started

Q1: Encourage students to think how transport will be necessary for them to do things in the next five years, e.g. study in a different town or city, study or work abroad.

Exploring the skills

Q2: Write the first part of the example sentences on the board ('This is the park…'). Add a second column with the last part of the sentences in random order. Students match the parts. Show that the second part, ('where we like to play'), gives more precise information. The reader knows that the park is special because the writer likes to play there. Give a quick definition of a clause: a group of words that includes a verb and a subject. Sometimes it can stand on its own as a complete sentence. Underline the clause on the board (e.g. 'where we like to play') and ask students to identify the verb and the subject in each of the example sentences.

Give extra support by asking students to complete **worksheet 9.3** on relative pronouns.

Give extra challenge by asking students to identify the clause, verb and subject in each of the sentences in the **Exploring the skills** section.

Add examples of relative clauses that are 'non-defining'. These are clauses where the extra information is not essential and could be left out. Identify the examples of non-defining relative clauses in the text in the Student's Book. (Defining: '…the boat I arrived on'. Non-defining: 'The ferry, which was quite small,…)

Q3: Ask students to identify which of the relative clauses in the text are non-defining, or not essential to the sentence, and which are defining. Point out to students that in the sentence 'This is the boat I arrived on.' the relative pronoun (that) has been omitted.

Give extra support by reminding students that non-defining relative clauses can often be spotted because they are 'sandwiched' in between commas. For example: 'The hotel, which was in the town centre, was really noisy.' Here, 'which was in the town centre' can be deleted and the sentence still makes sense. Give some other examples:

* My friend, who lives far from school, has to come to school by car.
* In Beijing, where people still commute by bicycle, there are bicycle lanes.

Q4: Show students that, in part **d)**, you can delete 'that': 'These are the tickets ~~that~~ we need for the plane.'

> **Give extra challenge** by telling students that when the *that/which/who/whom* is the object of the clause, you can delete it. For example:
> - The bus ticket ~~which~~ I couldn't find cost $5.
> - The railway tracks ~~that~~ men laid over 100 years ago have finally disintegrated.
> - The children ~~whom~~ I see on my way to work carry rucksacks.

Developing the skills

Q6: Encourage students to bring in a photo or photos of a place they would like to visit or have already been to. Give students time to brainstorm adjectives to describe the place and the transport used to get there.

Q7–8: Break down the writing task by asking:

- what they are writing: an email to friends/family – hence tone will be informal
- why they are writing: to describe – hence likely to use lots of adjectives
- what they have to write about – *why* they went and *why* they chose the transport.

Q8: Remind students of informal openings and closings to emails: e.g. (openings) 'Hi…' and (closings) 'Take care…', 'See you soon…', etc. Point out the **Top tip**.

Tell students they will receive (extra) marks for using:

- relative pronouns/clauses
- a noun phrase
- at least five adjectives
- at least two connectives to make a compound or complex sentence.

Going further

> **Give extra support** for **Q9** by asking students to complete **worksheet 9.4** on connectives.

Q10–11: Break down this task by asking:

- what they are writing: an article for a school magazine – hence tone likely to be formal
- what they are writing about: the importance of a good transport system for young people.

This is a challenging writing task. Help students focus by asking them what a transport system is, i.e. an integrated system where the train is linked to the bus or to the airport/plane. What do *they* need? For example, do they need a lot of buses to get to school? Would it be helpful to have cheap or free bus passes for students? Do they need buses/trains to be able to carry bicycles so they can cycle home from the bus stop/train station?

> **Give extra support** by asking students to complete **worksheet 9.5** to help them plan their magazine article.

Assessment for learning	Ask students to write the magazine article in timed conditions (**Q11** in the Student's Book) using the notes they made for **worksheet 9.5**.
Further challenge	Ask students to check their own writing to make sure they have used varied sentence structures, including relative pronouns and a range of connectives.

Chapter 9
Transport

9.3 Problems with transport

Assessment objectives

S2 Demonstrate control of a range of vocabulary and grammatical structures

Speaking skills in focus
* Use a variety of grammatical structures accurately and effectively when speaking
* Vary the tense of verbs used according to the situation

Question types
* Discussing in pairs and groups
* Recording and analysing
* Expressing opinions

Differentiated learning outcomes
* All students should use simple structures when speaking and usually attempt to use the appropriate verb tense.
* Most students should use simple structures securely and attempt to use some variety of sentence structures and verb tenses when speaking.
* Some students should consistently use a variety of sentence structures and complex verb tenses appropriately and accurately when speaking.

Resources
* **Student's Book**: Section 9.3
* **Audio track**: 9.1
* **Video clip**: see 'Getting started'
* **Worksheet**: 9.6
* **Workbook**: Section 5.2

Getting started

Introduce the theme of problems of transport with this short **video clip** of traffic congestion in Old Delhi, India from 2019. Search for 'Daily life in India: Chaotic traffic of Old Delhi, India on Youtube (2:09 minutes). Remind students that this is one example of congestion and there are many examples worldwide. Remind them that Delhi, which contains Old and New Delhi, is the second-wealthiest city in India.

Q1: Ask students to define 'pollution' and 'congestion' – both side-effects of transport, especially the car. Together with students build up a word bank of associated vocabulary on the board. For example:

be stuck in a traffic jam – dense exhaust fumes – CO_2 emissions – greenhouse effect – road construction – damage the environment – to be/get caught in rush hour traffic.

Introduce the idea of your carbon footprint: when you use electricity for air conditioning or petrol for your car; these things produce carbon dioxide, which is a greenhouse gas. Your carbon footprint is the total amount of carbon dioxide you release into the air. If you always drive or fly a lot, or use a lot of electricity, you will have a big carbon footprint, which is bad for the planet. To understand this phrase, ask students to think of walking in the sand and the footprints they leave. You also leave a carbon footprint, which you can't see but which has an effect on the earth. Tell students to calculate their carbon footprint using an online calculator. Search for 'calculator carbon footprint'.

Exploring the skills

Stress that using different tenses correctly will help students speak (and write) more fluently and naturally.

Q2–3: Ask individual students to read aloud the sentences. As a class ask students to identify the tenses, underlining the verbs in each sentence. Students should spot that the last bubble contains conditional sentences; explain that this describes things that *might* happen, rather than things that *will* happen.

Give extra challenge by asking students to rephrase the last bubble using future tenses (i.e. 'If we don't have a good transport system, we won't have all the things...' etc.).

Give extra challenge by asking pairs to talk about how their parents went to school 30 years ago, how people came to school ten years ago and how they come now. Ask

Q4: Encourage discussion. Remind students of phrases used to give your opinions, such as 'In my view…', 'I think…', 'In my opinion…', 'I suppose that…'.

Q5: Read through the questions with the students. Play **audio track 9.1** all the way through without stopping. Students can make notes if they like. Play the audio track again up to where Luca says 'so I was very late for my lesson'. Ask students for the answers (orally) to **Q5**.

Q6: Ask students to read through the incomplete sentences first and their possible endings. Then play **audio track 9.1** again. Check answers orally. Explain to students that the speakers use a variety of structures and tenses.

Give extra challenge by asking students to use 'unless' to make as many sentences as they can about solutions to congestion (making complex sentences). For example:
- 'Unless we all use public transport, the problem of congestion will not get better.'
- 'Unless we ban cars in city centres, the problem of congestion will just get worse.'

Developing the skills

Q8: First elicit the main point of view of the text with students – that buses provide cheap and practical public transport that doesn't cause as much pollution as cars. Then encourage students to discuss whether they agree with the point of view.

Q9: Remind students of the functions of connectives (see Student's Book Section 9.2) for showing reason/cause and effect, contrast and further information. Model the skill of constructing sentences using connectives. Show that connectives can go at the beginning or in the middle of sentences. For example:
- '*Even though* the bus is cheap, it is much slower than the train *because* it gets caught in traffic.' (contrast/cause and effect)
- 'I use the bus to get to school *because* it stops right outside the school gates.' (reason/cause and effect)
- '*Although* the bus is cheap, it does not run as frequently as the train.' (contrast)
- 'I tend to chat to my friends *when* I get the bus to school.' (further information)

Q10: Allow students time to research ideas on the internet for homework to find out information such as how much pollution a car/plane causes. If you have not done so yet, ask students to find out their carbon footprint using the search terms given.

Q11–12: Put students in pairs, Student A and Student B. Student A asks the questions in **a)** for the relevant form of transport chosen by Student B. Ask students to check whether they use complex sentences for each of their answers to the questions in the bullet points in a) when they play back their recording. Challenge them to have a dialogue that is longer than two or three minutes.

Going further

Give extra support for **Q14** by asking students to complete **worksheet 9.6**.

Assessment for learning	Ask students to work in groups. Each person gives their opinions about the best and worst forms of transport and then the other members of the group say whether they agree or disagree with them. Remind students to give reasons for their opinions. Groups should reach an agreement if possible and present their ideas to the class.
Further challenge	Record the feedback to the class, and have students discuss a) the ideas and b) whether the speaker used a good variety of structures, including sentence structures and variations in the verb tenses.

Where will we go and how will we get there?

Assessment objectives

L3 Demonstrate understanding of the connections between ideas, opinions and attitudes

L4 Demonstrate understanding of what is implied but not directly stated

Listening skills in focus
- Understand connections and differences between related ideas
- Understand what is implied but not directly stated in a formal spoken text

Question types
- Multiple choice
- Listening for clues
- True/False questions

Differentiated learning outcomes

- All students should understand a few connections and differences between related ideas, and attempt to answer multiple-choice questions relating to literal meaning.
- Most students should understand some connections and differences between related ideas and answer multiple-choice questions competently. They should attempt to understand what is implied but not actually stated.
- Some students should securely understand connections and differences between related ideas and answer multiple-choice questions accurately, including those that test inference.

Resources
- **Student's Book**: Section 9.4
- **Audio tracks**: 9.2–9.4
- **Worksheet**: 9.7
- **Workbook**: Section 4.2* Section 4.6

The audio for Workbook Section 4.2 contains some more complex vocabulary such as 'monstrosity', 'blob' and 'carving'. Please support students by pre-teaching this vocabulary before they listen to the recording.

Getting started

Introduce the theme of possible solutions to transport issues by asking students to discuss the questions in **Q1** in pairs.

Q2: Make sure students have looked at the photos as the listening comprehension in **Q3** talks about the three forms of transport shown.

Exploring the skills

Q3: Play **audio track 9.2** all the way through without stopping. Make sure students give a reason for why they think their choice is likely to be the most successful.

Q4: Ask students to write sentences **a)–i)** in their notebooks. Give them time to identify key words. Play the audio track again, stopping at intervals so that students have time to note down true/false for each statement as well as make notes for why an answer is false. Instruct the students to check their answers. Play the audio track again without stopping. Get feedback, making sure students give reasons why they think an answer was false.

Developing the skills

Q5 highlights the use of synonyms and asks students to think of different ways in which information could be presented.

Teach the **Language booster** vocabulary either before or after the first listening. Do it *before* to pre-teach the vocabulary and boost confidence; do it *after* if you want to encourage students to listen carefully and guess answers from context.

Q6: Ask students to look at the photos, in pairs, and discuss what they think they will hear. Next, ask them to read through the questions, then feedback to the class on whether their ideas of what they may hear have changed. Then play **audio track 9.3** all the way through without stopping. Play the track again, pausing to allow students time to answer questions. Play it a third time all the way through without stopping.

> **Give extra challenge** by asking students to make educated guesses at possible answers (through world knowledge and vocabulary knowledge) before playing **audio track 9.3** for the first time.

Q7–8: Show students a photo of a rocket launching into space. Introduce/revise vocabulary from **Chapter 2, Exploration,** and create a word bank of vocabulary associated with space exploration, e.g.

> *launch a rocket – crewed/uncrewed flight – space programme – outer space – satellite – spacecraft – space junk – space station – enter/leave the Earth's atmosphere – without gravity.*

Play **audio track 9.4** three times:

* the first time without stopping
* the second time stopping to give students time to make notes of answers – adapt the length of time given according to students' experience and ability
* the third time without stopping so students can check answers.

> **Give extra challenge** by asking students to write down other things scientists are hoping to find on other planets.

Going further

Give students the example of someone saying, 'I feel hot and cold, and my stomach feels as if it's in a knot'. This might tell us different things in different situations. For example, just before a big football match it might indicate someone being nervous about the match. If they were about to phone the doctor, then the words might mean they feel sick. Show that inference is about forming opinions (what you think) by using all the available clues from contexts and meanings (e.g. photos, gestures, intonation, context, use of strong positive or negative vocabulary).

> **Give extra support** for **Q9** by asking students to complete only the first column of the table in **worksheet 9.7**.
>
> **Give extra challenge** by asking students to complete the table in **worksheet 9.7** columns 1 and 2, to help them come to a conclusion about the speaker's attitude to space travel.

Assessment for learning	Ask students to write a paragraph (100 words) giving their opinions about whether they would like to travel into space. They should then write five 'true/false' questions based on their paragraph.
	Ask students, working in pairs, to read aloud their paragraph and the questions. Partners say whether the questions are true or false. They discuss the reasons for their answers, and consider how well they understood the differences between related ideas.

Further challenge	Ask students to produce a monologue transcript of 200 words offering an opinion on whether money spent on space travel is well spent or not. The paragraph must include opinion that is implied and not directly stated. In pairs, students should listen to each other's monologues and consider whether a positive or negative view is being given, discussing how they can tell.

Chapter 9
Transport

Resources needed for this chapter

- **Student's Book**: Chapter 10
- **Worksheets**: 10.1–10.2
- **Audio tracks**: 10.1–10.3
- **Workbook**: see suggestions in 'Resources' panel of individual sections

The big picture

Allow students to look at the photos and read the topic introduction, which talks about the importance of clothing, fashion and the rich cultural diversity represented by fashion around the world.

It is important to stress that different cultures view fashion differently. Avoid students making judgments about what they consider 'cool' or 'acceptable' versus what is 'weird' or 'strange'. Encourage students to focus on the artistic diversity represented by fashion around the world and stress its importance as a form of self-expression.

Discuss the following quote: 'Style never goes out of fashion.' What does this mean? Encourage students to attempt a definition that defines the difference between the words 'fashion' and 'style'.

Notes on photos

Most of the photos are general fashion photos, illustrating different types of fashion from across the world. There are a few specific aspects you might want to mention:

- *Top middle:* a portrait of a warrior from the Maasai Mara in Kenya
- *Left middle:* the black and white photo shows five men's styles from an international fashion show held in London, UK, in 1967
- *Left bottom:* musicians in traditional dress for the annual elephant festival in Jaipur, India
- *Centre:* African American hip hop dancers

Thinking big

As your group works through this chapter, create a word bank for clothes, fashion and style. Give time for students to add these words to their personal notebook or journal, along with any other words relating to this topic that they come across.

Q1: Having set the tone for the chapter, get students to focus more closely on the photos in **The big picture**. Ask students to pick two that they find most interesting and to form questions they would like to ask about each photo, focusing on detail and context. Question prompts are provided in the Student's Book.

Q2: Students should now consider their own preferences for an item of clothing, shoes or jewellery that has proved lucky or is special to them in some way. They should also consider how their choice of clothing or style of dress reflects their culture. The focus is on building on students' prior knowledge as well as personal exploration and developing vocabulary.

Q3: The fashion quotes in the Student's Book have a strong language focus. Encourage students to discuss quotes:

- What did the speaker mean?
- What do you know about the speaker and what is your opinion of them?
- Do you agree/disagree with the quote? Why?

During students' discussions, circulate and note if students have misunderstood any language or the philosophical meaning of a quote.

'Be yourself!' – Putting on a fashion show

Check students' understanding of 'fashion shows' and what they mean in your context. Brainstorm with students some of the issues around fashion shows:

* very skinny models and the connection between fashion and eating disorders
* use of fur and hides of endangered species
* discrimination based on size and weight
* use of underage models
* promoting sweatshop brands
* low pay for long hours.

Ask students to think about this statement on fashion. Which aspects of this statement do they agree with and which do they disagree with? Why?

'Fashion is an art of personal self-expression, not an excuse to be pretty, popular or charismatic.'

Alternatively, ask students to discuss this statement:

'Fashion is just as important to boys and men as it is to girls and women.'

Then ask students to jot down a statement of about 100 words that best describes their attitude and practical response to fashion that is all around them.

Mention that the fashion show they are about to organise will be different. Students will organise this show themselves and present clothes that represent their own style and opinions on fashion. Remind them that 'fashion' can include such items as sportswear.

Q1: Read the flyer with students, checking all key words and meaning as you go along. Then get students to summarise the flyer by simply highlighting information that is most relevant to them.

Draw students' attention to the negative issues they must avoid and pay particular attention to the bullet points that have impressed judges in the past.

Q2: Clarify steps that students will need to follow to begin planning for their fashion show. Remind them that this is a unique opportunity to showcase all the vocabulary and ideas they have been gathering over the course of this chapter.

Assist students with the prompts provided in the Student's Book. Grouping allows opportunities for differentiation so it is possible to partner more fluent speakers with less fluent ones.

Allow students to copy and paste images or photographs if they are not skilled at sketching and drawing.

Focus on the presenting and writing aspects of the fashion show. Give advice on the description of the outfit and why it is innovative, versatile or practical. Encourage students to think about the following learning points from this chapter:

* choosing *specific nouns and adjectives* that best describe clothing accurately
* demonstrating their knowledge of *sporting and culturally inspired clothing*
* using *persuasive language* both formally and informally to have an impact on their audience
* using *emotional language* that persuades their audience to 'buy into' their ideas and opinions on fashion.

Chapter 10
Fashion

10.1 Fashion and fabric

Assessment objectives

R1 Demonstrate understanding of specific factual information

R3 Identify and select details for a specific purpose

Reading skills in focus

- Find facts and details from complex texts that present information in different forms
- Understand and use information presented in different forms

Question types

- Reading flow charts and diagrams
- Note-taking
- Text comprehension

Differentiated learning outcomes

- All students should show a basic understanding of diagrams and timelines, and pick out simple details from them.
- Most students should show a general understanding of diagrams and timelines, and pick out relevant details from them.
- Some students should demonstrate a thorough understanding of diagrams and timelines, and should be able to select and use relevant information successfully.

Resources

- **Student's Book**: Section 10.1
- **Workbook**: Section 1.1

Getting started

Q1: Activities in **The big picture** and **Thinking big** should have set the tone for fashion as a great outlet for creativity and artistic expression. Ask students to consider when and where being 'in fashion' could have negative effects. Draw attention to the preposition 'in' as this is often misused by English as a Second Language students. Contrast this with 'out of fashion'. Suggest to students other phrases for the fashion word bank such as:

anti-fashion – fashion-conscious – fashion victim – fashion item – fashion accessory.

Have a short class discussion about the negative effects of fashion. This might include ideas like overspending on fashion, being a 'victim' of fashion, low self-esteem based on fashion needs, celebrities as positive or negative role-models for fashion, etc.

Now direct students to jot down their own thoughts on the prompts in the bullet points in **Q1**.

Exploring the skills

Ask students when and where they come across maps, tables, flow charts, diagrams and timelines in their study of other subjects. Check students' understanding of these words for visual elements within texts.

Do these add key information to help them understand a text? How? Elicit students' experience of texts in science, geography, food technology or design technology that focus on describing processes.

Q2: Allow students time to study the flow chart, which shows the life cycle of a T-shirt. Draw their attention to the prompts in the bullet points on the next page and the advice about reading and understanding different forms of information. Make sure students have understood the purpose and direction of the flow chart before they attempt **Q2** and teach any unfamiliar vocabulary, e.g. *harvested, woven, dyed, packaged, marketed*. Showing pictures (e.g. cotton being harvested, cloth being woven) can help to illustrate each stage.

Q3: Ask students what they know about the origins of silk to generate interest in the text 'How Silk is Made'. Encourage students to present their understanding of the process. Knowledge may vary depending on their familiarity with silk as a fabric. It would be helpful to bring in a sample of silk, both natural and artificial silk, so that students can see and feel the different qualities. Bring in some other fabrics as well so that they can feel the different textures, e.g. denim, linen, cotton, nylon and canvas.

As students read the text, refer them to the **Glossary** box to help them with unfamiliar words. Draw their attention to the diagram explaining how silk is made as they read and point out that it contains information that they will need in order to answer the comprehension questions. Be sensitive to the fact that vegans do not wear silk and that some students may therefore may not be comfortable with the process described.

Developing the skills

Check students' understanding of timelines. Why do authors and historians use them? Clarify that timelines cover long periods of historical time, highlighting key periods or dates and how they are related to each other.

Q4: Explain that the history of silk is long and varied. A timeline is therefore useful to highlight particular periods of interest that might appear in the text they are reading.

Some of the vocabulary in the text 'The Story of Silk' will be unfamiliar to students, but they may be able to elicit the meaning from the context. Let students read it through once and then check and help them with any unknown words. Ask students if they've heard of the Silk Road and discuss what it was (a major trade route across countries in Asia and the Middle East.) It would be useful to source a map to help illustrate this. Point out any key on the map, and discuss how the map shows different features such as countries, cities, seas and roads.

> **Give extra support** by explicitly drawing attention to how and where the timeline links to the first date in the text. Draw attention to how the dates work backwards when they are 'BC', i.e. the larger the number, the earlier the date is.
>
> **Give extra challenge** by asking students to research the Silk Road. Ask them to name some of the main cities and countries that the Silk Road passed through.

Going further

Tell students that simplifying complex texts that include diagrams, maps and dates in their own words can be a useful skill in any subject (e.g. when revising). Explain that this involves looking at various parts of the diagram or map, relating it to the text.

Q5: This activity involves students using the information they have learned earlier in the lesson and presenting this as a poster for a younger audience. Ask students to look again at the diagrams and texts about silk and cotton production and to choose one of these for their project.

Students will need to decide on the key pieces of information and to adapt the language used. Remind students that, as it is for a younger readership, the poster needs to be colourful and clear. Students must cover the prompts provided in the Student's Book.

Assessment for learning	When students have completed their posters, ask them to work in pairs to assess each other's work using criteria that they discuss and decide on together, e.g. main points included, language suitability, inclusion of suitable graphics.

Further challenge	For further extension, ask students to research a topic of their own choice, e.g. how nylon is made, and present it as a poster with clear, useful diagrams for their own age group.

Assessment objectives

W3 Use a range of appropriate grammatical structures and vocabulary

Writing skills in focus
- Use a range of appropriate vocabulary effectively in writing
- Use formal and informal vocabulary appropriately

Question types
- Multiple matching
- Informal writing
- Writing a letter
- Persuasive writing

Differentiated learning outcomes
- All students should use simple vocabulary with some awareness of the need to adjust the level of formality.
- Most students should use straightforward vocabulary securely and attempt to use more sophisticated vocabulary; they should show an awareness of the need to adjust the level of formality.
- Some students should use a wide range and variety of vocabulary and demonstrate the ability to adjust the level of formality as required.

Resources
- **Student's Book**: Section 10.2
- **Worksheets**: 10.1, 10.2
- **Workbook**: Section 2.3 Section 2.4 Section 3.1

Getting started

Q1: This simple matching exercise is designed to increase students' knowledge of fashion and clothing items that are referred to in various descriptions of fashion. The visual matching is useful and you could get students to bring in appropriate fashion magazines of their own to label and annotate. This could form a class display for use throughout this chapter.

Exploring the skills

Explain to students that a wide and varied vocabulary is the key to sounding like an expert on any subject. Both teachers and students will be familiar with the language of education, discussed in Chapter 4, but there is also a range of specialist vocabulary to do with fashion. The focus of this section is, therefore, to sound like an expert on fashion by using appropriate vocabulary, as well as learning to adapt the style of writing according to the purpose and the audience: informal or formal.

Much of the vocabulary in this section may be new to students so draw their attention to the tips in the bullet points to encourage them to elicit meaning from context.

Q2–Q3: Before students look at the social media post, have a class discussion about how language can be adjusted depending on the audience and the level of formality required. Ask students what sort of language they might expect to read in a social media post, thinking about both the vocabulary that might be used and the sentence structures, punctuation, etc.

When they've read the post and checked their understanding of the key terms, draw their attention to the **Language booster**, which highlights some of the features of writer's informal style.

Developing the skills

Discuss the purpose of social media posts and why they are examples of writing in an informal friendly style. The matching task in the **Language booster** will help to expand students' vocabulary for the next task.

Q4: Students can either choose a photo from the internet or use one of themselves but make sure that they feel comfortable doing so and that the photo is appropriate for class discussion. The objective of this exercise is for students to recognise the difference between a formal and informal style of writing, rather than promoting a fashion statement.

Going further

Q5: Remind students that the way we speak is not always the way we write. When writing, we make different word choices and make allowances for who our readers are and what our purpose is in writing.

> **Give extra support** by modelling casual, friendly language often used in blogs or social media posts, e.g. the use of the imperative to draw attention, as in *'Make yourself comfortable* – time for a history lesson!' or *'Pay attention* – interesting historical fact coming up!'
>
> **Give extra challenge** by getting students to notice the frequent use of idioms in blogs. 'Get yourself a pair of these retro Greek sandals at just $19.99 – they *are to die for!* A great buy you won't regret and one that lets you put *your best foot forward!'* 'To die for' is an idiom that means the sandals are highly desirable – almost worth dying for, although that is, of course, an exaggeration. 'Put your best foot forward' is an idiom that means to present the best side of oneself.

Q6: Ask students to jot down some words and phrases to do with school uniforms or dress codes in different settings, such as your school. They should come up with examples such as 'uniform', 'fitting in', 'restrictive', 'rules and regulations'. Ask them to think not only about clothes and shoes, but also aspects or appearance such as hairstyles, use of make-up and wearing of jewellery.

Then ask students to write a well-structured, persuasive argument to the principal/boss on dress code. Hand out **worksheet 10.2**, which provides a template for the letter.

To prepare students for interesting vocabulary and persuasive arguments they could add about the origins of denim, consider introducing **worksheet 10.1**.

> **Give extra support** for **Q6** by explaining in advance some of the techniques used in the examples given in the bullet points in the Student's Book, e.g. using lists of three, citing celebrities or important people, giving reassurance.

Assessment for learning	Ask students to demonstrate and develop their knowledge of current fashions by first discussing what particular items are called, e.g. *skinny jeans, capri pants, sneakers, Mohawk, rat's tail, ponytail.* Students could label their own images A, B, C, etc., and then mask them to play a game which allows them to test one another. Once again, pictures with sticky labels are helpful.

Further challenge	Supplement **Q6** by asking students to write a short, informal email to a friend on the topic of school uniform, using idioms as well as a casual, informal conversational style.
	Ask students to revisit their letter from **Q6** and to think of other techniques that would be useful for writing a persuasive letter. What persuasive techniques could they use? (Refer them back to Chapter 8 and the techniques mentioned there, such as acknowledging the other person's point of view, using strong, positive language, etc.)

10.3 Clothes and culture

Assessment objectives

S2 Demonstrate control of a range of vocabulary and grammatical structures

Speaking skills in focus
* Use the right words when speaking about culture and clothing
* Use more specialised vocabulary appropriately

Question types
* Note-taking
* Preparing and giving a talk
* Using correct pronunciation
* Asking and answering questions

Differentiated learning outcomes
* All students should use some straightforward vocabulary about clothing and fashion.
* Most students should use a reasonable range of specialist vocabulary about clothing and fashion.
* Some students should use a good range of specialist vocabulary to express ideas with some precision.

Resources
* **Student's Book**: Section 10.3

Getting started

Start by writing the following key question on the board: 'What is culture?' Check students' understanding of the word 'culture' and ask them to identify the cultures that are most visible around them in their part of the world. Explain that fashion is one aspect of culture and is constantly influenced by other aspects: language, food, art, literature, music, ideas and beliefs.

Q1: In pairs, students consider questions from the prompts provided. Suggest that one student takes notes for the other as they listen to each other's ideas. Alternatively, allow students to jot down some thoughts before sharing them with their partners.

Exploring the skills

Q2: Reiterate that a strong vocabulary to describe fashion is necessary to talk knowledgeably about the link between culture and clothing. Ask students to match the items of culture-specific clothing shown with the specialist name for it.

Q3: In groups of three, have students write down some of the vocabulary items provided to use for a drawing game. In turns, students should quickly draw one of the clothing items from the list while the others guess what it is. The student who is drawing is not allowed to speak or write; instead they should draw quickly to illustrate the item. Set a time limit of 30 seconds for each drawing.

Give extra support for **Q3** by providing less confident students with pictures showing examples of the items in the list to help them understand and draw them.

Give extra challenge for **Q3** by getting students to write their own lists of fashion words for members of the opposing team to draw.

Ask students to note words that they are unable to draw for further investigation using a dictionary. Gather these words together for later clarification.

Q4: Students should now add words describing other items of headwear and styles of clothing, either from their own region or elsewhere in the world.

Developing the skills

Q5: Alongside students, read the text which explains some reasons for wearing different types of clothing. Clarify any difficult ideas presented, e.g. 'clothing can represent who we are, what we believe and even how we worship.'

Chapter 10
Fashion

Q6–9: Build students' understanding of the complex ideas in this text in preparation for the short talk to the class. Use this opportunity to promote intercultural understanding in the classroom. Encourage students to investigate the origins of various forms of clothing in their own cultures and those of others. Focus on the similarities and differences as well as the richness created by culture and clothing. Encourage students to take notes on the clothing and culture of their region. Focus on the following factors that influence clothing:

* gender
* climate and geographical location
* the needs of a particular lifestyle
* to show group membership
* special ceremonies
* joy and sorrow.

Give extra support for **Q8** by allowing students to collaborate extensively on choices of clothing for their talk and division of responsibilities for regions / cultures / occasions, etc. Suggest that bringing in real items would provide an effective 'show and tell' talk that allows students to illustrate various details of the clothing. Offer options of using a series of detailed photographs instead.

Give extra challenge for **Q9** by getting students to prepare a TV fashion show script or voiceover for their chosen items of clothing, using a range of accurate and authentic vocabulary with all new words adequately defined. All five 'Wh' questions – *what, when, who, where, why* (and *how*) – must be covered for each item of clothing.

Going further

This section focuses on pronunciation, specifically intonation. Explain to students that correct intonation makes it easier to be understood and improves fluency, and that the intonation heard in questions varies depending on the kind of question.

Q10: Listen to the audio and elicit from students whether the intonation is falling or rising in each case. If necessary, model some other questions to check that they can hear and understand the difference between falling and rising intonation. Then ask them to read through the **Top Tip**, which clarifies which is used, when.

Q11–12: Listen to the audio as a class and make sure that students notice the intonation used by the presenter when he asks questions. Get students to prepare their own questions and to practise speaking them aloud with the correct intonation.

Q13: Divide the class into groups of about four students each. Some of the groups (Group As) should argue in favour of people wearing branded sportwear while the others (Group Bs) are against people wearing branded sportswear. Suggest that they think about brands of sports clothing that they know, how the brands are advertised, cost and availability, relative importance for younger and older people, etc. After discussing and writing notes, each group should give a short talk while the other groups listen and prepare questions. At the end of the talk, they should then ask the questions using the correct intonation.

Assessment for learning	Elicit from students how they might speak differently for different audiences. Get them to role-play in pairs: (a) talking to a friend about buying a much-wanted brand of new sneakers; (b) explaining to a parent why they need money for these new sneakers; and (c) a trader selling a pair of sneakers to a customer. Ask some students to present their role-plays. The other students should identify increasing levels of formality in these talks and give feedback to the speakers.
Further challenge	Ask students to make notes during the role-plays above and draw up a list of phrases / vocabulary used in the three contexts to show the various levels of formality / style. They can use three columns headed: 'Very informal', 'Quite informal', 'Very formal'. They should then add to these lists themselves. Stress they should be on the lookout for idioms and conversational phrases.

Assessment objectives

L1 Demonstrate understanding of specific information
L2 Demonstrate understanding of speakers' ideas, opinions and attitudes
L4 Demonstrate understanding of what is implied but not directly stated

Listening skills in focus
* Understand how to listen effectively to fellow students
* Understand and select detailed information spoken by fellow students
* Understand what is implied but not stated in a conversation

Question types
* Note-taking
* Giving a talk
* Multiple choice
* Listening for detail
* Listening for implied meaning

Differentiated learning outcomes

* All students should listen politely to fellow students, then understand and pick out a few required details in a conversation. They should show some understanding at a literal level.
* Most students should listen attentively to fellow students, understand and pick out most of the required details, and should show some understanding of implied meanings in a conversation.
* Some students should listen effectively to fellow students, understand and pick out nearly all the required details and should show confident understanding of implied meanings in a conversation.

Resources
* **Student's Book**: Section 10.4
* **Audio tracks**: 10.3–10.5
* **Workbook**: Section 1.2 Section 4.2* Section 4.6

The audio for Workbook Section 4.2 contains some more complex vocabulary such as 'monstrosity', 'blob' and 'carving'. Please support students by pre-teaching this vocabulary before they listen to the recording.

Getting started

Remind students of some of the negative aspects of the fashion industry discussed earlier at the start of section **10.1**. Refer to the key idea of 'exploitation' of people or the environment in order to 'pay the price' of fashion.

Q1: Check students' familiarity with issues such as environmental damage caused by some aspects of the fashion industry, and people being exploited in clothing factories.

Put students into pairs or groups of three. Each group should choose one of the issues outlined in the bullet points and brainstorm what they know. Encourage students to jot down key words and phrases that help them communicate their ideas more clearly.

The groups should then present their ideas while the other groups listen and feed back with comments and questions. Each listening group should pose further research questions for the speakers to investigate.

Exploring the skills

Get students to focus on all the listening skills they were required to use in **Q1**. Ask them to brainstorm these skills and write them on the board. Then direct them to the bullet points in the Student's Book. Compare the lists and discuss.

Q2: Explain to the students that the audio track is going to feature three voices: a presenter, an activist/protestor from an environmental rights group called Earth Friends and a representative of the fashion industry. They will be discussing fast fashion. Before listening to the track, ask students what viewpoint they might expect to hear from each of the contributors. Tell the students to scan the questions and the multiple-choice options *before* the audio starts. Now play **audio track 10.3**.

Give extra support by talking students through all the questions and explaining all the choices in the multiple-choice questions. Check understanding of words such as *brands, fur, activist, uncaring, realistic*.

Q3–4: Students should read through the comprehension questions before audio **10.3** is played a second time. Allow students to work in pairs and discuss their responses. Play the audio one more time for students to check their answers.

Developing the skills

Ask students what they already know about sweatshops. Clarify the meaning of the word 'sweatshop' and explain that this is an informal term for a factory where people work long hours for little pay, often in dangerous or unhealthy conditions. Encourage a class discussion, which you may decide to continue at the end of the lesson when students have worked through the tasks.

Q5–6: Divide the class into As and Bs and pair each student A with a student B. Each pair reads the corresponding set of 'Fast Facts About Fashion'. Facts 1–4 = Group A and Facts 5–8 = Group B. This allows students to do some individual work and some paired work. Remind students that they must focus on explaining the meanings of key words in bold. They must be ready to summarise information provided in their own words.

> **Give extra support** by offering dictionary support for the key words in the 'Fast Facts About Fashion'.
>
> **Give extra challenge** by getting students in both groups to put each of the key words in bold into a sentence of their own related to the environment or fashion.

Going further

Revise students' understandings of *implied* meaning, and what it means to read or listen 'between the lines'. Revisit the idea of there being different points of view for different people depending on their role or what they know about an issue. Remind them that the views of the fashion industry representative were very different from those of the environmental protestor on **audio track 10.3**.

Q7: Introduce **audio track 10.4**, in which two students start a conversation about sweatshops. Give students half a minute to look at questions **a)** to **d)** before listening to the first part of the conversation. Play the recording a second time after another pause of 30 seconds, giving students time to look through their answers and decide which questions need attention. Discuss students' answers to the questions.

Q8: Now introduce **audio track 10.5**, which repeats the first part of the conversation and then moves on to discussing what they could do to campaign against sweatshops. Students should read the questions before listening. Students should then check their answers and 'star' the ones where they had to listen for implied meaning.

Assessment for learning	Suggest another resource on the subject of fast fashion or sweatshops, e.g. a magazine feature or an audio or video clip from YouTube. It could be chosen by students or selected by the teacher. In pairs, students should devise their own questions for one another based on the resource. Answers must be single words or phrases no longer than three words.
	Afterwards students should go through their answers and discuss them with one another. Students can then self-assess to decide together how they could have improved their listening skills. Alternatively, do this as a class if listening facilities are limited.
Further challenge	Give students opportunities to role-play a discussion on the cost of fashion, which should include a parent, a teacher and two students. You might consider suggesting that the discussion focus on just one aspect of this topic, such as how the fashion industry could be encouraged to be more environmentally conscious.
	At this level, students should be able to incorporate a wide range of vocabulary and implied meanings into their conversation. Other students should watch and afterwards give feedback on points where inference was needed by one of the role-play group.

Resources needed for this chapter

- **Student's Book**: Chapter 11
- **Worksheets**: 11.1–11.8
- **Workbook**: see suggestion in 'Resources' panel of individual sections
- **Audio tracks**: 11.1–11.5
- **Video clips**: see suggestion in in section 11.1

Thinking big

Q1: Get feedback from students and start to create a word bank of words and phrases associated with different forms of entertainment. Encourage students to give examples of both actively taking part in, as well as watching, entertainment, e.g.

go to a show/put on a show – go to a concert/be a member of a band – go to the cinema/ make a video – support football – watch football on TV – be a member of the local team – play video games - post photos on social media.

Q2: Each explanation should only take 30 seconds/one minute. Invite a few students to give their short talk in front of the class explaining their usual form of entertainment.

Q3: Ask students to present their pie charts to the rest of the class and to discuss the balance between studying and relaxing or playing. Do your students have a healthy balance between the two? Ask your students what they do while they are relaxing/playing? Do they spend a lot of time on their screens? Explain 'screen time' if needed. Students will debate screen time and how good it is for young people in the big task at the end of the chapter.

Q4: Encourage discussion. Before students form groups, make sure everyone understands the key words and phrases in the quotation, e.g. what is meant by 'to make a distinction between' and 'know the first thing about'. If necessary, rephrase the quotation to make it easier to understand. For example, 'Anyone who claims that education and entertainment are totally separate things knows nothing about either.'

Photo notes

Working clockwise, the photos show:

- people partying at a frenetic pop concert
- people watching a women's football match
- boys playing video games
- three women watching their favourite TV programme
- a young man reading a book
- *Centre:* a ballet dancer waiting to go on stage.

<table>
<tr><td>**The big task**</td><td>**Debate on how good for you screen time is**</td></tr>
</table>

Students should do the *big task* once they have completed all four sections of the chapter.

Q1: Make sure you first work with students to break down the question:

* What do you need to produce? = a debate
* Subject = whether lots of screen time is good for you or not.

Discuss what 'screen time' means (e.g. time spent using a device, such as a smartphone, TV or tablet). Students must therefore argue either *for* or *against* lots of screen time.

Work with students to discuss why 'I don't own a smartphone' is not a relevant argument. What one person does is not relevant, important or interesting unless that person can show that they are an example of what happens on a wider scale in their country or community. Similarly, statements such as 'I don't like xxx' are not relevant or interesting to the debate as they only express one opinion.

Arguments for lots of screen time	Arguments against lots of screen time	Irrelevant arguments
There's lots of educational stuff online. You can do research for your studies online.	Too much screen time can result in bad posture, eye strain or neck pain.	I don't own a smartphone.
Can keep in touch with and chat to friends.	A lot of screen time can affect your sleep.	
Learning strategies to manage screen time is an essential skill.	Too much screen time takes time away from sports which keep you active and healthy.	
Young people need to learn to be smart consumers and choose good quality content.	The ability to spot advertisements and know how advertisements works is an important life skill for teenagers.	
Good quality apps, TV show, movies, etc. can help teenagers understand real-world issues.	When disasters happen and there is lots of distressing news, this can upset teenagers.	

Q3: A debate is a challenging and stylised form of public speaking, but as a task type, it fosters many skills such as critical thinking, teamwork, questioning, persuasion and research, as well as the skill of public speaking. The tone of a debate is always formal. Make sure students understand that a debate is a competition between two teams to present their arguments and oppose the arguments of the other team.

You will need to help students to coordinate their arguments so that if Group 2 says 'a lot of screen time can affect your sleep' then Group 1 can answer by saying 'if you avoid digital media an hour before bedtime, you'll sleep well'.

Make sure that students take turns to speak – and that each person speaks for no longer than one minute.

Remind students that they will need to support their arguments with:

* statistics – e.g. '50% of people say…'
* examples – e.g. 'For example, young people often come in and…'
* expert opinions/quotes – e.g. 'As Gandhi says…'

Assessment objectives

R1 Demonstrate understanding of specific factual information

R2 Demonstrate understanding of connections between ideas, opinions and attitudes

R3 Identify and select details for a specific purpose

R4 Demonstrate understanding of implied meaning

Reading skills in focus

* Understand and select relevant information
* Identify points for and against a point of view in a text
* Recognise a point of view when it is implied and not directly stated

Question types

* Text reading
* Multiple matching
* Identifying arguments for or against

Differentiated learning outcomes

* All students should locate some of the required details in a straightforward text, identify one or two of the main points for or against a viewpoint, and understand some literal meaning in the text.
* Most students should locate most of the required details in a text, identify and understand the main points for and against a viewpoint, and infer some of the writer's implied meaning.
* Some students should correctly locate required details in a text, fully identify and understand the points for and against a viewpoint, and infer the writer's implied meaning with some accuracy.

Resources

* **Student's Book**: Section 11.1
* **Video clips**: see 'Developing the skills'
* **Worksheet**: 11.1
* **Workbook**: Section 1.2

Getting started

Ask students for names of different types of music, e.g. garage, rap, classical, soul, jazz, disco, etc. Build up a word bank of words associated with music, for example:

> *musician – recording studio – record label – play in a band/orchestra – be a (number one) hit – listen to the charts – be a fan of X – go to rehearsals.*

Exploring the skills

Q1: Ask students what 'streaming' music means and the impact it has had on music. (Streaming means accessing music via a streaming service and people are more likely to listen to single songs by an artist and then move on to another song by another artist rather than listening to complete albums as they did in the past.)

Q3: Discuss the meaning of the word 'democracy', which appears in the text. 'Democracy' can mean different things but here in this context it means 'the practice or spirit of social equality'.

Give extra support by introducing some of the more difficult vocabulary: *download music, piracy, earn royalties, etc.*

Give extra challenge by asking students which of the arguments (for or against) they find the most persuasive and why.

Developing the skills

Introduce *supporting* arguments by writing the following example sentence on the board: 'People think that learning a musical instrument is fun. _____ many people believe that it makes you more intelligent.'

Show that 'is fun' is a positive reason in favour of learning an instrument and that 'making you more intelligent' is also a positive reason. Ask students to complete the sentence to see if they know phrases to *support* arguments such as 'moreover,' 'furthermore', etc. Do the same for an opposing argument.

Introduce the theme of classical music by asking students to name all the instruments they know. If possible, show them a photo or video clip of a classical orchestra to make it easier to identify the instruments, e.g. horns, trumpets, violins, clarinets. Include all the various sections, i.e. woodwind, strings, percussion, brass, conductor.

Show students the MITOGEN YouTube **video** of the BBC's end credits for the 1990 Italia World Cup which features Pavarotti singing 'Nessun dorma', which was used as the theme tune for the World Cup in 1990. (3:17 minutes). Remind students that the classical piece, *Carmina Burana* by Carl Orff, has also been used by *The X Factor*.

Q4: Write the following sentence on the board: 'Classical music is still relevant to young people today'. This is the theme of the next two questions. Ask students to underline and analyse the different parts of the sentence before attempting **Q4**. Break the title down into sections: classical music (What is it?); still relevant (What does 'relevant' mean?); young people (Who are they? What is their experience of classical music?).

Give extra support by asking students to write sentences using each of the synonyms for 'relevant' or ask students to look the words up in the dictionary and write example sentences on the board.

Q5: Tell students that the introduction and the conclusion will not necessarily give you a reason for or against – they will introduce a topic saying why there are different opinions and sum up at the end. Ask students to identify which paragraph/s is the Introduction (Paragraph A) and which is the conclusion (Paragraphs F and G).

Give extra support by going through the article with students and underlining the phrases that support and oppose arguments.

Give extra challenge by setting **Q6**: this question is fairly challenging so go through the example before setting this question.

Going further

Give extra challenge for **Q8** by asking pairs to talk about a karaoke evening, school concert or rock concert they have been to. Tell students to:
* avoid saying it was 'good' or 'bad'
* think of strong verbs or adjectives that describe the event
* take turns to guess how their partner felt about their evening.

Assessment for learning	Ask students to write letters to their local council asking for money to support *either* their local/school youth orchestras *or* folk music in their culture. Pairs should comment on their first drafts. Teachers should mark the final letter allocating marks for: • use of details and facts to support a viewpoint • sentence structures • general level of formality.
Further challenge	Ask students to bring in reviews of concerts or plays from a local paper; in pairs, they should analyse them to produce a list of bullet points giving reasons why the reviewer did or did not like the piece. Pairs should mark one another's work.

Chapter 11
Entertainment

Assessment objectives

W1 Communicate information, ideas and opinions

Writing skills in focus
* Communicate information clearly and accurately
* Use punctuation of speech correctly
* Use a wide range of punctuation correctly and effectively

Question types
* Writing a short story
* Punctuation awareness
* Formal writing
* Writing a review
* Writing an interview

Differentiated learning outcomes
* All students should write in simple sentence structures and punctuate them so that meaning can be generally understood.
* Most students should write in simple structures accurately, sometimes attempting more sophisticated structures, such as direct speech, where errors will occur.
* Some students should write using some variety of structures, including direct speech, using a wide range of punctuation correctly to make meaning clear.

Resources
* **Student's Book**: Section 11.2
* **Worksheets**: 11.2–11.4
* **Workbook**: Section 2.5

Getting started

Q1: Ask students for basic categories of books, e.g. fiction and non-fiction. Make sure students understand they should think of *all* different types of reading texts – not just novels. The aim is to enlarge and enhance their vocabulary, e.g. directories, encyclopaedias, reports, diaries, posters, websites, flyers, instruction manuals, advertisements and graphic novels, as well as all the different types of fiction, such as thrillers, science fiction, romantic fiction, historical novels, plays, poems, rhymes, riddles, jokes.

Give extra challenge by asking students to group the various forms of reading into different categories.

Q2: All your students – even if they are unenthusiastic and believe otherwise – will spend a lot of time reading during their day. Things they read include their school textbooks, signs and notices, posters/advertisements, social media and websites.

Exploring the skills

Lead into **Q4** by telling students you are going to make a 'quotation mark sandwich'. Ask one student an easy question. Write their answer on the board. Tell the students that what someone says is the filling in the sandwich. Add the quotation marks – tell students that these are the two pieces of bread that go around the filling. You need both pieces of bread or otherwise the filling will fall out. When the spoken words come first, the additional punctuation (e.g. commas, question marks) also needs to go inside the sandwich – so inside the quotation marks.

* Example: 'What is your name?' my teacher asked.
* 'My name is Bassem,' he answered.

Q5: Remind students to use paragraphs when writing their text and to use a new line for each new person speaking when writing direct speech.

Give extra support by asking students to complete **worksheet 11.2**.

Give extra challenge by asking pairs of students to make up a disagreement between a parent and a child arguing about doing their homework. After they have created the dialogue, they should go back and ensure there is correct punctuation.

Developing the skills

Q6: Write the sentences on the board and ask students to correct them, explaining each time whether it is apostrophe for omission (contraction) or possession, and whether the owner is singular or plural. Before adding the punctuation, ask students if the sentences are easy to understand or not. Remind them that punctuation helps the reader understand what is written and makes communication easier.

Q7: Introduce the extract by showing students the covers of Anthony Horowitz's books from the Alex Rider series. Explain that the main character is a young spy called Alex Rider. Ask students to think carefully about their punctuation. They can decide, for example, whether they want to use an exclamation mark or a comma at the end of what someone says in direct speech – both are correct, but using different punctuation marks can subtly change the meaning. Using punctuation correctly is important for clear written communication.

Give extra support by asking students to complete **worksheet 11.3** on apostrophes.

Give extra challenge by asking students to write new sentences using apostrophes.

Going further

Go through the example sentences that use semicolons and colons. Point out that there is no comma before 'and' when you use a colon to introduce a list of items. Give extra practice by asking students to complete **worksheet 11.4** on semicolons. Semicolons are used less frequently now but it's still useful for students to know why they are used in case they come across them while reading.

Tell students that punctuation adds meaning to their writing. Often you can punctuate in different ways and all will be correct. The difference will be the meaning. Demonstrate this by saying the following:

* 'Really!' – The exclamation mark implies that someone shouts the word and is upset, angry or exasperated.
* 'Really?' – The question mark implies that someone is surprised about something or has to think about something in a different way.
* 'Really.' – The full stop implies that there is not much emotion.
* 'Really,…' – The comma implies that there is more text to come.

The same is true for pairs of commas and brackets. They are both correct and can both be used to add more information to a sentence. The difference is in the meaning.

Q11–12: These questions challenge the students to put their punctuation skills into use when writing. Tell them that punctuation is one of the last things they should check when writing. First, they need to plan or brainstorm ideas for their review or interview, then write it out in draft – and finally check their punctuation.

Q11: Put students in pairs to ask and answer questions about the books they are going to review. They should ask 'What do you think?' to get a summary opinion about their chosen book, which they can use as a comment for the end of the review.

Give extra challenge by asking students to do **Q12**.

Assessment for learning	Copy an extract from a book with some dialogue, but omit the punctuation. Ask students to write in the punctuation and then mark their own by comparing it with the original text. Ask them to identify places where two different ways of punctuating were correct.
Further challenge	Give students a piece of prose to read aloud in pairs. Each pair should decide how to use the punctuation to help them with their reading aloud. Remind them that to sound fluent and natural, they need to show they can use a range of punctuation to help make their meaning clear.

11.3 Television

Assessment objectives

S3 Develop responses and maintain communication

Speaking skills in focus
* Disagree politely in a conversation
* Keep conversation going by rephrasing what the previous speaker said

Question types
* Conducting surveys
* Role-plays

Differentiated learning outcomes

* All students should give some responses and, with support, take part in a conversation, trying to make disagreements polite and respectful.
* Most students should take part in a conversation, being ready to disagree politely and respond appropriately. They should sometimes try to make use of rephrasing.
* Some students should sustain a conversation and contribute at some length, using points of disagreement as a means to further the conversation, and using rephrasing to assist the other speaker.

Resources
* **Student's Book**: Section 11.3
* **Audio tracks**: 11.1, 11.2
* **Worksheets**: 11.5, 11.6
* **Workbook**: Section 5

Getting started

Start by asking students who watches TV and how? Is it via a streaming service? Then ask students 'What are the most popular types of TV programmes at the moment?' Write students' answers on the board. Agree a list of the five most popular types of programmes. Encourage discussion and disagreement. Remind students to be *polite* when they disagree (e.g. 'Mmm. I'm not sure. What about…?'). Ask several students to come to the front to tick the type of programme they watch the most.

Create a word bank with some generic phrases for watching TV, e.g. *streaming service, binge watch, advert-free, TV ads, box set, listing, to check a programme/show on the TV listings, watch xxx channel, to pay a monthly subscription, this season, the season finale.* Students should add these phrases to their own word banks.

Ask questions about the example bar chart in the Student's Book to make sure students understand what a bar chart is, for example: What types of programmes are the most popular? And the least popular?

Ask students to draw a bar chart similar to the one in the Student's Book, showing the most popular kinds of TV programme among students in the class. Students will need to build on the answers to **Q1**, taking a survey of students to determine which types of programme to include.

Additional activity: In pairs, students prepare a short questionnaire (five questions) on 'going on holiday', e.g. 'Where do you usually go on holiday?', 'What activities do you do on holiday?', 'Who do you go with?', 'How do you travel there?', 'Where would you like to go on holiday?' Students conduct a class survey and prepare a presentation on the topic. Their presentation must include a bar chart showing the information gathered from one of the questions, e.g. the five most popular destinations/methods of transport/activities. To encourage students to understand the wider use of bar charts, ask: 'Which school subjects use bar charts?' (Possible answers: maths, geography, business studies, economics) Then ask: 'What sort of information do they usually contain?' (Possible answers: financial, population growth, online use).

Exploring the skills

Emphasise that when having a conversation with another person students should *expand* on the conversation by expressing their own opinions, and that their opinions may often be different from those of the other speaker. Model this by saying something contentious such as 'MTV is boring'. Ask students how they would disagree politely. Remind them of the phrase(s) they used in **Getting started**.

In feedback to **Q2**, emphasise that one way of being polite is to acknowledge the other person's viewpoint (without necessarily agreeing with it). Ask students which of the phrases do that ('I take your point but...', 'I see what you mean but...').

> **Give extra challenge** by asking students to think of other polite ways of acknowledging the other speaker's opinion without agreeing with it e.g. 'That's a valid point but...' or 'I know many people share that view but...'

Q3: Play **audio track 11.1** all the way through the first time; stop after each conversation the second time. Ask students to complete **worksheet 11.5** after each conversation. Students can use the worksheet to discuss which of the phrases are used to disagree. All of the phrases used are polite. Each person cleverly manages to disagree or not do what the other person wants but without upsetting them.

Q4–5: Ask students to listen again to the audio this time paying attention to the intonation of the speakers, in particular when the speakers are politely disagreeing. Then ask students to fill in the table. This will help students think about context and when to use which phrase.

Developing the skills

Q6: Allocate roles A to D. Give students a few minutes to read their card and work out what they're going to say before starting the conversation.

> **Give extra support** by putting all Student As together, Student Bs together, etc. to decide on the phrases they could use to disagree politely before groups reconvene.

Q7: Students repeat task 6 but this time as themselves.

Q8: Make sure students understand what 'screen time' means. This term is glossed in the **Glossary** box on the previous page.

> **Give extra support** by writing the phrases for disagreeing politely on the board so that students can refer to them while speaking.

Going further

Ask different pairs of students to model the examples and discuss the techniques used. *Rephrasing* is a particularly good but challenging technique for keeping a conversation going. Explain it as trying to be a mirror to what your partner has said. You don't have to agree with what the person says, but rephrasing shows you have understood the meaning. The rephrasing can be more than one word.

In order to practise the technique of rephrasing, you need to have a wide vocabulary. Encourage students to add lists of synonyms to their notebook. For example:

* Person A: Last night's match was <u>exciting</u>.
* Person B: Yes, the last few minutes were <u>electrifying</u>.
* Person A: Yes, I was <u>on the edge of my seat</u>.

Ask students to complete **worksheet 11.6**, which practises synonyms for some of the vocabulary related to television and entertainment.

> **Give extra support** for **Q13** by writing 'Wh' question words on the board: *What? Why? When? Where? How?*
>
> **Give extra support** to students by asking them to practise using only particular phrases to agree or disagree politely with the other speaker.

Assessment for learning	Ask students to conduct their conversations (**Q13**) in pairs. Their partner should use the list of devices being practised, and tick them off as they hear them used.
Further challenge	Pairs of students could present their conversation to the class. Remind them they should also be using the rephrasing and other techniques to keep the conversation going. The rest of the class could listen out for the techniques used.

11.4 Film

Assessment objectives

L1 Demonstrate understanding of specific information
L2 Demonstrate understanding of speakers' ideas, opinions and attitudes
L3 Demonstrate understanding of the connections between ideas, opinions and attitudes

Listening skills in focus
* Understand and select facts in both formal and informal spoken texts
* Recognise and understand opinions and attitudes in a more formal dialogue

Question types
* Gap-fill
* Note-taking
* Discerning fact from opinion

Differentiated learning outcomes

* All students should understand and select a few required facts and recognise an opinion in straightforward informal and formal texts.
* Most students should understand and select some required facts and should both recognise and understand opinions in both informal and formal texts.
* Some students should understand and select nearly all required facts, and should recognise and understand more sophisticated opinions in a wide range of spoken texts, including complex formal texts.

Resources
* **Student's Book**: Section 11.4
* **Audio tracks**: 11.3–11.5
* **Worksheets**: 11.7–11.9
* **Workbook**: Section 1.1

Getting started

Before starting remind students that the question: 'Have you seen xxx (yet)?' uses the present perfect form. Together with several students, model different question forms to ask for their opinions on a film of your choice, e.g.

* What did you think?
* What is your opinion about it?
* Did you like it?
* What did you like exactly? Why did you like it?
* Why didn't you like it?

Q1: Ask students to move around the class asking ten students whether they have seen a particular film. Get feedback afterwards from individual students to say what their chosen film was and what people thought about it. As individual students tell the rest of the class what friends thought about their chosen film, write a list of vocabulary associated with film on the board, for example:

go to see a movie – download/stream a movie – the star of the movie – it features big stars/ action scenes – in the first shot/scene – I liked the chase scene/the acting/the director – to shoot a movie – to release a movie – to be a blockbuster.

Exploring the skills

Remind students about facts and opinions, and the difference between them. Ask students to write facts or opinions about the films they discussed in **Getting started**. Remind students that adjectives and adverbs are likely to make a sentence an opinion.

Q2: This listening text is an informal dialogue between two friends. Point out to students that it mixes facts with opinions (just as facts and opinions are usually mixed in formal texts).

Developing the skills

Introduce the theme of Nollywood by asking where the biggest centre for making movies is. The students are likely to tell you Hollywood and/or Bollywood. Tell them that Nollywood (Nigeria's Hollywood) started in the mid 1980s and has been growing ever since. Point out the photo of a shop selling a huge selection of DVDs. Nollywood movies are made for the home DVD market (there are cinemas, but most Nigerians prefer watching DVDs at home). Themes in Nollywood movies include romance, history, folklore, betrayal, revenge and murder.

Q3: Play the listening (**audio track 11.4**) twice. The second time you should stop after each paragraph to give students time to write down the facts.

> **Give extra support** by asking students to complete **worksheet 11.7**. This worksheet focuses on the facts contained in the monologue.

The audio track contains a mixture of facts and opinion. 'Nollywood is incredibly prolific' is an opinion, whereas 'Nollywood usually makes about 2500 films annually' is a fact. You could write both sentences on the board and ask students to identify which is fact and which is opinion – and why. Similarly, the claim that Nollywood makes movies 'at an astonishing rate' is an opinion – what is astonishing to one person will be normal to the next. Ask students to identify the adjectives and adverbs, and tell them that it is often these that make sentences into opinions.

> **Q5–8**: The listening in **audio track 11.5** is quite long. **Give extra support** by playing the audio track in sections. Draw students' attention to phrases the film critic uses that indicate opinion (e.g. 'in my view', 'for me').
>
> **Give extra support** by asking students, either before or after playing the listening, to complete **worksheet 11.8**. You can use it either to teach or to test vocabulary associated with film.

Going further

Language booster: Introduce adjectives to describe films by naming a well-known movie in your culture and then asking students to describe it using one adjective. Introduce the idea of hyphenated (or compound) adjectives. Stress that sentences with hyphenated adjectives are likely to contain strong opinions.

Q9: This pairwork activity is a lead-in to the group work of **Q10/11**.

> **Give extra challenge** by asking students to look at film (or video game) reviews and find other hyphenated or extreme adjectives.

Q10–11: If it is appropriate (and there is time), you can watch a film as a class – classic films such as *Star Wars*, *Harry Potter*, *Titanic* or *War Horse* might be suitable. Students should then take turns to rate the film at the end. The star rating is an evaluative comment that should always come at the end of a film review, as it is the reviewer's *overall verdict* on the film.

> **Give extra challenge** by asking students to use some of the hyphenated adjectives from the **Language booster**.

Assessment for learning	Ask students to write a review of a film – see **worksheet 11.9**, which gives students a basic structure for writing a film review. In groups of four, students should read aloud their review. Others should listen and note three facts they are given about the film, as well as the reviewer's overall opinion of the film.
Further challenge	Ask students find a review of a film on the internet. They should then listen and prepare a summary with bullet points: five facts and a sentence of opinion. They should then add star ratings to show whether this is a film the class would like. Pin the findings up in a class display so everyone can look and get some recommended viewings. (As teacher you might want to check they all pick reviews of different films and films that are age-appropriate.)

Resources needed for this chapter

- **Student's Book**: Chapter 12
- **Worksheets**: 12.1–12.4
- **Workbook**: see suggestions in 'Resources' panel of individual sections
- **Audio tracks**: 12.1–12.7
- **Video clips**: see suggestions in sections 12.1, 12.3 and 12.4

The big picture

Write a timeline on the board with numbers 0, 10, 20, etc., up to 100. Tell students that it shows a lifespan. Ask students what the names for each stage of life are, e.g. 0–1 baby; 2–3 toddler; 4–12 child; 10–20 adolescence; 13–19, teenager … etc. There may be different views as to the ages of adolescence, adulthood, middle age, old age, etc. so encourage discussion.

Thinking big

Q1–3: Students should look closely at the photos to talk about both what they are able to do and what they are expected to do at each age. In many cultures increased independence also involves increased responsibility for household chores and for supporting the family.

Take advantage of students' interest to talk about the rights and responsibilities that they will get at certain ages, for example: 'When I am 18, I can vote, I can learn to drive a car.' Encourage discussion of the best and the worst things about being young/old (**Q3**).

Explore with students the different meanings that age has in different cultures. For example:

- In some societies, childhood is a relatively short period of time – as soon as children can work, they are allocated responsibilities such as helping with day-to-day chores. In other societies childhood is seen as a time when children should play and learn and aren't expected to work until they've finished their formal education.
- In some societies, age commands authority and respect (as shown, for example, in the photo of Shangana warriors gathered around their tribal chief in South Africa). On the other hand, in other countries older people may be made to feel no longer useful, or there may be issues around how to care for older people in society.

<table>
<tr><td>**The big task**</td><td># Rights and responsibilities in youth and old age</td></tr>
</table>

Students should do the *big task* once they have completed all four sections of the chapter.

Q1: Write the various opinions given in the Student's Book that will form the focus of the possible presentations. In addition to those in the Student's Book you could include:

* 'Older people don't need a lot of company – it doesn't matter if they are on their own a lot, and they aren't really interested in communicating with younger people.'
* 'Children shouldn't focus too much on a particular talent or skill, even if they are good at it. It is more important to go to school and get a general education.'

After discussing in pairs, ask students to underline the key words in each statement. Break down each statement with students.

After researching and planning the presentation, more confident students should concentrate on the tone of the presentation. All presentations should be formal, but encourage students to think about whether they want to be more detached and factual (they will need more statistics for this) or more impassioned (they will need to give more opinions for this), or whether they wish to achieve a balance between the two extremes. All presentations benefit from clear visuals (e.g. photos, charts).

Allocate time to each group/pair to give their presentation to the rest of the class. Each person should be given time to talk.

As well as marks for the content of each presentation, you could give marks for accuracy of English, variety of sentence structure used, tone, stress, pauses for effect and repetition for effect (to practise the main teaching aims of sections 12.2 and 12.3).

Draw up a list of about four or five of the criteria you will use and present it to the students at the outset. Then use the list to assess each presentation and give feedback at the end.

Power for the young and the old

Assessment objectives

R2 Demonstrate understanding of the connections between ideas, opinions and attitudes

R4 Demonstrate understanding of implied meaning

Reading skills in focus
* Recognise both facts and opinions in different types and lengths of text
* Understand how the use of language may suggest a viewpoint

Question types
* Open-response questions
* Text comprehension

Differentiated learning outcomes

* All students should recognise and understand some simple facts and opinions from straightforward texts, with very little awareness of how language may suggest a viewpoint.
* Most students should recognise and understand facts and opinions in different kinds of texts, with some awareness of how language may suggest a viewpoint.
* Some students should recognise and understand facts and opinions in a wide range of texts, with a clear understanding of how language may suggest a viewpoint.

Resources
* **Student's Book**: Section 12.1
* **Video clip**: see 'Getting started'
* **Workbook**: Section 1.1 Section 1.2

Getting started

Q1: To foster interest and engagement with the theme of the lesson, first show the YouTube clip 'Why Young People Should Vote'. Other video clips can also be shown later in the lesson – for example, by searching for the YouTube clips 'The Power of the Youth Vote', 'Should 16-year-olds be allowed to vote?' or 'Why should youth be allowed to vote?'

Discuss the video clip with students, or ask them what they already know and think about voting age and responsibilities of young people. Write a list of associated vocabulary on the board:

be elected to the school council – take part in decisions on – express opinions – be involved in decision-making– do what you are told – be in charge – be able to vote – be represented by – be responsible for running/doing something.

Exploring the skills

Q2: Explain that even though it's not written in the first person, the text in the box is written by someone with a viewpoint, so students need to identify the author's opinion. The first paragraph makes it clear that the author agrees with campaigners who want to lower the voting age.

Make sure that students understand the meaning of 'should be allowed', i.e. that young people need to be given the right to vote.

Give extra support by highlighting the phrases which express the author's opinion by writing them on the board. Also write key vocabulary such as *campaigners, opportunities, shape their future, responsible positions, the chance to...* and check students' understanding before they answer the questions.

Give extra challenge by asking students to research voting ages around the world and find out the minimum voting ages of ten different countries.

Q3–8: Give students plenty of time to complete these questions because they include a lot of key vocabulary, facts and discussion points. The focus of these exercises should be on distinguishing opinion from fact so make sure that students understand the difference and how to recognise it in a text.

Students can work in pairs but allow for whole-class feedback at regular intervals. Encourage students to take notes as they discuss each point, which they can refer back to during the wider discussion. Make sure that students give answers in their own words rather than quoting from the text.

Q9: Now put students into small groups in order to widen the discussion. They may need to do some initial research about the voting age of their country. Encourage them to take notes about the pros and cons of voting in general, as well as the pros and cons of lowering the voting age. Ask each group to feed back to the class.

Give extra challenge by asking students to list arguments for and against lowering the voting age to 16 and to present their arguments in a debate.

Developing the skills

Q10–12: Much of this discussion is founded on the idea of *democracy*, which is a system that promotes the notion that people discuss problems (dialogue) and are given the opportunity to say what they think (and therefore vote) as well as understand the views of others. Discuss possible alternative systems of government.

Going further

Q13: Ask students to describe the image in their mind of a 'mob' or an 'audience' or a 'congregation'. Then ask if the words are positive or negative. Point out that sometimes the same word can be positive or negative for different people, e.g. 'congregation' might be positive to a Christian, but it may not necessarily be positive for someone of a different faith or of no faith.

Give extra challenge for **Q14** by asking students whether the idea that young people without work don't do anything for society is a common view (or misconception) in their society. Discuss unemployment figures for young people.

Q15: Together with students, before they complete the table for **Q15**, identify all the verbs in the first text. Ask students whether verbs such as 'hanging around' and 'wasting time' are positive or negative.

Then do the same for all the adjectives in the second text. Ask students whether adjectives such as 'disgusted', 'vast', 'hard-working', 'conscientious' and 'courteous' are positive or negative.

Q16: Tell students that 'summing up' is giving an overall view – *usually in one sentence.*

Assessment for learning	Ask students to write a short (50-word) paragraph giving their opinion of young people and how they spend their leisure time nowadays, using at least two verbs, two adverbs, and two adjectives. In pairs, students should swap texts and identify the verbs, adverbs and adjectives, saying whether they are positive or negative. Then they should sum up their partner's opinion.

Further challenge	Ask students to bring in newspaper reviews of plays, films or concerts, or sports reviews and highlight the words that imply a viewpoint. Working in small groups, students should tell one another about their review and explain how the writer has expressed their viewpoint on the play / film / concert / match.

Assessment objectives

W1 Communicate information, ideas and opinions

W4 Use appropriate register and style for the given purpose and audience

Writing skills in focus

* Choose the correct tone and style for different readers and different situations

Question types

* Long writing questions
* Multiple matching
* Writing instructions

Differentiated learning outcomes

* All students should show some awareness of purpose and reader in their writing.
* Most students should show some awareness of purpose and reader, and attempt to adapt their style accordingly in their writing.
* Some students should show a strong understanding of purpose and reader, and adapt their style confidently as required.

Resources

* **Student's Book**: Section 12.2
* **Worksheets**: 12.1–12.3
* **Workbook**: Section 3.1

Getting started

Q1: The focus of this lesson is to show how writing is adapted according to its purpose and its target readership. Students will be familiar with lots of different writing styles – from formal articles to informal blogs and social media posts – but they need to identify what it is that changes the tone from formal to informal in order for them to use the same techniques in their own writing.

Start by discussing specific websites, blogs and social media posts and eliciting from students the purpose of each one and how the styles differ between them.

Exploring the skills

Achieving the correct *tone* is a higher-level skill. Every written document (and spoken language) will have a tone – even if it is a note or an official document. Tone goes beyond formal and informal – for example, you could have a formal letter with an impersonal tone or a formal letter with an impassioned tone. Examples of tone include serious, friendly, cheeky, rude, impassioned, aggressive and ironic.

Students should not assume that informal writing is any easier than formal writing. Formal writing is often characterised by 'turns of phrase' (e.g. 'Please find attached…') that are easy to memorise. Informal writing is often characterised by wit, humour, idioms and verbal wordplay such as jokes and puns.

> **Give extra support** by asking students to complete **worksheet 12.1** on tone and style.

Q2: Ask students to read through the text once to get the general gist of the post. They may not understand all the vocabulary first time round but should be able to elicit some of it from context. They should then do the **Language booster** matching exercise to help with some of the unfamiliar words. Support them with any other unfamiliar vocabulary. Students should then read the post again for full understanding.

Q3: Pre-teach some of the vocabulary such as *citizens, digital revolution, income, gender, proportion, decrease, steeply, method, isolation, make up for.*

Q4: Ask students to identify the facts and the opinions in the article. Elicit from students that the article is nearly all factual. Students should be able to judge that the tone is formal. The use of statistics also keeps the tone serious and informed.

On the other hand, the writer of the blog post uses an informal style, addressing her readers as though they are friends. She writes from her own experience and talks about her feelings and opinions. She uses a lot of exclamation marks and informal language (eg. *she's really into…, hooked*)

Discuss the reasons for the difference between the two types of text: they serve a different purpose. This is because a blog is an informal space where you write your opinions. An article (for a newspaper or magazine) is more formal, should be well researched and based on facts, although often authors of articles use facts in order to give their own opinion.

Q5: Students should discuss these questions in pairs and then feed back to the whole class.

Developing the skills

Q6: Students consider the topic and purpose of a blog they may write. Discuss with them what tone of writing would be appropriate for their chosen topic?

Give extra support by allowing students time to complete a concept map summarising the content and tone of their blog. Use **worksheet 12.2** as the basis for this.

Q7–8: Students should do the matching exercise to help with phrases appropriate for different forms of writing. They then plan two letters, one to a teacher and one to a friend. Together with students discuss the *tone* of both letters. The letter to the teacher should be formal and serious; the one to the friend, informal and possibly funny. Also discuss the *format* of the message to a friend: a letter may not be appropriate as it may be more usual to send a text or direct message on a social media site. If they want to send a text, the message should be very short and can use abbreviations, but stress that in any exam situation they should not use 'text language' (e.g. abbreviations) at all – unless the question asks for it.

Tell students to use their imaginations for reasons why they had to miss school. Even if it is a funny reason, it must be explained in a serious way to the teacher and may only be explained in a funny way to the friend.

Give extra support by asking students to complete **worksheet 12.3**.

Going further

Q10–11: Discuss the different approaches in the extracts about internet safety. Students may well have personal experience of trying to help older relatives with digital technology so allow them to share their ideas and experiences.

To make this exercise clear, ask students to think about the difference between a seven-year-old and a 70-year-old in terms of ability to read and understand. Elicit from students that someone older is likely to have read a lot and so be able to understand and read very well. However, someone older may well have much less experience of the internet or the computer, so they will need that language to be explained thoroughly. On the other hand, the child may be less fluent in reading and have less general knowledge, but they may have already had a lot of exposure to the internet. Note that although we tend to assume that young people like things to be fun and interesting, so do older people.

Assessment for learning	Ask students to write a note to their parent / guardian explaining why they have had to go out unexpectedly to a friend's house. They should explain that they will be back by 6pm in time for supper and to help their parents/guardian with domestic tasks.
	Remind them to include features of an informal style. When it is marked, these features should be commented upon in the teacher's feedback.

Further challenge	Ask students to follow up on the previous exercise by writing a letter of thanks to the parent of your friend: the student has to be inventive and think of a reason, following on from the previous imagined event.
	Remind students that the tone and style of this letter will be very different from the last activity. When it is marked, pay particular attention to the difference in style and tone. Able students could write their own critique of how they have adapted the style.

12.3 Growing up

Assessment objectives

S3 Develop responses and maintain communication
S4 Demonstrate control of pronunciation and intonation

Speaking skills in focus
- Speak clearly and use the correct stress when speaking
- Vary your tone to interest the listener

Question types
- Discussing in pairs
- Active listening
- Recording and analysing
- Giving a presentation

Differentiated learning outcomes
- All students should speak briefly in response to others, with limited accuracy in pronunciation and little variation in intonation.
- Most students should speak clearly and at a reasonable length in response to others, showing competence in pronunciation and some variation in intonation.
- Some students should respond to others confidently and at length, with clear pronunciation and variation of tone to interest the listener.

Resources
- **Student's Book**. Section 12.3
- **Audio tracks**: 12.1–12.3
- **Video clip**: see 'Getting started'

Getting started

Introduce the theme of coming of age by asking students to watch the National Geographic YouTube video 'Girl's Rite of Passage' (4:39 minutes) about coming of age in the Apache community and its meaning.

Exploring the skills

Q2: Prior to playing the listening, discuss with students how they would feel on the day of their coming-of-age ceremony. Write the words that students say on the board. Play **audio track 12.1** all the way through. Play the track again, pausing after each person to allow students enough time to write down words to describe how the people feel. Afterwards ask students how they knew what the people were feeling. Try to get students to talk about:

- *how* people say things
- *stress* – the emphasis put on certain parts of words and parts of the sentence
- the *speed* at which they say something – which may indicate nervousness, urgency, etc.
- how *high* their voice is, and whether intonation is rising or falling
- *tone* – the attitude they are trying to convey.

Q3: List the techniques given in **Exploring the skills** on the board. Give examples of each technique. Play **audio track 12.2**. Get students to identify the stress on 'amazing', the pause before 'wow' and the repetition of 'amazing'.

Give extra challenge by asking students to discuss the different coming-of-age ceremonies and decide which one is the most interesting and why. They should also broaden the discussion to ways in which the ceremonies are similar to coming-of-age ceremonies in their culture and community.

Q4: Discuss a few ideas with students before asking them to work in pairs. Situations of being treated like an adult and being treated responsibly will change from one culture to another. Situations may include being allowed to travel independently, having a debit card, earning their own money, being allowed to sit with the adults when eating, and so on. Allocate time to allow each student to present their ideas to the class, as this is a good opportunity for each student to talk about what happened and how they felt.

Q5–6: Get feedback after students have talked in pairs. Write vocabulary of feelings on the board, e.g. *feel exhilarated – amazed – terrified – worried – calm*.

Encourage them to talk about what happens to their body in times of stress, e.g. *my heart beat like a drum – my stomach was churning – I felt sick – I had butterflies in my tummy/stomach*.

> **Give extra challenge** by asking students in pairs to talk about a time when they had to do something that made them feel nervous or anxious. Students should describe how they felt to their partner. They should think in particular about the words they will stress and their tone of voice. They can record what they say and then listen to check they have used stress, pauses, repetition, tone, etc.

Developing the skills

Q7–8: Learning to drive, leaving home and getting married are all huge steps in growing up. Introduce the theme of this section by asking students how old they have to be to do each of these things. Get feedback after students have talked in pairs. Encourage all students to be as ambitious as they wish in terms of their hopes and plans for the future.

Q9: Remind students of the techniques for adding interest: stress, variation of speed and tone, pausing for extra effect, use of repetition for extra emphasis. All three of the speakers are excited and animated/passionate about what they think – even the last speaker, who doesn't want to get married, feels strongly.

> **Give extra challenge** by asking three students to read out the comments, putting as much expression into their delivery as they can. Ask other students to praise the positive aspects of the speakers' delivery and to identify the techniques used.

Q10–11: Play **audio track 12.3** all the way through and get students to understand what Eliza's news is – that she has passed her driving test. Point out that Eliza is so excited that she speaks quickly – so quickly that her friend cannot understand her. Play the track again, pausing after each couple of lines and asking students to identify words stressed in each line of dialogue (e.g. 'SO happy', 'SO scary'. Ask them to identify the pausing (e.g. 'I've passed/my driving test') and the repetition (e.g. 'I've passed, I've passed…') as well as the vocabulary (e.g. 'amazing', 'hooray').

Going further

Q12–13: Go round the class listening to students as they speak. Tell them you will be listening for stress, tone, pausing for dramatic effect, repetition and general variation in tone to interest the listener.

Assessment for learning	Ask students to prepare a presentation on a coming-of-age ceremony in their country or about a ceremony in another country that interests them. Students will need to: • research the information • mix factual information with their own opinions • give the presentation to the class. Tell students you will allocate marks (a) for content and research, and (b) for clarity (i.e. stress, tone, pausing for dramatic effect, repetition, and so on).
Further challenge	Ask students to do the above task, but discuss with them in advance how they can make the talk interesting. Elicit content and ideas, as well as ways of bringing variety and expression to their delivery. Afterwards students should peer assess one another's presentations using these criteria in their spoken feedback.

Chapter 12
Young and old

Assessment objectives

L1   Demonstrate understanding of specific information

L2   Demonstrate understanding of speakers' ideas, opinions and attitudes

Listening skills in focus

* Recognise and understand ideas, opinions and attitudes
* Answer multiple-choice questions about ideas
* Recognise connections between ideas
* Understand what is implied but not actually said in a formal interview

Question types

* Multiple choice
* Listening for detail

Differentiated learning outcomes

* All students should understand opinions expressed simply in straightforward spoken texts, and answer some multiple-choice questions about literal meanings of what is said.
* Most students should understand opinions expressed in a range of spoken texts, and answer multiple-choice questions competently, showing some understanding of implied meaning.
* Some students should securely understand opinions expressed in a wide range of spoken texts, and answer multiple-choice questions accurately, including those requiring good understanding of implicit meaning.

Resources

* **Student's Book**: Section 12.4
* **Audio tracks**: 12.4–12.7
* **Video clip**: see 'Getting started'
* **Worksheet**: 12.4
* **Workbook**: Sections 4.4–4.6

Getting started

Introduce the theme of child prodigies by searching the YouTube video clip of Momiji Nishiya winning her gold medal at the Olympic Games in Tokyo when she was just 13 years old (1:48 minutes).

Child prodigies are young people who show talent at an early age. Think of a young champion in your country or one that students will know. You could choose someone in the community who has done extraordinarily well at something. Build up a word bank on the board of vocabulary associated with the theme:

to be pushed from a young age – to be talented at something – to dedicate your life to something – to be awarded a perfect score for something – to show talent for something – to break a record – to set a world record – to be a champion.

Exploring the skills

Most students will be familiar with the multiple-choice format. Make sure you stress that if they don't know the answer, they should *always* guess – they will (usually) have a one in three or one in four chance of answering correctly.

Q2: Play **audio track 12.4** all the way through. Play the track again, pausing after the first sentence to allow students to answer the multiple-choice question. Elicit the answer and together with the students read the text about key words to listen for.

Q3–4: Ask students to read through the multiple-choice questions and to underline the key vocabulary in each answer option before playing the listening passage.

Play **audio track 12.5** all the way through. Students should point to the relevant photo as the speaker talks about each person. Play the track again, pausing after the information about each child and allowing students time to answer each question. Play the track again all the way through for students to check their answers.

> **Give extra challenge** by asking students before listening to guess how old each child was when they set the records (Jordan Romero 15; Jessica Watson 16; Inge Sorensen 12). Ask them to research whether they still hold these records.

Developing the skills

The theme of the first listening passage of this section is achievements of older people. To personalise this section, ask students to name older people they know and admire. Encourage them to discuss what the person has done, how old they are, etc.

Q5: Ask students to choose four of the words and to write a sentence for each word.

Q6: Students should know a marathon is 26 miles and 385 yards or 42.195 kilometres.

Q7: The answers to this question are in the excerpt of the article shown in Q6.

Q8: Make sure students read through the questions and underline the key words in each option before playing the listening passage. Discuss with students the words that they have underlined. Play **audio track 12.6** all the way through without stopping. Play the track again, pausing to allow students time to answer questions. Play the track once more all the way through without stopping so that they can check their answers.

> **Give extra challenge** by asking students to discuss the following questions in pairs:
> * Which of the activities described so far in the chapter would they most/least like to try (i.e. marathon running, diving, sailing, climbing)?
> * Which activity do they think is the most amazing?
> * What do they think about the achievements described?

Going further

Q9: Refer back to the discussions you had about the stages of life, in the **Thinking big** section at the start of Chapter 12. Also remind students of timelines, which they came across in Chapter 10.1. Once pairs have drawn their timeline, they can compare it with the timelines of other pairs and discuss any differences.

Q10–12: The listening passage in **audio track 12.7** is quite long and challenging. Students should prepare by doing the **Language booster** first. Play the audio all the way through first for students to get the general gist of the conversation. Students should then read through the questions of **Q11** before listening again. Check whether they need any help with unfamiliar words.

It may be helpful to pause the audio after each stage of life has been discussed to give students time to answer the questions.

> **Give extra support** by asking students to complete **worksheet 12.4**, which will help them with the vocabulary in the listening passage. You could hand out the worksheet, and then play the passage again, asking students to put their hands up when they hear the words on the worksheet. Ask students to write a sentence for each word for homework.

Assessment for learning	Ask students, working in pairs, to tell one another about three key moments in their lives so far, spread out about four years apart (allow five minutes for this). Afterwards, they should make notes on the three key moments (allow four minutes) and then check if they listened accurately (about five minutes). Times may need to be adapted according to students' abilities. Also some preparation time may be required.
Further challenge	As above, but as well as noting the memory/event, students should make a note about their partner's attitude to each event/state of mind at the time. Ask students to write down two or three words that suggest attitude or feelings. They should then check and compare how carefully they listened to each other. They then feed back to the class on how they used inference.

Assessment objectives

R1 Demonstrate understanding of specific factual information

R2 Demonstrate understanding of the connections between the ideas, opinions and attitudes

R4 Demonstrate understanding of implied meaning

Question types

* Text reading
* Multiple matching

Differentiated learning outcomes

* All students should skim read and scan well enough to pick out a few required details, and should understand simple information at a literal level.

* Most students should skim read and scan competently, and pick out most of the required details. They should sometimes understand things that are implied but not written.

* Some students should skim read and scan effectively, and pick out nearly all the required details. They should usually understand things that are implied but not written.

Resources

* **Student's Book**:
  Chapter 13, Answering short text reading questions
  Sample Answers: short text reading questions
* **Worksheets**: 13.1–13.3
* **Workbook**:
  Section 1.1
  Section 1.2

Open-response reading questions: step by step

Explain that for open-response questions students have to pick out details from a short text in order to answer questions and then write brief, concise answers – each one a single word or phrase, not a sentence. Also explain that open-response questions use text types that the students are familiar with.

Step 1: Ask students to brainstorm the types of reading texts they have come across during this course, or from elsewhere. Write these on a board. The final list should include: advertisement, brochure, leaflet, guide, report, manual, instructions, report, newspaper/magazine article. Reassure students that even if their experience of some texts is mainly in their mother tongue, that can still be helpful to them.

Step 2: Explain that it is important to read through all the questions very quickly before they start answering them. It can help them get a sense of the whole text. It can also sometimes prevent them giving wrong answers when the answers are found in the order they appear in the text.

Step 3: Explain that the reading skills they need to use are the ability to *skim read* and to *scan*. Explain that *skimming* is a great way to help them get the 'gist' – the overall meaning – of a piece of writing, without having to read it all slowly and carefully. *Scanning* is looking closer and picking out the exact information or detail that you want. So you *skim* over a piece of writing to find the chunk of text where the required information is likely to be, and then *scan* to pick it out.

Students may be aware of the phrase 'skim the surface', which may help them remember the difference between skimming and scanning. Also many students will be aware of the word 'scan' when applied to computer software, which can 'scan' for and pick out viruses.

Students should be made to feel confident that they already use the skills, maybe in their first language as well as in English. Ask students, in pairs, to list as many situations in real life where they have to find out details without reading every word of a text as they can, and then share these with the class. For example, when they use a website to find out the date of a concert, they would not read every word of that website. Ensure their lists include familiar situations, e.g. using a contents page in a recipe book or a contacts list on a mobile phone.

Using a webpage, ask students to list the features they would use to help them find any detail they needed. During feedback, ensure the following are included: website 'menu', headings, subheadings, important or key words to scan for.

Remind students that they can make use of the key question words – *Who? When? Where? What? How?* – to help them search for the right kind of information. Ask them to produce lists of possible sorts of answers to these questions. For example, *When…?* requires a date or a day or a time.

Before they tackle **Practise an open-response question**, ask students individually or in pairs to list a step-by-step approach to how they will tackle it. Tell them to have three sections: before/during/after writing answers. Then ask them to compare their lists with the **REMEMBER TO** bullet points in Chapter 13.

Practise an open-response question

You may choose to have the students complete all the practice reading questions in one sitting, perhaps as a last-minute revision exercise. Alternatively, you may choose to do each question separately and focus on it. Whichever route you choose, a study of the marking guidance afterwards will greatly help students to understand more clearly what they should be aiming to do.

For extra practice, students could make up five new questions about the 'Where have all the bees gone?' article in the Student's Book and then see how quickly they can answer their partner's questions. They could try to make the questions trickier – but each one should still only have one word or a short phrase as its answer.

After students have completed **Practise an open-response question**, invite them to discuss their responses in pairs, using these prompts:

* Compare and then agree on your answers to all the questions.
* Did all the answers appear in the text in the same order as in the questions? How can this help you?
* Can you make any of the answers shorter? Keeping answers as short as possible saves you time and might stop you writing the answer incorrectly.

The student as marker

Go through the marking guidance below with the students, drawing attention to the comments in the final column. The students can then use the marking guidance to mark the sample answers for **Practise an open-response reading question** on **worksheet 13.1**. Ask students, working in pairs, to discuss and agree their marks. They should then compare their marks and comments with those given on **worksheet 13.2**. Check that they correctly identified those answers that failed to score full marks and that they understood the reasons why.

Students can then mark their own answers, using the marking guidance on the next page. Alternatively, as teacher, you may decide to use the marking guidance to support and enhance your own marking, perhaps referring to it closely when returning students' work to them.

Using the Sample answers

In Chapter 13 Sample answers (at the back of the Student's Book), there are two more sample answers to the **Practise an open-response question**. Your students can practise marking these and so improve their understanding about how to produce a good answer. See the **Introduction** to this Teacher Guide for more guidance on using the sample answers and marking guidance.

Answer		Mark	Comment
1	50 million	1 mark	*Also accept 'half' or 50% as this means the same.* *You can write numbers as numerals or as words.*
2	threatens crop production	1 mark	*Accept threatens crops/the production of crops.*
3	food	1 mark	*Also accept new food sources / new plants and flowers.*
4	insecticides	1 mark	*Do not accept 'chemicals' or 'herbicides'.*
5	renting them	1 mark	*Accept 'renting to other people'.*
6	i) fuel ii) equipment iii) controlling bugs iv) queen bees	**Give ONE mark EACH, up to a maximum of 3 marks**	
	TOTAL	8 marks	

Handy tips

As a final task, ask students to draw up a list of 'Handy tips' to help them when they do a reading question like this. This is a useful last-minute revision activity. Here is one to start them off:

Handy tips for an open-response reading question

- Check that you keep the answers as short as you can.

Multiple-matching reading question: step by step

Steps 1–3: Ask students to highlight the similarities and differences between an open-response question and a multiple-matching question, by reading Chapter 13 in the Student's Book. They should decide that the skills are much the same, but the format of longer multiple-matching questions is different and some inference is required. Also, the questions are not in the order of the text.

Step 4: Remind students to check their answers and stress they can use A, B, C and D more than once.

Step 5: Using inference will improve students' general comprehension. Give them confidence that this is not a difficult skill by illustrating simple inference we use in daily life – for example, if you are waiting for examination results, and a boy comes into the room smiling and waving a piece of paper, you might infer that he has got some good results, without him actually saying anything at all. In other words, 'inferring' means 'reading the signs/clues'.

After completing **Practise a multiple-matching reading question**, students can be given the following prompts to discuss in pairs:

- Compare and then agree on your answers to all the questions.
- There were no subheadings here, so what 'key words' did you use to help you find the answers?
- Did you ever have to look out for words that meant the same as the key words (i.e. synonyms)?
- Did all the answers appear in the text in the same order as in the questions? How did this complicate things?

The student as marker

Go through the marking guidance below with the students and, as before, draw attention to the comments in the final column.

The students can then use the marking guidance to mark the sample answers for **Practise a multiple-matching reading question** also shown on **worksheet 13.1**. Ask students, working in pairs, to discuss and agree their marks. They should compare their marks and comments with those given in **worksheet 13.3**. Check that they correctly identified those answers that failed to score full marks and that they understood the reasons why.

Students can then mark their own answers, using the marking guidance below. Alternatively, as teacher, you may decide to use the marking guidance to enhance your own marking, perhaps referring to it when returning students' work to them.

Using the Sample answers

In Chapter 13 Sample answers (at the back of the Student's Book), there are two more sample answers to the **Practise a multiple-matching reading question**. Your students can practise marking these and so increase their familiarity with the marking guidance. See the **Introduction** to this Teacher's Guide for more guidance on using the sample answers and marking guidance.

Handy tips

As a final task, ask students to draw up a list of 'Handy tips' to help them when they do a reading question like this. This is a useful last-minute revision activity. Here is one to start them off:

Handy tips for a multiple-matching reading question
* The answers are not in the order of the text.

Practice multiple-matching reading question – Marking guidance

Answer	Mark	Comment
a) **B**	1 mark	*A's top was the wrong size, but **B**'s trousers were too small ('they didn't even fit my little sister').*
b) **C**	1 mark	*His work is **voluntary** which means he isn't paid.*
c) **B**	1 mark	*A meets up online, **C** plays football with friends and goes out in the evenings, **D** no mention of friends.* 'going shopping with my friends is a good way for us to actually meet up in person'.
d) **D**	1 mark	*A had a long delay in getting his money back, but **D** did not get a refund.* 'A leather handbag I ordered turned out to be just plastic but the company wouldn't return my money'.
e) **A**	1 mark	*D does not buy things in shops, but we don't know if she goes every day.* *A works in a shop for two hours **every morning**.*
f) **C**	1 mark	*The rest of them talk about problems but **C** does not mention any.*
g) **A**	1 mark	*A comments:* I don't want to waste money on petrol and parking when I'm shopping.' **B** and **C** have to pay for petrol and **D** does not mention.
h) **C**	1 mark	*C buys online and collects what he has bought from the shop where he can change it for something else.*
i) **A**	1 mark	*A contacts his friends through social media. The other young people all enjoy going out with their friends.*
TOTAL	9 marks	

Chapter 14 Answering note-taking questions

Assessment objectives

R1 Demonstrate understanding of specific factual information
R2 Demonstrate understanding of the connections between the ideas, opinions and attitudes
R3 Identify and select details for a specific purpose

Question types

* Note-taking

Differentiated learning outcomes

* All students should select a few facts and details, showing a little understanding of the details and the connections between them.
* Most students should select some relevant details, showing some understanding of the details and the connections between them.
* Some students should select most of the required details, showing a secure understanding of the details and the connections between them.

Resources

* **Student's Book**:
  Chapter 14, Answering note-taking questions
  Sample answers: Note-taking questions
* **Worksheets**: 14.1, 14.2
* **Workbook**:
  Section 1.1
  Section 1.2
  Section 1.3

Note-taking questions: step by step

Build up students' confidence by reminding them that in the practice questions to follow, the text they will be taking notes from are similar to the types of texts they have been reading in the Student's Book – chosen with their interests and level of ability in mind. Also remind them that there are headings, which indicate the sort of information students should be looking for, and all the practice students have had in skimming and scanning texts will make this straightforward. Finally, they need to write concise notes, which is also a skill that they have already practised.

Step 1: Stress to the students the importance of getting an overall grasp of the text and the headings they before they write anything. This involves skim reading the text and making a mental note of any title, subheadings, pictures, topic sentences of paragraphs or any other clues. If students lack confidence in this skill, offer extra practice from the Workbook, or review relevant sections in the Student's Book. Quick practice can be offered, e.g. by asking students to look at the Contents page of any text book and asking questions such as, 'Where would I look to find out about X?' Pairs of students can be asked to make up a series of such questions for one another.

Step 2: All students will need to develop their own way of approaching these kind of questions, but the colour-coding system is useful as it is time-saving and helps to sort out what detail goes under which heading. It is important that students understand that the details they need may be spread throughout the text, and that they are probably not in the same order as the headings they are given. Step 2 offers an additional exercise to practise this system of identifying the relevant details.

Step 3: The next stage involves writing the notes, ensuring they are as brief as possible and entering them under the correct heading. Point out that time saved here by keeping the notes relevant and concise will reduce the time needed for the next stage: checking the notes.

It is also worth stressing that these notes do not have to be in students' own words, although more confident students may find it saves time if they do rephrase some.

Step 4:   This step offers extra practice in ways of keeping notes as concise as possible. The main methods are:

- delete all the examples
- omit any unnecessary detail
- omit any irrelevant opinions, emotions or comparisons
- use one word which sums up a longer phrase.

Using the practice question

See the **Practise an open-response question** section in Chapter 13 of the Teacher's Guide for more guidance on whether to have students complete all the practice questions in one sitting, or to tackle individual questions one by one.

After completing the practice note-taking question, students could discuss their responses in pairs with these prompts:

- Explain how you used your skills in skimming and scanning to find the details you needed.
- Did you keep your notes brief? How could some of them be made even briefer?
- Check that your answers are clear and easy to read.

The student as marker

Go through the marking guidance on the following page with the students, drawing attention to the comments in italics.

The students can then use the marking guidance to mark the sample answers for the practice note-taking question, shown in **worksheet 14.1**. Ask students, working in pairs, to discuss and agree their marks. They should then compare their marks and comments with those given in **worksheet 14.2**. Check that they correctly identified where the sample answers failed to score full marks and understood the reasons why.

Students can then mark their own answers, using the marking guidance on the next page. Alternatively, as teacher, you may decide to use the marking guidance to support and enhance your own marking, perhaps referring to it closely when returning students' work to them.

Using the Sample answers

In Chapter 14 Sample answer (at the back of the Student's Book), there is one more sample answer to the note-taking question. Your students can practise marking this and so improve their understanding about how to produce a good answer. See the **Introduction** to this Teacher Guide for more guidance on using the sample answers and marking guidance.

Handy tips

As a final task, ask students to draw up a list of 'Handy tips' to help them when they do a note-taking question like this. This is a useful last-minute revision activity. Here is one tip to start them off:

Handy tips for note-taking questions

- Don't waste time writing out sentences.

Practise a note-taking question – Marking guidance

Add the number of correct answers to give a total out of 7.

Remember that in note-taking questions assess understanding of content (reading and understanding) and not language. Do not subtract any marks for punctuation or spelling mistakes. Answers should be brief, but do not penalise if answers are in sentences (the student has only wasted time writing sentences). Correct responses can only get a mark if they are recorded under the correct subheading.

Answer	Comment
How the present way of life for the Inuits is different from the past • Live across many countries (now) • Kill animals with guns (now) • Live in permanent/more solid buildings (now) • Use petrol-driven vehicles (now) • Make rings and necklaces (out of stone/bone) to sell (now)	*Give one mark each up to a maximum of **3 marks**.* *Give the mark if the answer means the same, e.g. 'make jewellery out of bones to earn a living' / generate income.*
	Marks: 1 mark each up to 3 marks
What will not change for many Inuits in the future • Their main food source – the sea • The Inuit language • Values and ways of life • The Arctic Winter Games • Their sense of identity • Still live in (the frozen) Arctic regions of Canada, Greenland and Alaska	*Give one mark each up to a maximum of **4 marks**.* *Add the two marks together to give a total out of **7 marks**.* *Don't accept the idea of hunting because although their main food source will continue to be the sea, we do not know if they will continue to hunt sea creatures / find their own food source.* *'the frozen' is not necessary but the idea of the 'Arctic' is important so should be in the answer for the mark.* *Accept – 'Arctic regions of countries like Alaska' / 'in Arctic regions or countries'.*
	Marks: 1 mark each up to 4 marks
	Total marks: 7 marks

Chapter 15 Answering multiple-choice reading questions

Assessment objectives

Reading

R1 Demonstrate understanding of specific factual information

R2 Demonstrate understanding of the connections between the ideas, opinions and attitudes

R3 Identify and select details for a specific purpose

R4 Demonstrate understanding of implied reading

Question types

* Multiple choice

Differentiated learning outcomes

* All students should pick out a few of the more obvious required details.
* Most students should pick out many of the details required.
* Some students should pick out nearly all the details required.

Resources

* **Student's Book**:
  Chapter 15, Answering multiple-choice reading questions
  Sample answers: Multiple-choice reading questions
* **Worksheet**: 15.1, 15.2
* **Workbook**:
  Section 1.1–1.3
  Section 2.1–2.5
  Section 3.3

Exploring the questions

Multiple-choice questions involve studying a text that will assess students' reading and selection skills. Students have to answer each question by choosing the correct answer from a choice of a few different options.

Build up the students' confidence by reassuring them that they regularly make choices from a series of options in everyday life. Spend a few minutes brainstorming these occasions, which may well take place in their first language, such as:

* Choosing where to go on a family day out
* Choosing what to do with friends at the weekend
* Choosing what to wear for a party

Go on to reassure them that they have already practised their skimming, scanning skills in different chapters, such as Chapter 1.1. There is no imagination or originality of ideas involved; students must keep very strictly to the ideas in the text. As they work through the following steps, ensure they recognise that these are the skills that will be tested when answering multiple-choice questions.

Step 1: This step offers general guidance to students on understanding what they need to do to address this type of question appropriately. It reassures them that they are being tested on the same skills as on other types of reading texts, but that the way they are expected to identify the correct answer is slightly different.

Step 2: For this step students are informed as to the types of question that they might be asked in multiple-choice questions and reminded that they are very familiar with both the question words and the required answers.

Draw their attention to 'what' comprehension questions by reminding them that the answer will be a fact, an explanation or information about something. Ask them to prepare ten questions to ask a partner beginning with 'what'.

Similarly, draw their attention to 'how' questions by reminding them that the answer will be a manner of doing something, or else a condition or quality. Ask them to prepare five questions to ask a partner beginning with 'how'.

Step 3: For the purpose of understanding the meaning of a word or words in a line or paragraph, first ask students to make a list of pronouns and then ask them to give examples of who the pronouns could refer to, for example 'she' could refer to a mother or a sister.

Next, identify with your students what the pronoun 'it' can mean or refer to in a piece of text, as this can cause misunderstandings. Give them the opportunity to look at sentences in which 'it' is used as a subject or object and discuss how this pronoun is used to avoid the repetition of verbs or nouns or verb/noun phrases.

To take the above one step further, ask the students to identify the purpose of a paragraph which centres around a pronoun or a noun or person. This is explored in section 3.1 of the Student's Book.

Step 4: The ability to understand inferred or implied meaning is also key when answering multiple-choice questions. Brainstorm with the class what could be inferred or implied by different situations or comments for example:

Andreas has a great tan. / I asked Juan about his job interview and he gave me a huge smile. / It was a good holiday but I have paid less for accommodation, I must admit.

Step 5: Ensure students realise that multiple-choice questions can include one testing students' ability to identify the purpose of a text. Brainstorm with the class what types of things people write, for example books, articles, blogs, emails and why they write them, for example to give information, to persuade the reader to do something, to explain, etc.

Using the practice question

The student as marker

To help students become familiar with multiple-choice questions, distribute **worksheet 15.1** and ask them to complete it for further practice in the skills required. Students can then compare their marks and comments with those shown in **worksheet 15.2**.

Students can choose to mark their own responses or one another's work, using the advice on the next page. Alternatively, as teacher, you may decide to use the marking guidance to support and enhance your own marking of the practice question, perhaps referring to it closely when returning students' work to them.

Using the Sample answers

In the Sample Answers for Chapter 15: multiple-choice reading questions (at the back of the Student's Book), there are more sample answers to multiple-choice questions. Your students can practise marking these.

Handy tips

As a final task, ask students to draw up a list of 'Handy tips' to help them with multiple-choice reading questions. This can be done as a class, brainstorming ideas together, as a group, pair or individual activity. It may also be a useful last-minute revision activity. Here is one tip to start them off:

Handy tips for multiple-choice reading questions

- You can sometimes use common sense to identify the least possible answer.

Practice multiple-choice reading questions – Marking guidance

Scuba diving blog

Question	Answer	Mark
1	C	0 The candidate has not understood what 'the latter refers to. *The correct answer is B.*
2	A	1
3	B	1
4	B	0 They paid for some of the training but not all of it. *The correct answer is A.*
5	A	0 Although she had to get a medical fitness certificate, she does not say that being fit enough is an issue for other people to consider. *The correct answer is B.*
6	B	1
		3 marks out of a possible 6 marks

Practice multiple-choice reading questions

My cat speaks sign language with her tail

Question	Answer	Mark
1	B	1
2	A	0 It was not stated that she was surprised that such a degree was possible but it is clear that she didn't know what career this would lead to. *The correct answer is C.*
3	B	1
4	C	1
5	B	1
6	A	0 She says it would be great if everyone did but thinks it's unlikely. *The correct answer is C.*
		Total: 4 marks out of a possible 6 marks

Chapter 16 Answering informal writing questions

Assessment objectives

W1 Communicate information, ideas and opinions
W2 Organise ideas into coherent text using a range of linking devices
W3 Use a range of appropriate grammatical structures and vocabulary
W4 Use appropriate register and style for the given purpose and audience

Question types

- Informal writing questions

Differentiated learning outcomes

- All students should present some straightforward explanation and description; they should use simple structures in their writing, display a basic range of vocabulary and punctuation, and tend to use the same tone and style regardless of reader and purpose.

- Most students should explain and describe clearly; they should use some different structures to give variety to their writing, display a fair range of vocabulary and punctuation with some accuracy, and mostly adopt an informal tone and style for the reader and purpose.

- Some students should explain effectively and describe in some detail; they should use a wide variety of structures and vocabulary to good effect, use punctuation accurately and to clarify meaning, and always adopt a suitable informal tone and style for the reader and purpose.

Resources

- **Student's Book**:
  Chapter 16, Answering informal writing questions
  Sample answers: Informal writing question

- **Worksheet**: 16.1–16.4

- **Workbook**:
  Section 3.1

Exploring the questions

This section gives students practice in completing an informal writing task. Remind students that in writing tasks, writing is expected to be of a certain length and both content and language are assessed. They should therefore check the recommended length of writing from the start. This will be clearer when they come to look at the marking guidance later on.

Tell students to check the recommended length of the writing. Explain that if students have plenty of practice in writing informally in a timed situation, this will help them to learn how to pace themselves. Point out that writing much more than the recommended amount could be counter-productive. It may even mean there may not be enough time to write the minimum amount for the next question. Also, as the piece is marked for the quality of the writing, a much longer piece could create a sense of long-windedness. Remind the students that they must leave enough time at the end for checking and reviewing their work.

Explain that an 'explain or describe' type of writing question has a specific form, purpose and reader. They will learn to identify this. It is also informal. So, for example, it could be an email to a friend, to explain or describe something or to give an account of an event.

To help explain what is involved in this writing question, and to assist students in deciding on a plan of action, Chapter 16 shows an example exam-style informal writing task and goes through it step by step.

An informal writing question to explain or describe

Step 1: Students will need to revise the terms 'form', 'reader' and 'purpose' and what they mean in this context. Discuss how informal writing differs from other types of writing, reminding students that they need to use an informal style and tone and informal language.

Step 2: These kinds of questions can make use of a picture as a stimulus for writing. Emphasise that the picture is to help give ideas. Students do not have to use it – in fact, the sense of an individual voice with independent thinking is often the hallmark of a student who is a confident writer. On the other hand, students should not be afraid of using the suggestion – it has been designed as a valid idea and confident students should be well able to demonstrate some independence of thought through the treatment of the topic.

Step 3: As well as the picture, the exam-style question provides three bullet points: the 'prompts'. These prompts *must* be followed. The Student's Book suggests using the prompts as a way to structure the writing, i.e. as a framework for collecting and organising ideas. The exercises in the Student's Book will take more time than the student will actually have in an examination. Make it clear that this practice work is to help the student understand how to make use of the prompts. In the practice question at the end of the chapter the student should aim for greater speed.

Step 4: This step explains how ideas can be developed.

Step 5: This step focuses on the use of paragraphs and connectives within and between paragraphs. It includes some suggestions on how punctuation and pronouns can also help cohesion.

Using the practice question

You may choose to have the students complete the practice question at the end of the chapter as a last-minute revision exercise. A study of the marking guidance shown below will help students understand more clearly what they should be aiming to do.

After completing the informal writing question, the students can discuss their responses in pairs, with some or all of these prompts:

* Compare how you felt after writing an informal email to explain or describe.

* What use did each of you make of the picture when writing to describe or explain?

* Did you both make brief outline plans before you started writing? Compare your approaches and ask yourself: Did I use the best way to prepare? Should I make any changes to how I prepare for the writing exercise?

* Did you work to the best of your abilities and keep to the word limits? It is very important that you do not write too little, and if you write too much then you can waste valuable time.

* In these kinds of questions you are assessed on how accurate your grammar, your spelling and your punctuation are. Did you leave time to check through your work? You can make changes by clearly drawing a line through the wrong word, and writing the correct version above it.

* Read through each other's work. Tell one another about the best things about each piece, and also about any parts where the writing was less clear or more difficult to read.

The student as marker

To help students become familiar with how to answer these questions, give them a copy of the relevant marking guidance below, which they can later use to mark the sample answer to the practice question. Go through the guidance with students, ensuring they understand any difficult phrases/concepts.

* An additional sample answer is provided on **worksheet 16.1**, along with a marked-up version of it on **worksheet 16.2**. Ask students to mark this sample and then compare the marked-up version with their own marking.

Students can then mark their own responses or one another's work, using the appropriate marking guidance. Alternatively, as teacher, you may decide to use the marking guidance to support and enhance your own marking, perhaps referring to it closely when returning students' work to them.

Using the Sample answer

Chapter 16 Sample answer (at the back of the Student's Book) can be used to extend students' understanding of informal writing questions. Your students can practise by marking this and so improve their understanding about how to produce a good answer. See the **Introduction** to this Teacher's Guide for more guidance on using the sample answers and marking guidance.

Begin by reminding students that for any writing task they need to check how many questions need to be completed within the given time, as there may be more than one. So, if a student spends too much time on the first question, they risk running out of time to properly complete the second question. Should they run low on time for the two writing questions, they would be well advised to divide the remaining time in two, aiming to produce two shorter, but accurate, compositions. The importance of time management cannot be stressed enough.

You can then ask students to note down some features of the content and language of the Chapter 16 Sample answer (covering up the comments at the end) before comparing theirs with the marker's version.

Stress to the students that there is no 'right' or definitive way to make these notes. In fact, it will be interesting to compare the different features that different students identify. This will allow you to explain the subtleties of assessing compositions – it will be a matter of weighing up strengths and areas for development.

The same technique can be used when and if students assess one another's written responses to other writing questions on past papers. Photocopy the students' work, then ask partners to swap essays, mark and annotate them, and then hand them back. Highlighting pens may be used. Suggest that students identify three good features and three areas requiring improvement. The students then try to improve the work before handing it in to the teacher.

To vary the activity, choose two or three examples of responses from the class. Photocopy them but on a larger scale – say as A3-sized posters – and pin them on the wall. Give students a green and a red sticky note each, and invite them to identify a good feature (green) and a feature requiring improvement (red) in one of the essays. Then students stick them on the relevant poster with a line from the sticky note pointing to the feature.

Handy tips

As a final task, ask students to draw up a list of 'Handy tips', like the one below, to help them when they next do informal writing tasks like this. This can be done as a class, brainstorming ideas together, as a group, pair or individual activity. It may also be a useful last-minute revision activity.

Handy tips for informal writing questions

* Read the question carefully and underline words that tell you the form, reader and purpose.
* Open and close the email with friendly, informal greetings.
* Plan your content around the three question prompts.
* Add detail to develop some of your points.
* Maintain an informal style and tone throughout.

Marking guidance

The same instructions and the same marking guidance apply to both the informal and the formal writing questions.

You have to award each answer a mark for **Content** and a mark for **Language**.
* Content – out of 6 marks / Language – out of 9 marks
* Total – 15 marks.

Content means:

* Task fulfilment (how far the piece fulfils the task; awareness of purpose/reader)
* Development of ideas (details/examples given and how easy it is to read).

Language means:

* Range and accuracy (choice of words; sentence structures, grammar, spelling)
* Organisation (punctuation; paragraphs, overall cohesion, sequencing).

Notes:

* If the writing is considerably shorter than the recommended word length, it should be given 1–2 marks or less for Content for only partly fulfilling the task.
* If the writing is only partly relevant and therefore can be awarded only 1–2 marks for Content, the full range of marks for Language is still available.
* If the writing has nothing to do with the question, it should be given 0 marks for both Content and Language – even if it is good to read!

Marking guidance: Informal writing questions (same as Formal writing questions)

Mark (out of 6)	Content	Mark (out of 9)	Language
5, 6	Fulfils the task well and all content is relevant Excellent sense of the audience and purpose Develops ideas well with details/examples and uses own ideas in a convincing way Style and register is appropriate Text is the right length	7, 8, 9	Uses a variety of sentence structures successfully Uses a good range of vocabulary and idioms precisely and accurately No or few mistakes in accuracy If there are mistakes, these do not impact communication Well-constructed paragraphs, with good links inside and between them
3,4	Fulfils the task and the majority of the content is relevant Good sense of the reader and purpose Develops ideas well with details/examples Style and register is appropriate Text is the right length	4, 5, 6	Tries to use a variety of sentence structures Uses words precisely and may try to use idioms A few small mistakes in accuracy, but these do not usually impact communication Uses paragraphs correctly and may try to link ideas inside and between them
1, 2	Little or some of the writing fulfils the task and little or some of the writing is relevant Very little awareness of the reader and purpose Gives very few, if any, details/examples to develop ideas Style and register is not appropriate. Text is not long enough Tries to do the set task (1 mark)	1, 2, 3	Uses simple sentence structures but makes mistakes Meaning is not always clear Paragraphs not used properly if at all Very hard to understand because of all the mistakes (1 mark)
0	No attempt	0	Impossible to understand

Chapter 17 Answering formal writing questions

Assessment objectives

W1 Communicate information, ideas and opinions
W2 Organise ideas into coherent text using a range of linking devices
W3 Use a range of appropriate grammatical structures and vocabulary
W4 Use appropriate register and style for the given purpose and audience

Question types

* Formal writing questions

Differentiated learning outcomes

* All students should present some straightforward information and opinions / recommendations; they should use simple structures in their writing, display a basic range of vocabulary and punctuation, and tend to use the same tone and style regardless of reader and purpose.

* Most students should present information and opinions / recommendations clearly; they should use some different structures to give variety to their writing, display a fair range of vocabulary and punctuation with some accuracy, and mostly adopt a formal tone and style for the reader and purpose.

* Some students should present detailed information effectively and offer persuasive arguments / recommendations; they should use a wide variety of structures and vocabulary to good effect, use punctuation accurately and to clarify meaning, and effectively adopt a formal tone and style for the reader and purpose.

Resources

* **Student's Book**:
  Chapter 17, Answering formal writing questions
  Sample answers: Formal writing question

* **Worksheet**: 17.1–17.4

* **Workbook**:
  Section 3.1

Exploring the questions

This chapter gives students practice in completing a formal writing task. Remind students that in writing tasks, writing is expected to be of a certain length and both content and language are going to be assessed. This will be clearer when they come to look at the marking guidance later on.

Tell students to check the recommended length of the writing. Explain that if students have plenty of practice in writing formally in a timed situation, this will help them to learn how to pace themselves. Point out that writing much more than the recommended amount could be counter-productive. It may even mean there may not be enough time to write even the minimum amount for the previous question. Also, as the piece is marked for the quality of the writing, a much longer piece could create a sense of long-windedness. Remind the students that they must leave enough time at the end for checking and reviewing their work.

Explain that an 'argue/give opinions or report/make suggestions' type of writing question has a specific form, purpose and reader. It is formal: for example, an article or report for a newspaper, newsletter or magazine. It requires the student:

* *either* to argue points for and against a topic or to argue persuasively in favour of or against a viewpoint

* *or* to report on a situation, event or happening and make suggestions or recommendations (usually to improve things).

Emphasise to students that any formal writing they do should be noticeably different to their informal writing, in terms of style, tone and language used.

To help explain what is involved in a writing question, and to assist students in deciding on a plan of action. Chapter 17 shows an example exam-style formal writing task and goes through it step by step.

A formal writing question including opinion or argument

Step 1: Students will need to revise the terms 'form', 'reader' and 'purpose' and what they mean in this context. Discuss how formal writing differs from other types of writing, reminding students that they need to use a formal style and tone and formal language.

Step 2: Draw attention to the fact that the prompts for a formal writing question may be speech bubbles. These provide ideas that could be incorporated or simply used as inspiration. It is most important that students understand that in the example exam-style practice question they must *not* copy out the prompts but instead try to use their own words. The ideas should be referred to in some way, however.

Step 3: The Student's Book suggests using the speech bubbles as a way to structure the writing, using them as a framework for collecting and organising ideas. The exercises in the Student's Book will take more time than the student will actually have in an examination. Make it clear that the practice work is to help the student understand how to make use of the speech bubbles. In the practice question at the end of the chapter the student should aim for greater speed.

Step 4: This step explains how ideas can be developed.

Step 5: This step focuses on the use of connectives within and between paragraphs. It includes some suggestions on how punctuation and pronouns can also help cohesion.

The same steps are used when your students approach a question asking them to report or make suggestions for improvement. You may decide to ask students to do the practice question at the end of the Student's Book chapter on another day.

Using the practice question

You may choose to have the students complete the practice question in one sitting, perhaps as a last-minute revision exercise. A study of the marking guidance shown will help students understand more clearly what they should be aiming to do.

After completing the formal writing question, the students can discuss their responses in pairs, with some or all of these prompts:

* Compare how you felt after writing a formal article including opinion or argument.
* What use did each of you make of the speech bubbles when writing to include opinion or argument?
* Did you both make brief outline plans before you started writing? Compare your approaches and ask yourself: Did I use the best way to prepare? Should I make any changes to how I prepare for the writing exercise?
* Did you work to the best of your abilities and keep to the word limits? It is very important that you do not write too little, and if you write too much then you can waste valuable time.
* In these kinds of questions you are assessed on how accurate your grammar, your spelling and your punctuation are. Did you leave time to check through your work? You can make changes by clearly drawing a line through the wrong word and writing the correct version above it.
* Read through each other's work. Tell one another about the best things about each piece, and also about any parts where the writing was less clear.

The student as marker

To help students become familiar with how to answer these questions, give them a copy of the relevant marking guidance below, which they can later use to mark the sample answer to the practice question. Go through the guidance with students, ensuring they understand any difficult phrases/concepts.

* An additional sample answer is provided on **worksheet 17.1**, along with a marked-up version on **worksheet 17.2**. Again, students can mark this sample and then compare the marked-up version with their own marking.

Students can then mark their own responses or one another's work, using the appropriate marking guidance. Alternatively, as teacher, you may decide to use the marking guidance to support and enhance your own marking, perhaps referring to it closely when returning students' work to them.

Using the Sample answer

Chapter 17 Sample answer (at the back of the Student's Book) can be used to extend students' understanding of formal writing questions. Your students can practise marking these and so improve their understanding about how to produce a good answer. See the **Introduction** to this Teacher's Guide for more guidance on using the sample answers and marking guidance.

Begin by reminding students that ….that for any formal writing task, they need to check how many writing questions need to be completed before they start as there are often more than one. So, if a student spends too much time on the second question, it's possible that they didn't spend enough time on the first question. Should they run low on time and if the task includes two writing questions, they would be well advised to divide the remaining time in two, aiming to produce two shorter, but accurate, compositions. The importance of time management cannot be stressed enough.

You can then ask students to note down some features of the content and language of Chapter 17 Sample answer (covering up the comments at the end) before comparing theirs with the marker's version.

Stress to the students that there is no 'right' or definitive way to make these notes. In fact, it will be interesting to compare the different features that different students identify. This will allow you to explain the subtleties of assessing compositions – it will be a matter of weighing up strengths and weaknesses.

The same technique can be used when and if students assess one another's written responses to other writing questions on past papers. Photocopy the students' work, then ask partners to swap essays, mark and annotate them, and then hand them back. Highlighting pens may be used. Suggest that students identify three good features and three areas requiring improvement. The students then try to improve the work before handing it in to the teacher.

To vary the activity, choose two or three examples of responses from the class. Photocopy them but on a larger scale – say as A3-sized posters – and pin them on the wall. Give students a green and a red sticky note each, and invite them to identify a good feature (green) and a feature requiring improvement (red) in one of the essays. Then students stick them on the relevant poster with a line from the sticky note pointing to the feature.

Handy tips

As a final task, ask students to draw up a list of 'Handy tips' to help them, like the one below, when they next do formal writing tasks like this. This can be done as a class, brainstorming ideas together, as a group, pair or individual activity. It may also be a useful last-minute revision activity.

Handy tips for formal writing questions

* Read the question carefully and underline words that tell you the form, reader and purpose.
* Incorporate ideas from the speech bubbles but never just copy them out using the same words.
* Plan your content around your main points of argument or information.
* Add detail to develop some of your points.
* Maintain a formal style and tone throughout.
* If writing a report, include subheadings for your paragraphs if this helps organise your report.

Marking guidance

The same instructions and the same marking guidance apply to both the informal and the formal writing questions.

You have to award each answer a mark for **Content** and a mark for **Language**.

* Content – out of 6 marks / Language – out of 9 marks
* Total – 15 marks.

Content means:

* Task fulfilment (how far the piece fulfils the task; awareness of purpose/reader)
* Development of ideas (details/examples given and how easy it is to read).

Language means:

* Range and accuracy (choice of words; sentence structures, grammar, spelling)
* Organisation (punctuation; paragraphs, overall cohesion, sequencing).

Notes:

* If the writing is considerably shorter than the recommended word length, it should be given 1–2 marks or less for Content for only partly fulfilling the task.
* If the writing is only partly relevant and therefore can be awarded only 1–2 marks for Content, the full range of marks for Language is still available.
* If the writing has nothing to do with the question, it should be given 0 marks for both Content and Language – even if it is good to read!

Marking guidance: Formal writing questions (same as for Informal writing questions)

Mark (out of 6)	Content	Mark (out of 9)	Language
5, 6	Fulfils the task well and all content is relevant Excellent sense of the audience and purpose Develops ideas well with details/examples and uses own ideas in a convincing way Style and register is appropriate Text is the right length	7, 8, 9	Uses a variety of sentence structures successfully Uses a good range of vocabulary and idioms precisely and accurately No or few mistakes in accuracy If there are mistakes, these do not impact communication Well-constructed paragraphs, with good links inside and between them
3,4	Fulfils the task and the majority of the content is relevant Good sense of the reader and purpose Develops ideas well with details/examples Style and register is appropriate Text is the right length	4, 5, 6	Tries to use a variety of sentence structures Uses words precisely and may try to use idioms A few small mistakes in accuracy, but these do not usually impact communication Uses paragraphs correctly and may try to link ideas inside and between them
1, 2	Little or some of the writing fulfils the task and little or some of the writing is relevant Very little awareness of the reader and purpose Gives very few, if any, details/examples to develop ideas Style and register is not appropriate. Text is not long enough Tries to do the set task (1 mark)	1, 2, 3	Uses simple sentence structures but makes mistakes Meaning is not always clear Paragraphs not used properly if at all Very hard to understand because of all the mistakes (1 mark)
0	No attempt	0	Impossible to understand

Assessment objectives

L1 Demonstrate understanding of specific information
L2 Demonstrate understanding of ideas, opinions and attitudes
L3 Demonstrate understanding of the connections between ideas, opinions and attitudes
L4 Demonstrate understanding of what is implied but not directly stated.

Question types

* Multiple choice with visual prompts
* Multiple choice shorter questions
* Multiple choice gap-fill
* Multiple matching to speakers
* Multiple choice longer interview text

Differentiated learning outcomes

* All students should select and retrieve some of the required details, showing limited understanding of meaning and relevance. They should understand more obvious ideas, opinions and attitudes, recognising straightforward connections between related ideas.

* Most students should select and retrieve many of the required details, showing clear understanding of meaning and relevance. They should understand some ideas, opinions and attitudes, recognising some connections between related ideas. They should understand some inferred meaning but need support.

* Some students should consistently and reliably select and retrieve most of the required details, demonstrating secure understanding of meaning and relevance, including inferred meaning. They should consistently understand ideas, opinions and attitudes, recognising even subtle connections between related ideas.

Resources

* **Student's Book**: Chapter 18, Responding to listening questions Sample answers: Responding to listening questions
* **Audio tracks**: 18.1–18.5
* **Worksheet**: 18.1–18.6
* **Workbook**: Sections 4.1–4.6

Using the resources

The practice Listening questions can be used in their entirety for practice under timed conditions. Alternatively, they can be used as a teaching tool, by using the separate question sections to focus on the particular skills required. See below for some suggestions for this. If the practice questions are being used as a teaching tool, after completing each section, invite students to discuss their responses in pairs and agree on their answers.

The **REMEMBER TO... lists** may be used in the classroom. Ask the students to work in pairs or small groups and produce a **REMEMBER TO... list** for themselves. They can then compare their list with the ones in the Student's Book. In class feedback, ask students whether they had any extra points to make and encourage them to share these with one another. This activity could take place either before or after the practice questions are completed – or even both before *and* after.

Multiple-choice listening questions with visual prompts

Explain that in the exam-style practice question in the Student's Book, the format is six short monologues or dialogues. In each case, the students are asked to pick out some detail or information, and to answer a question, by selecting the correct visual answer. In an exam, there may be more or fewer questions.

In listening tasks, students hear each recording twice. If this is the case, it is crucial that they make proper use of the pause between each playing and each new question. Before playing the recording for the listening questions, discuss as a class how the pauses between speeches could be used. It may be useful to provide a copy of a transcript of a past or specimen paper. The recording asks the students to look at the questions and visuals.

Discuss how this might help. For example:

- It sets a context so that students will know the kind of vocabulary to expect.
- It sets a context because students can predict the possible answers by understanding what they see in the visuals.
- The key question words suggest the type of information they should listen for.
- They should underline key words in the question to help them focus on the exact detail they should listen out for.
- They should think about what is shown in each visual and predict possible vocabulary.

Discuss how the pauses *between* the two playings could be used – namely:

- to decide what (if anything) they missed
- in particular, to decide what they should listen out for during the second playing.

Discuss how the pause *after* the second playing could be used – namely:

- to check answers
- to make intelligent guesses at answers, if necessary
- to skim read the next question and prepare for it.

The student as marker

Understanding the marking guidance will benefit students enormously, as it will help them understand what is required in a listening task.

Talk the students through the marking guidance, drawing attention to the main issues. This may be done one question section at a time or as a whole.

Using the Sample answers

The marking guidance below can be used to mark the sample answers at the back of the Student's Book (Sample answer: multiple-choice listening questions with visual prompts). The comments and marks could be hidden. After the students have marked them, the final version can be presented and compared. This can be an individual, paired or even class activity.

An additional sample answer is provided in **worksheet 18.1**, along with a marked-up version of it in **worksheet 18.2**. Students can be asked first to mark this sample and then to compare the marked-up version with their own.

Marking guidance: Practice multiple-choice listening questions with visual prompts

Answer		Marks	Comment
1	B - a necklace	**1 mark**	She was going to get gold earrings but remembered her mum doesn't like gold.
2	B - the fashion museum	**1 mark**	They will go there in the morning and to the others in the afternoon.
3	C - the forest	**1 mark**	The forest was their parents' first idea.
4	A - the cafeteria	**1 mark**	It fell out of her bag when she had a sandwich in the cafeteria.
5	B - car is at garage	**1 mark**	They can't go for a drive because the car is still at the garage. Cleaning his room is mentioned but only as a result of Alan not being able to go out.
6	B - musical trio	**1 mark**	The musical trio are second as the replacement for the pianist, who is not well.

Shorter multiple-choice listening questions

Explain to students that in the example practice question, they will be listening to short dialogues or monologues, both formal and informal. No subject knowledge is expected of them.

Ensure that students understand exactly what the practice question entails. In the exam-style practice test, there are two questions per dialogue or monologue, each one with three answer options; only one will be the correct response.

There is further work on tackling multiple-choice questions in Chapters 7, 9 and 12. Invite students to explain how they tackle these questions. Elicit such points as:

* use pre-reading skills to decide what kind of detail they should listen out for
* underline key words or phrases to help give focus to their listening
* decide which of the three answer options is definitely wrong (if any)
* if all else fails, guess.

After students have completed this listening question, they could be invited to work in pairs and discuss the reasons for their choices; they should then decide on an agreed set of answers. The pairs could be put into groups of four and then compare their answers and reasoning.

The student as marker

Talk the students through the marking guidance below, drawing attention to the main issues. Students can use the marking guidance to mark the sample answers at the back of the Student's Book (Sample answer: shorter multiple-choice listening questions). The marker comments and marks could be hidden or reproduced blank. After the students have marked them, the final version can be presented and compared.

Marking guidance: Practise shorter multiple-choice listening questions

1	**B**	5	**B**	9	**B**
2	**C**	6	**A**	10	**C**
3	**B**	7	**C**		
4	**A**	8	**A**		

Gap-fill listening questions

In these types of questions, students have to pick out words and phrases to complete sentences or notes from listening to a spoken text (such as a semi-formal talk by one person).

Students should be reminded of the importance of taking advantage of the pauses and silences. In the exam-style practice question students will hear the speech twice. Remind them again of the pre-listening exercises they did in earlier chapters, for example in Chapter 4.4. Underlining key words again can help them focus and listen out for the precise information they need.

The student as marker

Talk the students through the marking guidance below, drawing attention to the main issues. Students can use the marking guidance to mark the sample answers at the back of the Student's Book (Sample answer: gap-fill listening questions). The marker comments and marks could be hidden

After the students have marked them, the final version can be presented and compared.

An additional sample answer is provided in **worksheet 18.3**, along with a marked-up version of it on **worksheet 18.4**. Students can be asked first to mark this sample and then to compare the marked-up version with their own.

1	B	Josh has been a National Champion 21 times.
2	A	Josh first became interested in chess when he was in a park.
3	A	Josh became an International Master at the age of 16.
4	A	*How to Win at Chess* was Josh's least successful book.
5	C	The writer recommends that people in general read *I am a Player not a Piece*.
6	B	*Chessmaster* is the second in a series of instructional videos.
7	C	Josh is dedicated to teaching chess because he wants to make his ideas available to everyone.
8	B	Josh was attracted to Tai Chi Chuan because of his interest in eastern philosophy.
9	B	Josh travels the world giving lectures on methods of learning, mental attitude and the psychology of competition.
10	A	Josh believes that people have to be prepared to face new challenges in order to be successful.

Matching speakers to statement listening questions

Ensure the students understand exactly what the question entails. Explain that in this example practice question in the Student's Book, student will listen to six short extracts spoken by six different speakers. Reassure them that the style will be semi-formal and on a topic of interest to their age group. The topics will not be too specialised, and questions will not assume any subject-based knowledge.

Invite the students to look at the sample question in the Student's Book. This shows a numbered list of speakers. Below that are eight statements, perhaps expressing an attitude, an opinion or emotion. Their task is to match the speaker to one of the statements, by selecting the letter corresponding to the statement next to the speaker. There are two extra letters which they do not need to use. This example question tests students' listening comprehension alone and they do not have to write any words or sentences.

Ask the students to suggest how they might use the pre-listening time in this activity. Elicit the following:

* Read the question very carefully and understand what to do.
* Read the list of statements and check their meanings.
* Underline key words in the statements – words they will listen out for, either as the word itself or a synonym or a phrase that paraphrases the words.

Choose one or two key words from the sample question and invite students to suggest other words connected in meaning they might listen out for.

Make sure students understand in this example question there will be two statements left over at the end that do not fit any of the speakers.

Remind students that they should never leave an answer box blank – even if they are making an educated guess, they will have a chance to answer correctly.

After students have completed this listening question, it would be helpful for them to discuss in pairs how they decided on their answers. Allow them to agree on their set of answers together and then have pairs explain their choices to the class. Answers can be checked using the marking guidance below.

The sample answer to this question can also be found at the back of the
Student's Book.

Marking guidance: Practise matching speaker to statement listening questions

Answer	Statement	
Speaker 1	B	I love my sport and want to play in international competitions.
Speaker 2	G	I have never liked sport, not when I was young, and not now.
Speaker 3	D	I have always enjoyed sport but it is definitely just a hobby for me.
Speaker 4	E	I am sorry that I do not do as much sport now as I did when younger.
Speaker 5	A	I enjoy sport because it keeps me fit and helps me make friends.
Speaker 6	C	I am really lucky because I am earning my living doing the sport I love.

These are the two extra statements that are left unused: **Statement F** (I used to hate sport but now I am really keen and will never stop.) and **Statement H** (My parents are both professional sports people and I grew up wanting to be exactly like them.).

Multiple-choice listening questions on longer interviews

 Explain to students that in the example question in the Student's Book, the text is an interview. It is a semi-formal or more academic discussion on a topic of general interest. No subject knowledge is expected of them.

Ensure that students understand exactly what the task entails. In the example practice question, the multiple-choice questions have three answers options; only one will be the correct response.

There is further work on tackling multiple-choice questions in Chapters 7, 9 and 12. Invite students to explain how they tackle these questions. Elicit such points as:

* use pre-reading skills to decide what kind of detail they should listen out for
* underline key words or phrases to help give focus to their listening
* decide which of the three answer options is definitely wrong (if any)
* if all else fails, make an educated guess.

The student as marker

Talk students through the marking guidance below drawing attention to the main issues. Students can use this to mark the sample answers at the back of the Student's Book (Sample answer: listening questions on longer interviews). The marker comments and marks could be hidden. After students have marked them, the final version can be presented and compared. This can be an individual, paired or class activity.

An additional sample answer is provided in **worksheet 18.5**, along with a marked-up version of it on **worksheet 18.6**. Students can be asked first to mark this sample and then to compare the marked-up version with their own.

Alternatively, after students have completed this listening question, they could be invited to work in pairs and discuss the reasons for their choices; they should then decide on an agreed set of answers. The pairs could be put into groups of four and then compare their answers and reasoning.

Marking guidance: Practice multiple-choice listening questions on longer interviews

1	**B**	5	**C**
2	**C**	6	**C**
3	**C**	7	**B**
4	**A**	8	**A**

Assessment objectives

S1 Communicate a range of ideas, facts and opinions
S2 Demonstrate control of a range of vocabulary and grammatical structures
S3 Develop responses and maintain communication
S4 Demonstrate control of pronunciation and intonation

Question types

* Speaking: short interview; giving a talk; discussion developing ideas in conversation

Differentiated learning outcomes

* All students should express simple ideas and opinions so that they are understood, using a limited range of structures and vocabulary; they should be reasonably good listeners, trying to respond appropriately to others; their pronunciation and use of stress patterns should be such that they can be understood.

* Most students should express some ideas and opinions clearly, offering examples to develop them satisfactorily and using some variety of structures and vocabulary; they should interact with others in conversation and help to produce a competent conversation using clear pronunciation and intonation.

* Some students should express complex or abstract ideas and opinions confidently, using effective examples to support them; they should employ a range of structures and vocabulary with precision and care; they should show sustained ability to maintain a conversation at some length, sometimes taking the initiative; their pronunciation and intonation should be effective at clarifying meaning and conveying subtleties of emotion.

Resources

* **Student's Book**: Chapter 19, Responding to speaking questions
* **Audio tracks**: 19.1–19.3
* Sample answers: speaking questions
* **Worksheets**: 19.1–19.4

Exploring exam-style questions

This chapter gives your students step-by-step guidance on how to answer speaking questions and helps them to prepare to take speaking tests. Exam-style speaking cards are included for them to practise answering interview questions and developing a discussion.

Speaking questions: step by step

Step 1: A speaking test may include an introduction and/or warm-up stage.. Students may find it strange that they have to be introduced by name by a teacher who knows them well; also that they have to hear all about the test procedure when they know it and have practised it several times. Explain that the format – the welcome, the introduction and the explanation of the test – is a fixed part of speaking tests.

Students may also feel uneasy about being recorded, so it is useful to practise this with them to help them feel more comfortable about it. Teachers should practise the formalities of recording with their students before they do the practice test so that by the time they take a formal test they will not be fazed by it.

Explain that warm-ups are a usual part of a speaking assessment and that a warm-up has two functions:

* to relax the student
* to allow the teacher to decide which speaking card is most suitable to offer.

Again, explain that this short section is actually of benefit to them.

Step 2: Explain to the student that speaking tests include a short interview, in which they are asked questions on a particular topic. Look at the example given in the Student's Book: Would having more money change a student's daily life? Have students role-play the parts of the interviewer and the student from the short exchange printed in the Student's Book. Then practise other interview topics with students.

Emphasise that although it is a short interview, it is an assessed part of the test and as such it is extremely important that the student speaks as much as possible. You should remember to allow them to respond to each question as fully as possible.

Reassure students that they should see the experience as a natural conversation. Reassure them that their teacher will not fire questions to which they are supposed to know the 'right answers'. In the conversation they are allowed to express their own ideas, thoughts and opinions. Nothing is 'right' or 'wrong' – they should concentrate on expressing themselves clearly, offering examples and developing their ideas well. Students should listen carefully and respond appropriately. Most students even enjoy the experience! They should put the fact that it is an assessment to the back of their mind.

Explain to students that they need to consider four main areas as they talk: grammar, vocabulary, pronunciation and the development of ideas.

Step 3: Explain that in a speaking test they will be asked to give a short talk on a particular topic. They are given some time to prepare. Explain that students are given a topic card, but before they start looking at speaking cards in detail, explain the importance of the preparation time. It may be worth spending a session with the class or small groups discussing how best to use this opportunity to prepare. Elicit such hints as:

- asking about words or ideas you don't understand on the card
- thinking of words or phrases specific to the topic
- going through the notes on the card and thinking quickly what you could say about each one.

3.1–3.2: This section explains the structure of a speaking card using an example topic: 'A useful birthday present'. As a class go through this example identifying the different features that are highlighted. As a practice, students should copy and fill in the chart to make notes to help them prepare for what they would say.

3.3: Remind students that in a formal assessment, they are not usually able to make written notes. Some students may be alarmed at this but reassure them that it is actually to their advantage *not* to make notes: the conversation should be natural and notes would make it sound unnatural. This section therefore gives them practice in preparing for a talk without notes, using another practice speaking card: 'Watching TV'. More confident students can do this in pairs or small groups, without notepaper and pencil. Less confident students could start off writing notes and discussing/comparing them, and then repeat the exercise another day, without making any notes.

Step 4: Go through the points in the Student's Book which help students understand how to structure the talk. Point out that they will have to discuss the advantages and disadvantages of the topic and look at the example transcript in which the speaker is discussing the pros and cons of receiving a new PC for their birthday. Model the response by reading the transcript out loud and ask students to do the same.

Explain that to finish the talk, students should summarise what they have said and add a personal opinion. Look at the next example transcript and again model the speaker's words. Invite students to give their own opinions on the subject and to practise giving a short summary to the class.

As the example speaking cards require the student to talk about advantages and disadvantages, it would be worth practising appropriate functional language; you could select a variety of general topics for this practice, such as the environment, eating habits, sport, holidays, hobbies, technology, etc.

If students are not used to giving short talks and feel more comfortable in a two-way discussion, reassure them by emphasising that this is their chance to demonstrate just how much range of language they have and how accurate they can be. Help to build up their confidence by first asking them to practise speaking on their own, in pairs and then in a small group. When you feel that they are ready, you could move onto asking them to give a short presentation on a topic to the whole class. Explain the benefits of them practising by themselves at home and recording themselves to listen back to assess their range, pronunciation and accuracy.

Step 5: Explain to students that speaking questions can also require further discussion on a topic. The interviewer asks questions to encourage students to further develop the topic of the short talk.

Work through sections 5.1 to 5.13 in the Student's Book, which uses examples from the topic 'daily life in the future'. This is in preparation for the practice interview at the end of the chapter, so refer to that as you discuss examples with the class to be sure that everything is covered and that students are fully prepared for the later task.

Use the activities to build awareness of how people interact with one another in natural conversations. It might be helpful to open up with a discussion of how we keep conversations going and what makes a good conversation:

* Does it need people to talk at great length?
* How important is it to be a good listener?
* How can you show you are a good listener?

Another activity could be to record a conversation between two friends, or to download one from the internet. This could be in English or, if the class has another shared language, in their first language. Invite pairs of students to analyse how the two people managed to keep the conversation going.

Make some suggestions about how people develop ideas in conversations. Again, real examples could be found on the TV – perhaps record a few minutes of a chat show or a news interview. If they have the technology, invite students to search the internet and record an interview or conversation themselves and bring it to class for discussion. Again, this could be done in their first language for less confident students, before applying the same observations to an English conversation.

If appropriate, ask a pair of students to sit in front of the class having a relaxed chat about 'what we did last weekend' or 'a film I saw last night'. The rest of the class can then discuss in pairs or brainstorm as a class which of the techniques to keep the conversation going they observed. You could video conversations for a more formal analysis. Or you could ask your class to record themselves in pairs and then write an analysis of how the conversation was sustained, along with ideas for improvement.

Using REMEMBER TO...

The REMEMBER TO... **list** at the end of Chapter 19 can be used as a simple revision exercise. Invite students as pairs or a class to come up with handy tips for success in the interview. They can compare their lists with the one in the Student's Book. Did they find new points not included in the list?

Using the practice speaking questions

The speaking card shown at the end of Chapter 19 provides an opportunity for students to practise the interview in its entirety, with the teacher conducting and marking it.

To give students more support and to prepare them for the practice interview, give them **worksheets 19.1** and **19.2.** The first three exercises in **worksheet 19.1** can be done in pairs. The final task on this worksheet involves students creating a topic card of their own, which students might find challenging.

Give students **worksheet 19.3**, which will give them further practice in the aspects of development and fluency.

The student as marker

To help students become familiar with how to produce a good answer when responding to exam-style speaking questions, give them a copy of the relevant marking guidance below. Go through the guidance with students, ensuring they understand any difficult phrases/concepts.

Marking guidance: for practice interview

Mark (out of 10)	Grammar	Vocabulary	Development and fluency	Pronunciation
9–10	Variety of structures used accurately and confidently throughout the conversation	Uses sophisticated vocabulary to explain complex and subtle ideas, linking the ideas with a range of appropriate linking devices	Keeps the conversation going and responds at some length to the other speaker. May introduce new ideas into the conversation and respond to a change of direction.	Clear pronunciation and intonation
7–8	Structures generally correct. Some errors in attempting complex sentences	Uses a fair range of vocabulary to explain ideas clearly	Responds to the other speaker well and takes part in a flowing conversation	Pronunciation and intonation generally clear
5–6	Uses straightforward structures well	Uses straightforward vocabulary to convey simple ideas	Responds to the other speaker but does not develop ideas. The other speaker has to keep the conversation going	Pronunciation and intonation not always clear, but can be understood
3–4	Very simple structures but with errors	Uses a limited vocabulary and hesitates or searches for words	Responds very briefly to the other speaker in a hesitant conversation. Some gaps and long pauses	Pronunciation and intonation cause some communication difficulty
1–2	Attempts to take part but little clear meaning	Uses a very limited vocabulary and cannot express ideas clearly at all	Responds so briefly and says so little that no real conversation can take place	Pronunciation and intonation difficult to understand
0	No real response	No real response	No real response	No real response

 Use the recording available online of Answer 3 (from the Sample answers at the back of the Student's Book) in which the speaker delivers the short talk and then responds to questions on the speaking topic card *Daily life in the future*. Students use the table shown in **worksheet 19.4** to assess the conversation using the marking guidance, deciding on marks for 'Grammar', 'Vocabulary', 'Development and fluency' and 'Pronunciation'. They should make a few notes in the 'Comments' column, perhaps jotting down some examples of words or phrases used by the student.

They can then compare their marks, either in pairs or in small groups, and reach some consensus. These agreed marks can then be discussed in class and compared with the marker's assessment in the Sample answers at the back of the Student's Book. Emphasise that the accuracy of their marking is not the issue here – but they should engage with the marking guidance and understand how to produce a good answer.

  You could also ask students to apply the marking guidance to the other two online recordings referred to in the Sample Answers (at the back of the Student's Book). They can then compare their thoughts with those in Student's Book. The guidance can also be used as a regular part of lessons for self-assessment.

Skimming and scanning

Look at the advertisement. It is from the 1980s. Skim and scan the advertisement, looking at the images and headings, to answer the following questions.

a) Which company designed, produced and distributed the BBC Microcomputer System?

b) What are the six ways you can use the BBC Microcomputer?

c) Which two pieces of equipment do you need to use this computer?

Now scan for these details:

d) How much does the BBC Microcomputer cost?

e) Where is it available?

Chapter 1
Technology

Computers for learning: listening for pros and cons

Listen to the conversations at the Chan home (**audio track 1.1**) and the parent–teacher meeting between the Chans and Ms Burroughs (**audio track 1.2**). List the pros (positives) and cons (negatives) that come out of this conversation regarding the use of computers for learning and computers as a distraction for students.

Pros/Positives (+)	Cons/Negatives (–)
Online homework is convenient for students.	Students are distracted by other activities online.
Laptops are now compulsory in some schools and students have access to internet resources for learning.	
	Schoolwork is an excuse for students to stay online, chatting, etc.

Underlying attitudes

Use this worksheet to explore the writer's underlying attitude to Zheng He. This means the writer's real attitude to Zheng He that is not obvious. Fill in the following table to analyse the various words and phrases used by the writer to describe Zheng He's voyages. Then complete the sentence below the table.

Words and phrases	Positive/negative	What the phrase suggests
Six centuries ago	Positive	China was busy exploring the world a long time before European countries began their travels.
Crossed	Positive or negative	
Dozens of		'Dozens of' suggests there were so many that they were impossible to count
The great power of		
Dynasty		'Dynasty' is a word associated with more than one emperor – it suggests that many emperors came from the same family. This means that family was very powerful.
Loaded with		
Spices, ivory, medicines		
Rare woods and pearls		
Expedition		
Ambitious		
Gift		
Amazing		

The writer's underlying attitude is that he/she ....

(a) is disappointed by Zheng He

(b) admires Zheng He

(c) is afraid of Zheng He

(d) is bored by Zheng He

Pros and cons of space exploration speech plan

Use the writing frame below to help you structure your arguments on *either* the advantages *or* disadvantages of space exploration.

Give examples in each paragraph to support your ideas.

Thank you for coming to listen to our talk on space exploration today.
What are the **advantages** / **disadvantages** (*delete one*) of space exploration? I would like to argue that ...

....

....

....

....

My major argument **for** / **against** (*delete one*) space exploration is that ....

....

....

....

Second, I would like to suggest that..

....

....

....

However/on the other hand,...

....

....

....

To sum up, ...

....

....

Therefore, overall I believe that...

....

....

Cooking vocabulary

1 Match each of the verbs used in cooking (in the left-hand column) with the correct definition from the right-hand column.

boil	**A**	add salt, pepper and other spices
fry	**B**	combine items or put one item together with another
stir	**C**	cook in very hot water
season	**D**	raise the temperature
grill	**E**	cook until the food becomes a darker colour
heat	**F**	move a spoon around in a liquid in order to mix it thoroughly
simmer	**G**	cook under direct heat or over a fire
add	**H**	cook in hot fat
brown	**I**	cook gently in a liquid below the boiling point

2 'Collocations' are words that are often used together, e.g. fried rice. There are many food collocations. Match the preparation style in the list below to the correct food. You can match the preparation style with more than one food.

Preparation	Food
ground	tomato
fresh	peanuts/ground nuts
roasted	almonds
dried	tuna
toasted	onion
chopped	garlic
fried	coffee
flaked	cumin
	plantain
	fish
	fruit

e.g. fried plantain   fried fish

....

....

....

....

....

....

Sentences

1 Find four sentences and four phrases in the exercise below. Write either **S** ('sentence') or **P** ('phrase') on the dotted lines.

a) We breathe in through our nose and exhale through our mouth. ....

b) information about the swimming schedule ....

c) jumping over the hurdles ....

d) You should wear comfortable clothing to do exercise. ....

e) I trained hard yesterday. ....

f) during my training session ....

g) Have you got any trainers? ....

h) running down the road ....

2 Make a sentence from each of the four phrases from question **1**.

1...

2...

3...

4...

3 Identify the subject and the main verb in the following sentences.

Sentence	Subject	Verb
a) I like going to the gym.		
b) We went to see the tennis match.		
c) Weights are used to increase muscle power and strength.		
d) Have they completed an introduction to the gym?		
e) At school we practise the 100 m race on the track.		
f) I didn't play badminton with them.		
g) Breathing heavily, Femi collapsed at the end of the race.		
h) Yoga makes you feel good.		

4 Now write four sentences about PE in your school. Label the subject and the verb in each one.

1...

2...

3...

4...

Compound sentences

Complete the following sentences using your own ideas.

1 We decided to get fit, so ....

    ....

2 She bought a pair of trainers and ....

    ....

3 Class 10 went to the Pilates classes, but ....

    ....

4 We could either run in the morning, or ....

    ....

5 You wanted to watch the match, so ....

    ....

6 I am a fan of gymnastics, so ....

    ....

7 I like watching boxing and ....

    ....

8 I would have gone running, but ....

    ....

9 The gym membership was expensive, but they must have thought it was worth it or ....

    ....

    ....

10 The article said we needed to exercise for 30 minutes a day, so ....

    ....

    ....

Writing frame

Title

....

How to play

....

....

....

....

....

....

....

What to wear

....

....

....

....

....

....

....

Why it is good for you

....

....

....

....

....

....

....

Malaria

1   Complete the dialogue. Complete the last line using your own ideas.

do a blood test	shivering	a really high fever
sleep under a mosquito net		tell you what medicine
What seems to be the problem?		take your temperature
by wearing long-sleeved tops		I've got a terrible headache

Patient: Good morning, doctor.

Doctor: Good morning. _____

Patient: Last night I had _____ and I could not stop _____.

Doctor: Okay. Let me _____ .

Doctor: Oh yes. I can see that you are very hot. You've got a temperature of 99 degrees. Was there anything else?

Patient: Yes, _____ . My head is pounding and I feel awful.

Doctor: Well, I think you've got malaria. But we need to _____ to make sure.

After the blood test results come back I will be able to _____ to take.

Patient: Thank you.

Doctor: You know you can prevent malaria. Where do you sleep?

Patient: In the bedroom.

Doctor: Do you use a mosquito net?

Patient: No.

Doctor: Well I advise you to _____. And do you go out at night?

Patient: Sometimes.

Doctor: Another way to prevent malaria is _____ and trousers after 5 pm.

Patient: Have you got any other advice?

Doctor: Yes, you could _____

Did you know?

- An estimated 219 million people had malaria in 2018.
- Seventy per cent of people who died of malaria were in 11 countries (ten in Africa, plus India.
- Half of the people in Africa who got malaria did not sleep under a mosquito net.
- The number of countries where there is no longer malaria is increasing.

(source: World Health Organisation World Malaria Report 2018)

Abstract nouns

1 Many abstract nouns are made by adding suffixes to the ends of words.

Example: participate → participation

> Here are some suffixes that can be used to make nouns.
>
> -ment   -tion   -ity   -ness   -sion   -dom   -ship

What suffixes would you add to the following words to make abstract nouns? Write your new words in the box below. Note that the spellings/endings might change.

1 satisfy ....

2 enjoy ....

3 determine ....

4 excite ....

5 generous ....

6 member ....

7 combine ....

8 aggressive ....

9 free ....

2 Complete the sentences with appropriate abstract nouns from exercise 1, or nouns of your choice.

1 I wanted to join the gym, so I asked about ....

2 I get a lot of .... from doing exercise.

3 You get a great sense of .... when you know you have done some exercise every day.

4 Being healthy is a .... of both eating well and doing regular exercise.

5 He only managed to get into the team through hard work and ....

6 If you want lots of .... and ...., go and watch a live football match.

3 What do these words mean for you?

Health is...

Happiness is ....

More brain facts: sentence matching

Look at the jumbled 'brain facts' below and match the half-sentences in the first column to their appropriate half in the other column.

The brain is over 75% water	is called the neocortex.
We blink 20 000 times a day	change rapidly. People learning to juggle showed brain changes in less than seven days.
Children who learn two languages before the age of five	the production of new neurons or brain cells.
Studies show that the brains of people who are learning new things	so a lack of sleep could actually decrease your ability to store memories and information.
Any mental activity results in	which means that the human brain itself, can feel no pain.
About 100 billion neurons	that gives us our position at the top of the food chain.
The brain sorts and stores memories while you sleep	make up the human brain.
There are no pain-receiving points in the brain	have a different brain structure from the children who learn only one.
The newest, most rational and logical part of the brain	so keeping the brain hydrated is very important while studying or exercising.
Brain researchers believe that it is the large neocortex	yet the world does not go dark each time because the brain keeps it bright and lit.

An online language learning school conducted a survey on difficulties that people face when learning a new language. The survey was conducted using 16 000 language learners across 150 countries. The pie chart below summarises the results. Study the pie chart and then answer the questions that follow.

What is the main difficulty that you experience when learning a new language?

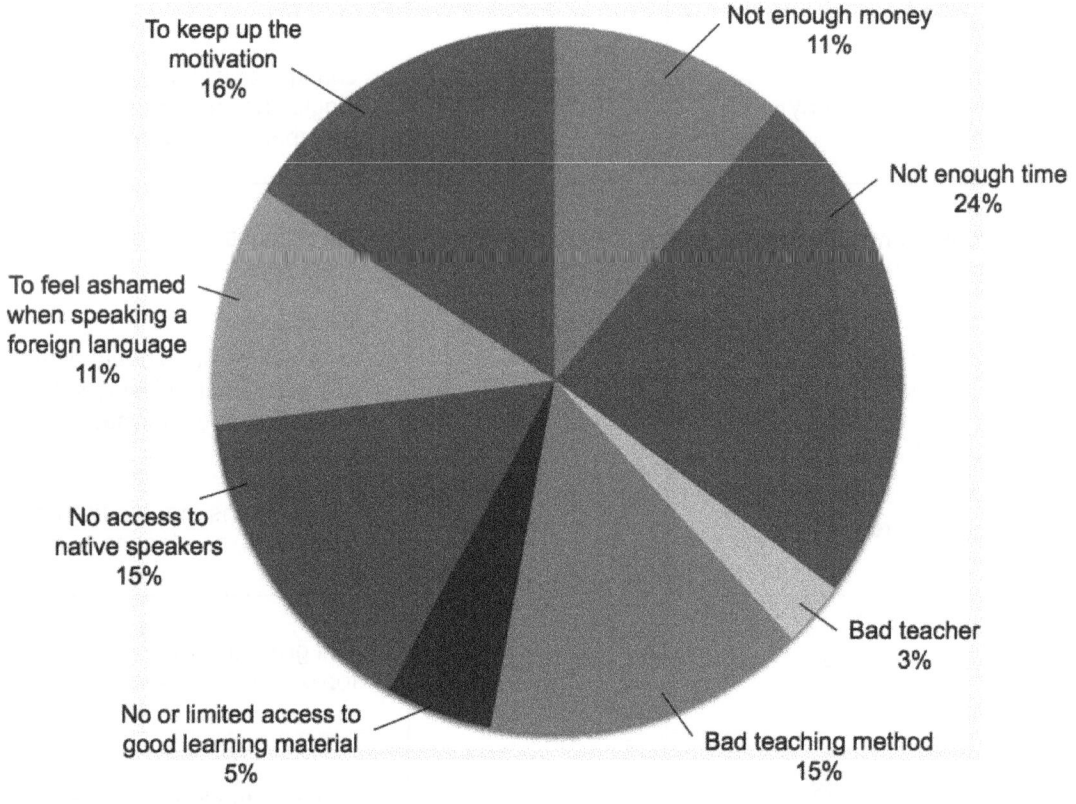

Of the people surveyed, 24% said ....

and 11% said ....

However, another 11% said ....

while 5% had ....

Fifteen % of learners suffered from ....

and 3% were affected by ....

Another 15% complained that they ....

although 16% admitted that they ....

Summarise the main problems faced by people learning a new language: ....

....

....

Writing to compare and contrast

Use the following writing frame with prompts to help you compare and contrast different aspects of schooling in ancient times to schooling today. Use some of the connectives provided to help you.

Introduction: Schools in general. What is different, what has changed?

Curriculum in schools in Ancient India / Egypt compared and contrasted with the curriculum today:

Both ancient Egypt and India had a curriculum that was strictly followed. **Although** Indian *gurus* combined several subjects together, Egyptian teachers taught only what was required for the student's profession or trade. **Nevertheless**, the curriculum in **both** ancient systems involved long hours of study at the teacher's house. Today, **however**, students and teachers go to a common place like a school or college. **In contrast**…

Contrasting connectives:		Comparing connectives:	
Yet… today…	However…	Similar to…. Just like….	
Although…	Even though…, though …	Compared to…	Just as…..
Both…	Nevertheless….	And…	Like….
In contrast…	In comparison….	Not only… but also…	
Despite…,	In spite of….		
On the other hand …	On the contrary…		

Learning styles in ancient India / Egypt compared to today:

....

....

....

Teachers in ancient India / Egypt contrasted with today's teachers:

....

....

....

Discipline in ancient Indian / Egyptian schools compared to today's schools:

....

....

....

Conclusion: Sum up which kind of schooling you prefer and why.

....

....

....

How the brain learns – focus on listening

Listen to **audio track 4.1** *and* watch the video, 'How the brain learns' by searching 'How the brain learns' on YouTube. Then answer the following questions.

1 What are the brain's microscopic cells called? ....

   How many of them exist?...

2 What happens to brain cells when you are learning something? ....

   ....

3 What impact do emotions have on our learning? ....

   ....

4 When do we learn best? Why?...

   ....

5 a) Which important liquid do we need the most when we are learning? ....

   b) Name two negative effects of not having enough of this liquid.

      ....

      ....

6 Which foods does the brain need to maintain a good balance? ....

   ....

7 Which foods should we avoid? Why? ....

   ....

8 What are some effective ways of giving the brain a break? ....

   ....

   ....

   ....

9 Name two of the best conditions for learning?..

   ....

   ....

Listening for implied meaning

Watch the YouTube video of an interview between talk-show host Huckabee and world-famous educationalist Sir Ken Robinson. Pick out three examples of implied meaning. For each example, explain what the speaker really means in this context. We have given you two examples to start you off.

Example	Implied meaning
'An education system that simply just transfers data from one brain to another is not an education system, it's a data download!'	Implies that there is no creativity and no new ideas or talents expressed in this type of education
'Joining me now is a person who understands something about it...'	Understatement – Ken Robinson is a world expert on creativity and education, and has lectured and written books about it.

For extra challenge, pick out two examples of how both speakers use humour and irony – stating the obvious to draw attention to it. In the second column explain why they use it.

Example of how speakers use humour and irony	Why they use it

Big task: schools of the future

You should already have presented your ideas for the 'Ideal school of the Future.' You will now take on the role of a journalist who has attended the presentation. Write a newspaper article that does the following:

1 outlines and describes the key features of the school of the future designed by students

2 states the importance of funding such a project within the local community.

An outline structure is given below for you to follow or adapt.

Introduction:

What, when, who, where, why. Date of the presentation. Date of the Article. See the example below:

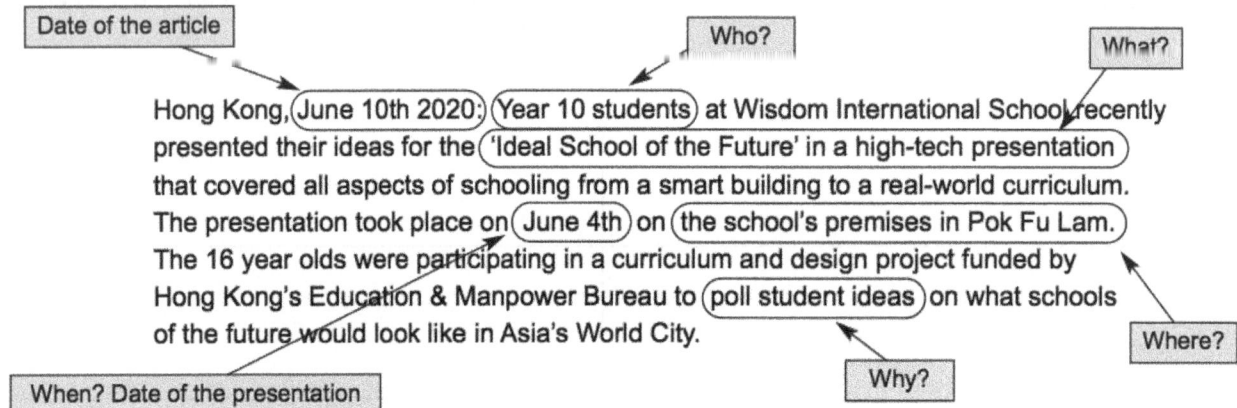

Content: area 1, e.g. the school building

* Describe what students did.
* Explain/comment on what was practical and worth funding.

Content: area 2, e.g. the new curriculum

* Describe what students did.
* Explain/comment on what was practical and worth funding.

Content: area 3, e.g. the roles of teachers, teaching and learning

* Describe what students did.
* Explain/comment on what was practical and worth funding.

Content: area 4, e.g. the rules and culture of the school

* Describe what students did.
* Explain/comment on what was practical and worth funding.

Quotes:

* Include responses of some members of the audience.
* Interview quotes from key listeners, e.g. the education secretary, the principal, chair of the parent–teacher association.

Conclusion:

* Give a summary of good ideas from the presentation and suggestions for the ones worth funding.
* Come up with a phrase that sums up the school design project, such as '*By the kids, for the kids! What better way to design a school?*'

Topic sentence and paragraphs

1 Identify the topic sentence and the supporting details in the following paragraphs.

a) A recent China–America basketball match descended into a fight. Witnesses said first there was a foul on a US player. After that, the audience threw water bottles. Then a spectator threw a chair. Finally, the players and coaches were forced to quit the match early. (A foul is something that someone does in a sport that is not allowed according to the rules.)

Topic sentence	Supporting details

b) Almost three and a half million women and girls now play football in the UK. For a long time there was no professional female league and the UK lost many of its top players, who were tempted to go to the US where they could earn money for playing football. Consequently, in 2009, women's football in the UK created its own professional league.

Topic sentence	Supporting details

2 Write your own paragraph about an athlete or sport. Make sure it has a topic sentence and then two or three supporting details.

Topic sentence: ....

....

....

Supporting details: ....

....

....

....

....

....

Connectives

1 What connectives could be used to connect these sentences? Keep the sentences as separate sentences but add connectives to make them sound better together.

A She earns her salary. She earns money from the organisation that sponsors her.

She earns her salary. Moreover, she earns money from the organisation that sponsors her.

B The opening ceremony was cancelled. Everybody got a refund on their tickets.

....

C You are not allowed to join the club. You can become a temporary member.

....

D He won the gold medal. He broke the world record.

....

E Cricket is very popular in India and Pakistan. The press reports that there is corruption.

....

F He did not train hard. He came last in the race.

....

G I come home from school. I do my homework. I watch football highlights until supper.

....

2 Insert an appropriate connective to fill the gaps in the text below.

The Olympic Games attracts the best athletes from over 200 countries in the world.

.... (*cause and effect*), many people consider the Olympic Games to be the most important sporting event in the world. .... (*add information*) for most athletes, nothing can compare to the idea of winning a gold medal at the Olympic Games.

.... (*contrast*) there are regular reports of dishonest officials during the Olympic Games. .... (*add information*) in the eighties there were protests against the Olympic Games for political reasons. .... (*cause and effect*), the Olympic Games has also had a reasonable number of criticisms and challenges.

3 Write a sentence of your own using the following connectives.

Moreover, ...

However, ...

Main idea and supporting facts

You have agreed to write an article describing a recent sports competition for the school magazine. Use the writing frame below to note down your ideas for the article.

Topic sentence

For example: The Inter-regional School Football Championships were the most exciting event in this year's school sports calendar.

....

....

....

First main idea	**Supporting fact**
For example: where/when the event took place	

Second main idea	**Supporting fact**
For example: what happened	

Third main idea	**Supporting fact**
For example: what people liked or disliked most/least	

Introducing examples

1 Join the following opinions (from the left-hand boxes) to an example that backs it up (in the right-hand boxes), using one of the phrases in the middle.

1 Talent shows encourage young people to sing or dance or play an instrument.		**A** I notice that singers win every year. Plus there are no heavy-metal bands and very few ballad singers. In fact, the judges nearly always base their opinions on whether an act will 'sell' well in the charts.
2 You never achieve fame that lasts a long time through a talent competition.	*For example,*	**B** last Saturday night during the *Got Talent* final, I first went skateboarding with my friends and then we rented a movie and watched it together while eating popcorn.
3 Talent shows only reproduce a certain type of act.	*To give you an example,*	**C** I had a small part in the school play last year and I had to attend rehearsals twice a week after school for about four months and on Saturdays for the last four weeks.
4 Performing in a play is a lot of work.	*Let me illustrate:*	**D** I was asked to offer flowers and to thank the town chief for Independence Day last year and I tripped up and then forgot what I had to say.
5 I never watch the talent contests because I think they are boring.	*For instance,*	**E** the winner last year made one album that was a success – but then we haven't heard from her since.
6 I find going on stage makes me nervous.		**F** when the guitarist played last year, requests for guitar lessons doubled in our school.

2 Now back up these opinions with examples of your own.

The *Got Talent* competitions encourage young and old to sing and dance.

For example, ...

....

....

The judges on the *Got Talent* competitions are useless.

For example, ...

....

....

Rephrasing

1 Match the comments to the rephrasing comment.

1 She can't sing at all.	**a)** Yes – I laughed so much I nearly cried.
2 I really enjoyed the last film – it was so exciting.	**b)** I agree. I cried in the last scene where the heroine dies.
3 The judges are useless.	**c)** It's true there's a lot of shooting.
4 The clown act was hilarious.	**d)** Mmm. I couldn't stop watching her.
5 The film was really sad.	**e)** I couldn't agree more. The lights didn't come on and you couldn't hear what any of the actors were saying.
6 The video game was completely mindless.	**f)** It's true that their comments are fair.
7 The latest school play was badly produced.	**g)** Yes, I was on the edge of my seat.
8 Her performance was mesmerising.	**h)** Yes, it's not strategic and you don't get to make many decisions.
9 The latest *Call of Duty* video is violent.	**i)** Yes, her top notes are all off key.
10 The judges seemed open-minded.	**j)** I agree – they never make any constructive comments.

2 Now rephrase these comments.

Going to the theatre is only for rich people.

....

....

The latest film is really scary.

....

....

Facts and opinions

Write down **three** facts and **three** opinions about a product you know or have seen advertised.

My product is ....

Fact 1 ....

....

....

Fact 2 ....

....

....

Fact 3 ....

....

....

Opinion 1 ....

....

....

Opinion 2 ....

....

....

Opinion 3 ....

....

....

Skills

1 Tick the skills that you are good at.

- [ ] Typing
- [ ] Being accurate
- [ ] Looking after children/old people
- [ ] Being patient
- [ ] Juggling lots of different projects
- [ ] Painting
- [ ] Making things from metal/wood/fabric
- [ ] Sewing
- [ ] Cooking
- [ ] Organising
- [ ] Persuading
- [ ] Influencing
- [ ] Explaining
- [ ] Observing (detail)
- [ ] Teaching
- [ ] Presenting things

- [ ] Analysing things
- [ ] Arranging things
- [ ] Designing
- [ ] Researching
- [ ] Reading
- [ ] Making decisions
- [ ] Being innovative
- [ ] Seeing alternatives
- [ ] Motivating others
- [ ] Listening to others
- [ ] Repairing things
- [ ] Speaking
- [ ] Giving advice
- [ ] Being physically active/fit
- [ ] Running
- [ ] Helping others
- [ ] Interviewing people
- [ ] Looking after animals
- [ ] Growing plants

- [ ] Selling things
- [ ] Writing
- [ ] Being polite
- [ ] Taking risks
- [ ] Memorising things
- [ ] Copying
- [ ] Writing
- [ ] Finding information
- [ ] Measuring
- [ ] Calculating
- [ ] Estimating
- [ ] Managing money
- [ ] Computers
- [ ] Learning
- [ ] Asking questions
- [ ] Working out answers to problems
- [ ] Observing detail
- [ ] Concentrating

2 Imagine you are the following people. What skills do you think you are good at?

Carpenter: ....

....

Member of parliament/government representative: ....

....

Web developer: ....

....

3 Write a short paragraph about your skills. Use the following phrases.

I am good at ....

....

I think I can offer these skills ....

....

I believe I have excellent .... skills because ....

....

Facts or opinions?

1   Identify the facts and the opinions. Tick the appropriate column on the right.

		Fact	Opinion
A	Being a journalist is lots of fun.		
B	You interview people when you are a journalist.		
C	Being a computer engineer is a fulfilling career.		
D	Being a member of parliament is a rewarding job.		
E	The majority of taxi drivers own their own cars.		
F	My sister applied for the post of water engineer.		
G	My brother got an interview to be a nurse at the local hospital.		
H	You earn money while learning skills when you are an apprentice.		
I	I think public relations pays a lot.		
J	Teaching has a good career structure.		

2   Now write **one fact** about each of the following jobs.

Food buyer for a store: ....

....

Tailor: ....

....

Lawyer: ....

....

3   Write **one opinion** about each of the following jobs.

Doctor: ....

....

Gardener:...

....

Sales assistant:...

....

A career in event planning

1 Listen to the video 'Event planning careers: creative jobs for organised people' and complete the form below.

Name of person:	
Industry she works in:	
Three things you have to do to be an event planner:	1 2 3
Event planning is a great job for someone who …	1 2 3

2 Now answer the following questions.

What do you think Jessica's attitude to event planning is?

....

....

....

Why do you think this? Give three things she says about event planning that prove her attitude:

1 ....

....

2 ....

....

3 ....

....

Chapter 6
Work

1 Match the idiom to its meaning.

1	to be rushed off your feet	**a)**	to enjoy something so much it is one of the best moments in your life
2	to not look back	**b)**	to be very annoying
3	to have the time of your life	**c)**	to be much better than the others
4	to turn something on its head	**d)**	to be extremely busy
5	to be a pain in the neck	**e)**	to find out the true reason for something
6	to be head and shoulders above the rest	**f)**	to be well-informed and mentally sharp
7	to be on the ball	**g)**	to change the situation – make a bad situation good (or make a good situation bad)
8	to get to the bottom of things	**h)**	to not think about things that happened in the past

2 Choose **two** of the idioms and use each one in a sentence.

1 ....

....

2 ....

....

3 Underline the idioms in the following sentences and find out their meaning using a dictionary.

a) He had not revised for his maths exam but he made a stab at answering every question.

Meaning: ....

b) Chang felt down in the dumps because no one had replied to his job application letters.

Meaning: ....

c) I am sure she will get the job – she usually gets what she wants in life.

Meaning: ....

d) Maryam met the deadline by the skin of her teeth.

Meaning: ....

Letter of application

Complete the letter of application with appropriate words and phrases from the box.

look forward to hearing from you	convince you of	clients
typing skills	undertaken	company
greeting	speed and accuracy	speaking skills
apply for	Sir/Madam	took on the post of
part-time	With reference to	excellent working knowledge

12 Main St
Mamponteng
Kwabre East

1st May 2022

The Director
More Marketing Services
High St
Kumasi

Dear **(1)** .... ,

(2) .... your advertisement in *The Graphic*, I am writing to

(3) .... the post of **(4)** .... clerical assistant.

At present I am in my final year at Osei Tutu International School where I am an active member on the school council. During this last year, I **(5)** .... Secretary and have **(6)** .... all the clerical duties for the group. I believe I have good

(7) .... as I type up the notes from the meetings promptly and often receive compliments on the 8) .... of my work.

I also help to run the school newsletter for which I edit articles and I have

(9) .... of several software programmes including InDesign. For example, in the latest edition I helped to make cuts to articles so that the newsletter remained two pages.

My teachers tell me that I am polite and that I speak well in public. I am often chosen to show visitors around the school. I believe that I could use my **(10)** .... successfully when talking to and **(11)** .... potential

(12) .... for your **(13)** ....

(14) I .... in the near future and hope to have the opportunity to

(15) .... my enthusiasm for this post.

Yours faithfully

Akosua

Magazine article

Complete this writing frame to help you plan your magazine article.

Intended reader:

* who is going to read the text: ....

* what the purpose of the article is: ....

Therefore the **tone of my article** will be: ....

Introduction of self and scheme:

....

....

....

Where/when placement took place:

....

....

Who you worked with:

....

....

What you saw/heard and learned:

....

....

....

What skills you used/practised:

....

....

....

Overall impression:

....

....

....

....

Stress and intonation

1   Underline the parts of the words that you would stress in the following sentences and questions.

    a) What do you do?

    b) I work full-time as a biomedical engineer.

    c) I'm self-employed. I run my own software business.

    d) I work part-time as a teacher in a local school.

    e) I do some voluntary work with a local charity that looks after elderly people with dementia.

    f) What skills do you think you can bring to the job?

    g) I've got three months' experience of working as a sales assistant.

    h) I think I am good at persuading people. For example, I managed to convince the school to serve healthy snacks at the canteen.

    i) I believe I can offer strong research skills as I am good at observing detail and recording it accurately.

    j) I think I would make a good candidate for the student placement scheme as I enjoy learning things.

2   Read aloud the following sentences, changing your intonation for each situation.

    a) 'I got an interview.'

       • You are annoyed (you didn't want one).
       • You are surprised – you weren't expecting one.
       • You find it wonderful.

    b) 'I work part-time and study part-time.'

       • You are annoyed – you want to study full-time.
       • You are fed up – you are finding it hard to juggle work and study.
       • You find it wonderful.

    c) 'I passed the exam.'

       • You are surprised because you thought you failed.
       • You find it annoying because you passed the exam but you didn't get a place at your chosen college.
       • You are pleased because you worked hard and you think you deserve it.

Chapter 6
Work

A career in biomedical engineering

1 Listen to the video and complete the form below.

Name of person:	
Industry she works in:	
Two examples of biomedical engineering:	1 2
Three interests you need for biomedical engineering:	1 2 3

2 Now answer the following questions.

What do you think Amy's attitude to biomedical engineering is?

....

....

....

What skills do you think you need to be a biomedical engineer?

1 ....

....

2 ....

....

3 ....

....

Spotting key words

Here are some more questions. Remember to read them carefully and underline key words BEFORE the recording is played to you. The transcript of the recording (audio track 7.1) is provided to help you read along while you are listening.

a) What is the problem that the conservation organisation the World Wide Fund for Nature is concerned about?

    ....

    ....

b) In what year did countries in Europe make a promise to prevent the extinction of certain animals?

    ....

c) What is the reason wildlife organisations fear that the situation might get even worse in years to come?

    ....

    ....

Transcript

There is a real problem facing us. The numbers of birds, animals, **marine** and fresh water creatures have **declined** by almost one third, according to the World Wide Fund for Nature, a conservation organisation. Most of the blame for this terrible situation lies with human beings. Humankind has been responsible for this through **habitat** destruction and pollution.

Many wildlife organisations say that the promise made by European Union countries in 2002 to stop the **extinction** of certain **species** by 2010, has still not been met. They feel that the situation is likely to get worse as climate change continues to affect the destruction of various kinds of animals.

Glossary

marine – to do with the sea or ocean

declined – reduced, come down in number

habitat – the natural environment of an animal or plant

extinction – permanent disappearance

species – a distinct group of creatures having a set of common characteristics

Chapter 7
Environment and wildlife

Glossary

Listen out for these words in **audio tracks 7.3** and **7.4**. Play a game with your partner by taking it in turns to say the definition for a word chosen by your partner.

activist a person who works to bring about political, social or other changes by campaigning in public or working for an organisation

anthology a collection of writings by different writers published together in one book

carnivore an animal that eats meat

cheek by jowl if people or things are cheek by jowl with each other, they are very close to each other

claw one's way up achieve something with great determination and in spite of many difficulties

dedicate if someone has dedicated themselves to something, they have given a lot of time and effort to it because they think that it is important

disturb make someone feel upset or worried

Durga in the Hindu religion, the Goddess Durga is the mother of the universe and the power behind the work of creation, preservation and destruction of the world

Durrell, Gerald Gerald Durrell (1925–1995) was a British naturalist, zookeeper, conservationist and author. He wrote a number of books based on his life as an animal collector and naturalist.

face-off an argument or conflict that is intended to settle a dispute

Ganesh in the Hindu religion, Ganesh is one of the most popular gods. He is the son of Lord Siva and the Goddess Parvati, and he is usually shown with an elephant's head on a human body.

Hanuman in Hindu mythology, Hanuman is the monkey commander of the monkey army, one of the central figures in the epic *Ramayana*

hatch when a baby bird, insect or other animal hatches, it comes out of its egg by breaking the shell

Herriot, James James Herriot was the pen name of James Alfred Wight (1916–1995), a British veterinary surgeon and writer. He wrote a number of books about animals and their owners, including *All Creatures Great and Small*.

iconic important or impressive because it is a symbol of something

inviolate if something is inviolate, it has not been or cannot be harmed or affected by anything

kept vigil remain quietly in a place for a period of time because you are watching or protecting something

migratory a migratory bird, fish or animal is one that moves from one place to another every year

monumental very large and impressive and likely to be important for a long time

pitch if two opposing things or people are pitched (or pitted) against one another, they are in conflict

predator an animal that kills and eats other animals

profound very great or intense

protectress a female protector; a woman who protects you from being harmed

raise the profile (of someone or something) increase the attention someone or something gets

rehabilitate improve the condition of a building or place so that it can be used again

retaliatory if you take retaliatory action, you try to arm or annoy someone who has harmed or annoyed you

sanctuary a place where birds or animals are protected and allowed to live freely

tolerance allowing other people to say and do as they like, even if you do not agree or approve of it; allowing animals to live near you even if you do not like them

wane become gradually weaker or less, often so that it eventually disappears

Note-taking: Severn Suzuki's speech

Video clip, be2212's YouTube video 'The best Speech – Severn Suzuki' (6:49 minutes)

Listen to a speech given by 12-year-old Severn Suzuki in 1992 at The Earth Summit. She founded the Environmental Children's Organisation (ECO) at this young age. Severn Suzuki was said to be the 'girl who silenced the world for 6 minutes'. Take notes on what Severn Suzuki said about the following issues.

Holes in the ozone ....
....
....

Sick and disappearing wildlife ....
....
....

World poverty ....
....
....

Forests and deserts ....
....
....

Being a world family ....
....
....

Acting responsibly and sharing resources ....
....
....
....

Persuasive techniques used by Severn Suzuki

Listen to Severn Suzuki's speech once more (see **worksheet 7.3**). Notice that Severn Suzuki uses the following techniques with great expertise and passion as she challenges adults to listen to her.

After listening to the speech, fill in the blank boxes in the table below: give examples of her use of persuasive techniques and comment on the effect each has on her audience. Add any other techniques Suzuki uses.

Persuasive technique	Evidence/quote	Desired effect on audience
Rhetorical questions: Asking questions to which no answer is required. They are asked for dramatic effect.	'Can you imagine a world without any animals? Can we allow this to happen?'	Although the answer is obviously 'No!', it makes people think about the situation and want to find a solution.
Repetition: Stating a key idea or thought over and over again.		
Emotional use of language: Bringing in emotions like guilt, fear, etc.	'Losing my future' 'Starving children' 'I am afraid…'	
Lists of three or more: Lists three or four important things, facts or ideas that are closely linked.		Creates a sense of the many interconnected ideas or things that might be affected by environmental damage.
Challenging the adults: Tells the adults what they have to do.	'If you don't know how to fix it, please stop breaking it!'	

Summarising a text using notes

Read this text about carpet weaving and write some notes using the writing frame.

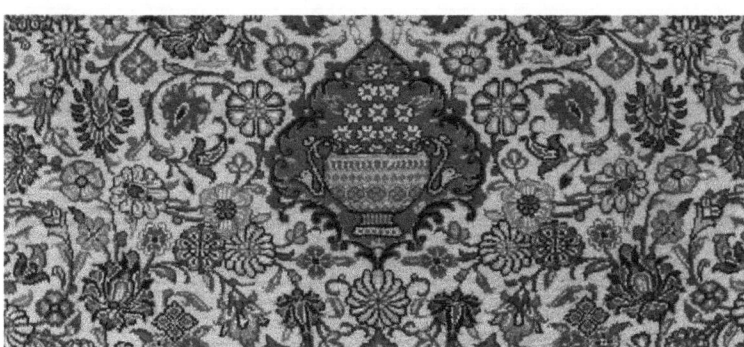

From 1600 to 1800 in the Islamic world, carpet weaving changed from a minor craft with patterns passed down from parents to children into a state-wide industry with patterns created in court workshops.

In this period, carpets were made in greater quantities than ever before. They were traded to Europe and the Far East where, too precious to be placed on the ground, they were used to cover furniture or hung on walls.

Very good quality carpets were in demand and collected by royal households. For example, in Iran the Shah (the king or ruler) decided to promote carpet weaving by asking all the silk merchants and weavers to move to Isfahan – the capital. The Shah then arranged to sell and send many of the carpets to the Kings and Queens of Spain, England and France.

Choose the best notes to sum up main idea of the first paragraph:

1 Carpets expensive 1600–1800

2 Carpet weaving admired/state sponsored industry 1600+

3 Lots of carpets traded 1600–1800

4 Carpet making was an industry in the Islamic world

The main idea of the second paragraph is (use notes) ....

....

....

....

The main idea of the third paragraph is (use notes) ....

....

....

....

Chapter 8
Culture and society

Summary of dialogue

Using your notes to the dialogue in **Going further**, in section 8.1 of the *Student's Book*, complete the sentences about the dialogue.

A girl and her father were discussing ....

....

....

....

The girl wanted to ....

....

because ....

....

The father recommended that ....

....

....

....

The girl maintained that ....

....

....

....

She added that...

....

....

....

The father suggested that ....

....

....

....

My culture and lifestyle

Complete the following table with your own ideas and opinions about your lifestyle.

One thing my culture values is.. ....
One thing my culture gives status to is ....
One thing my culture approves of is ....
One thing my culture rejects is ....
One thing my culture disapproves of is ....
One thing I reject is ....

Chapter 8
Culture and society

1 Replace the word in bold with its synonym.

fortunate	adore	deafening	freshly laundered
drowsy	giggle	brief	assist
huge	amazed	procession	filthy

I **like** [..] Independence Day.

You would be **surprised** [..] at all the things that happen.

The day starts with a **short** [..] prayer.

We don't wear our **dirty** [..] clothes.

We put on our **clean** [..] clothes.

I **help** [..] my younger brothers and sisters to get dressed.

We **laugh** [..] a lot.

We are **lucky** [..] because

the **parade** [..] goes past our door.

The drumming is **loud** [..].

Afterwards we eat a **big** [..] meal.

After 10pm I start to get **tired** [..].

2 Now rewrite this description of a festival using strong positive language.
You can change words and add adjectives and adverbs.

Independence Day happens every year. We all want to take part. We practise a lot to give a good performance. There is a school parade. There are lots of people and lots of noise. We walk past the flag. We wear costumes. An important person gives a speech. We give him/her some nice flowers. At home my family arrives and everyone greets each other. We all eat a nice meal. In the evening we watch the good firework display while drinking tea on the veranda.

....

....

....

....

....

....

....

Fact or opinion?

The following statements are a transcript for **audio track 8.1** used in **Q3**. Read them while listening to the text. Tick whether each one is a fact or an opinion. For those you describe as facts, write how you could prove they are a fact.

Statement	Fact	Opinion	How fact can be proved
The majority of people live in cities.	✓		Find out the numbers and percentage of the national population that lives in the major cities.
The overcrowding in our cities is terrible.			
Recently many people have moved to the cities.			
Health services are better in the cities than in the rural areas.			
There are more doctors and health centres in cities than in rural areas.			
Most people in villages have a mobile phone.			
Renting a room in a city is obviously more expensive than renting a room in a village.			
It is worth putting up with living in a town because I can go to Senior Secondary School.			
My auntie and uncle walk to the farm every morning.			
The conditions in the slums are awful – there are no toilets or running water.			

Facts and opinions

Complete the table with facts and opinions about your hometown. Try to change the facts into opinions.

- Example fact: 'My hometown has two senior secondary schools.'

- Example opinion: 'It's an advantage that there are two senior secondary schools in our town because ...'

My hometown   I live in ....
Fact 1:   ....
Fact 2:   ....
Fact 3:   ....
Opinion 1:   It's an advantage that ....   because ....
Opinion 2:   Another benefit is that ....   because ....
Opinion 3:   Although it is a shame that ....   Nevertheless ....

Facts and opinions

1 Decide whether each of the phrases below is a fact or an opinion and tick the appropriate column. Underline the phrase that signals the opinion, if there is one.

Statement	Fact	Opinion
1 In my view, going by bike is the cheapest option.		
2 When you travel by bike, you are saving the planet.		
3 In my opinion, it makes sense to make the area a car-free zone.		
4 I think the price of petrol is too high.		
5 It is likely that the majority of cars will be electric in 20 years' time.		
6 The highway is shut because of floods.		
7 I assume that most children walk to school.		
8 Walking to school encourages students to form good friendships.		
9 The train is more comfortable than the plane.		
10 In 2017 more students came to school by car than on foot.		

2 Now write one fact for each of the following means of transport. You can include numbers or percentages in your sentences, if you wish.

Car: ....

....

Bicycle:...

....

3 Write one opinion for each of the following means of transport.

Car: ....

....

Bicycle:...

....

Bus:...

....

Identifying an author's viewpoint

1 Complete the worksheet to explore the writer's opinion of the Trans-Siberian Railway. Use your dictionary to find out the meanings of the words and say whether the word is positive, negative or neutral.

Words and phrases	Meaning	Positive, negative or neutral
famous	very well known	positive
wonder about	think about, question	positive
adventure		
went beyond what I had expected		
the world		
opportunity		
vast		
beauty		
memories		
continue		
one of the very few		
on our planet		
absolutely anyone		

2 Complete the following sentence choosing the most appropriate word from the following list:
- amazement
- admiration
- terror
- inspiration.

The writer's underlying attitude to the Trans-Siberian Railway is one of:

....

1 Fill the gaps using a relative pronoun: **which, who, where** or **that**.

A commuter is someone **(1)** .... travels to work every day using a particular type of transport.

In China, **(2)** .... there is one bicycle for every household and **(3)** .... bicycle lanes are usual, most people traditionally commute by bike. However, this is not the only form of transport. You could also take the train. China's high-speed trains, **(4)** .... can reach top speeds of 300 km per hour, allow people **(5)** .... live in remote parts of a province to travel into the heart of their local city **(6)** .... most of the jobs and the money lie. For example, the Beijing–Tianjin Intercity line, **(7)** .... opened in 2008, reduced the 117-km commute between the cities to just 30 minutes.

2 Join the following sentences using **which, who, where** or **that**.

1   I live in a village. Most people in the village commute to work by bicycle.

   ....

2   There was a railway between Accra and Tema. It is no longer used.

   ....

3   We went to visit my aunties and uncles. They live in Beijing.

   ....

4   I booked a flight. It was cancelled

   ....

3 Use your own ideas to complete these sentences.

1   The High Speed Rail Project which ....

   ....

2   The bus conductor who ....

   ....

3   In my local town where ....

   ....

Chapter 9
Transport

Connectives

1   Complete the sentences with an appropriate connective from the box on the right. You will need to use two of the connectives in the box twice.

a) .... the bus takes longer, I prefer it because I can look out the windows.

b) .... high parking fees, most people use the car to get to work.

c) The high-speed rail link is important .... it means people can get into town in under 30 minutes.

d) I live in the suburbs .... I work in the centre of town

e) The high-speed rail link is quick .... it links into the bus network.

f) I was late for school .... it was raining and there were no buses on the roads.

g) .... I go to university I will cycle to my lectures.

h) I can't wait .... I go on holiday.

i) The flight attendant told us to fasten our seat belts .... landing.

j) .... booking the tickets in advance, we didn't get seats.

but

and

before

in spite of

although

because

when

until

2   Complete the following sentences with your own ideas.

a) Although the bus is cheap ....
....

b) When I have finished my exams ....
....

c) Despite rising petrol prices ....
....

Magazine article

Complete the writing frame to help you plan your magazine article.

Audience

- who is going to read the text: ....

- what the article is: ....

Therefore the **tone of my article** will be: ....

Introduction / description of what a transport system is

....

....

....

What the transport system is like at the moment

....

....

....

What this means for work / school / leisure

....

....

....

What improvements could be made

....

....

....

How improvements could improve young people's lives

....

....

....

Overall suggestions / conclusions

....

....

....

Chapter 9
Transport

Write notes in the writing frame to help you prepare for your conversation.

Introduction: where you live/where people want to get to

....

....

Different options available

....

....

Advantages of transport system 1	**Disadvantages of transport system 1**
Cost:	Cost: ....
Flexibility:	Flexibility: ....
Carbon emissions:	Carbon emissions: ....
Frequency:	Frequency: ....
Speed:	Speed: ....
Comfort:	Comfort: ....
Advantages of transport system 2	**Disadvantages of transport system 2**
Cost:	Cost: ....
Flexibility:	Flexibility: ....
Carbon emissions:	Carbon emissions: ....
Frequency:	Frequency: ....
Speed:	Speed: ....
Comfort:	Comfort: ....

Overall suggestions/conclusions

....

....

....

Inferring opinion

1 Complete the worksheet to explore the speaker's attitude to space travel. Use your dictionary to find out the meanings of the words in bold and say whether the word is positive or negative.

Words and phrases	Meaning	Positive or negative
dreamed of travelling up to the stars	dreaming is something you hope for in the future	positive – indicates hopes
this has now **become a reality**		
we can send spacecraft into **outer space**	space beyond Earth's atmosphere	
either with or without humans on board		positive – both options are a possibility
the main **desire** is for exploration		
there are also **commercial** reasons		
which is becoming a **popular** idea		
satellite telecommunications – which many of us **take for granted**	accept without question	
to **propel** the spacecraft	to cause something to move in a certain direction	
a great deal of **thrust**	power or force required to make a vehicle move	
and many other **features**		
hope to find out more about **other life forms**	other living things	
discover planets where we can find **precious minerals or metals**		
so we can all have the **opportunity** to		

2 Complete the following sentence choosing the most appropriate word from the following list:
- disappointing
- frightening
- wasteful
- inspirational.

The writer's underlying attitude is that space travel is ....

Denim

Read 'The story of denim' below and answer the questions.

The story of denim

In 1853, an ambitious 24-year-old German called Levi Strauss left New York for California with the intention of setting up a business there. Everyday goods were in short supply, and people struggled to find clothing and pots and pans in the Wild West. He carried with him huge rolls of cotton canvas that he thought would be useful for tents and wagon covers.

When Levi got there, he found that what people really needed was tough clothing that could survive the cruel life of the mines and factories. Levi cleverly turned the canvas he had brought into overalls for the miners and sold them at a profit. But the miners complained that the material was too rough and scratched their skin. Levi quickly substituted the canvas for a thick cotton from France called 'serge de Nîmes'. Not only was it strong, but it also felt soft on the skin. The material was later called 'denim' and the trousers and overalls made were called 'jeans'.

Miners then complained that their pockets tore off easily. In 1872, Levi joined up with an energetic tailor called Jacob Davis to add metal pins to all the key pressure points on the jeans and double-stitched pockets in thick cotton. They received a licence on 20 May 1873 and the 'Two-Horse' brand of jeans was launched. The advertisement showed horses unable to pull the material apart.

1 In which year did Levi Strauss come to California?...

2 What was his intention? ....

3 What was in short supply in the Wild West? ....

4 What did Levi do with the canvas he had brought with him? ....

5 What was the problem that miners faced with this material? ....

....

6 What material did Levi substitute for the canvas? ....

How did it acquire its new name or short form? ....

7 What innovation did Jacob Davis and Levi Strauss invent together? ....

8 Why did the advertisement show two horses trying to pull the material apart? ....

....

9 Write three words that would sum up three aspects of Levi Strauss's character.
Give an example in each case of the 'clue' you used to decide this:

a) ....

b) ....

c) ....

Writing a formal letter

When writing a formal letter that is also persuasive, it is important to present ideas in a logical, informed way. It is also a good idea to think about what the reader might see as problems in order to convince them that these can be overcome. Use the writing frame below to help you.

Date: ....

To: The Principal

Address of the school / organisation: ....

....

Dear ....,

Re: Reviewing the School Dress Code

Introduction: *Why you are writing.*

....

....

Paragraph 1: *Explain student views on the benefits / convenience of wearing denim.*

....

....

....

Paragraph 2: *Evidence that denim is popular with celebrities and VIPs.*

....

....

....

Paragraph 3: *Show understanding that there are concerns about extreme denim fashion. Offer reassurance that these concerns will be addressed.*

....

....

....

Conclusion: *Summarise your arguments and say that you're hoping for a favourable response. Offer to meet up to discuss further if required.*

....

....

....

Yours sincerely,

[Signature]

[Full Name]

[Email / contact information]

Phrases to introduce arguments

1 Finish the short paragraphs using a suitable phrase from the box.

firstly	secondly	on the one hand
moreover	furthermore	in contrast
however	on the other hand	in view of

1 There are many reasons to learn to play an instrument. It will teach you discipline – you will have to practise every day in order to be any good. .... it will help you to do better at your studies.

2 Shall we go to the concert this evening? Yes, I would like to go. .... I have football practice until 5 pm. Can we go after that?

3 It is easier to compose using technology nowadays. Firstly, you can download music you play to your computer, which will write it into notes electronically. .... you can easily play back and listen to what you have written.

2 Use a suitable phrase from the box to complete the paragraphs.

1 Johanna is a megastar – right? And you would expect a megaconcert – right? Wrong! I recently went to a Johanna concert and this is my opinion: .... I thought her singing was awesome – you could hear her very clearly and her playlist was amazing. .... she didn't come on until 11 o'clock, which meant two hours getting bored waiting and then a two-hour wait for the night bus home! .... my best mate Charley, who raves about Johanna, thought it wasn't so good either. She didn't get very good seats so she couldn't see her so well. .... my other mate, Noura, who managed to get good seats, told me she had the greatest time and it was definitely a night to remember. So .... the different reviews I would advise only go if you can afford good tickets and make sure you arrange for your parents to pick you up afterwards.

2 Using an electronic keyboard has many advantages: .... the electronic keyboard is much cheaper than a real piano. .... it takes up much less space. .... it is portable so if you are a member of a band, you can pack it up and take it to the rehearsal studio. .... if you are a composer, you can link what you play on your piano to a computer which can convert it to musical notes. .... it will never give you that authentic piano touch – the feeling of the keys as you hit the note.

3 Choose one of these two arguments and add another sentence to **SUPPORT** the argument: ....
....

Add another sentence to **OPPOSE** the argument: ....
....

Quotation marks and verbs of speaking

1 Join these sentences using a suitable phrase from the box.

begged	reminded	suggested	added
shouted	~~warned~~	complained	agreed

1 "Be careful. It could be dangerous," ......warned...... my mother.

2 "And don't forget to be home by nine," .... my Auntie.

3 "That's too early. I won't be able to see the end of the concert," .... my brother.

4 "Oh. Please let me stay out later," .... my brother.

5 "I could walk home with my friends," .... my brother.

6 "All right, as long as you phone me when it is finished," .... my mother.

7 "Remember to buy me a programme," my sister .... my brother.

8 "Thanks mum," .... my brother as he ran out the door and bounded down the stairs.

2 Write what each person says using direct speech. You will have to add the names of the speakers, use suitable verbs of speaking and add correct punctuation.

1 What shall we do for Book Week

"What shall we do for Book Week?" asked Mr Charles our English Teacher.

2 Let's do a book swap

(my friend) ....
....

3 And what about asking everyone to contribute one book to the library

(librarian) ....
....

4 Good idea

(the class) ....
....

5 What about inviting an author to come and speak

(Mrs Wu) ....
....

6 We could offer everyone a free book

(I) ....
....

7 Unfortunately we haven't got enough money to do that

(the head teacher) ....
....

Apostrophes

1 Write these short forms in full.

1 she'll	....	7 I'm	....
2 it's	....	8 you're	....
3 can't	....	9 she's	....
4 don't	....	10 how's	....
5 I've	....	11 won't	....
6 we're	....	12 I'd	....

2 Copy the message inserting the missing apostrophes.

Dear Esi,

Ive gone to grandmas
because she isnt very well.
Dont worry. Its not serious.
Ill be back by six.
Theres juice in the fridge.
Have some of Aunties soup.
Its in the pot.

See you later.

Mum

....
....
....
....
....
....
....
....

3 Insert the apostrophe in the correct place in the sentences.

Example: **We went to the library in Auntie's car.**

1 I found Charlenes schoolbooks on the floor.

2 Please return the twins books to the library.

3 I read my sisters magazine every month.

4 The teachers common room is very messy.

5 Mrs Hollingdales class is learning about apostrophes.

6 Unfortunately I ripped Karens book.

4 Make up three sentences using possession about what you can see around you.

Example: **Aruna's bag is on the floor.**

1 ....

2 ....

3 ....

Semicolons

Read the following tips about when to use semicolons.

> Semicolons can be used instead of a full stop to separate two sentences that are very closely linked. This means that:
>
> - sometimes semicolons replace a conjunction (joining word)
>
>   For example: *'I like science fiction but I don't like romance fiction.'*
>
>   could be written as: *'I like science fiction; I don't like romance fiction.'*
>
> - sometimes you can use semicolons before 'however'
>
>   For example: *'I am in favour of space exploration; however, I would prefer we reduce the budget.'*
>
> - you can use semicolons to separate longer items in a list.
>
>   For example: *'There are many things to do before we leave for space: we must check the space capsule; we have to train hard to make sure we are strong; we need to test the space suits.'*

Write out the following sentences inserting **either** semicolons **or** commas, and delete any conjunctions as necessary.

1   The Moon is 384 600 km away from Earth however sometimes it is nearer.

2   Mars has two moons but Jupiter has sixteen.

3   The International Space Station is 108.5 m long and 72.8 m wide it was built by the USA, Russia, Europe, Canada and Japan.

4   The International Space Station has been manned since 2000 and the astronauts do shifts of three to six months the plan is to keep it running until 2028.

5   Tests on astronauts have shown that during space missions the muscles become weakened and bones also lose calcium and the whole body can lose weight.

6   Laboratories inside the Space Station have hooks to keep boots firmly fixed so that scientists can keep still while conducting experiments while sleeping bags are anchored down to the sleeping platforms.

7   Tallulah wanted to become an astronaut however her parents preferred her to become a doctor.

8   The sky is full of satellites to receive and transmit television signals to transmit data on weather conditions to observe regions of the planet for military purposes to provide data for study on Earth about pollution to make a map of the stars and to keep track of the navigation of ships and aircraft.

Disagreeing politely

1 Listen to the short conversations and complete the dialogues with phrases that disagree politely.

---

1 A: Would you like to watch that new show?

  B: .... I'm finishing my book right now.

  A: No problem.

2 A: Would you like to come round tonight?

  B: .... finish a science project.

  ....?

  A: Yes – I'm not doing anything tomorrow. We could watch the international football match.
     It's Nigeria playing Cameroon. It's bound to be a good match.

3 A: I think that there are too many entertainment programmes on TV these days. It's all endless talent shows and unfunny sitcoms. Why aren't there more news or worthwhile discussion programmes?

  B: .... young people are not really interested in watching news or current events. .... all the nature programmes?
     You have to agree that they're educational and also entertaining.

4 A: Mum. Can I move the games console into my bedroom?

  B: ....

  .... you play enough video games already?

  A: Aargh, mum, I knew you would say that!

5 A: Would you like to buy a copy of the TV review?

  B: ....

  A: Okay.

6 A: People watch too much television.

  B: .... the more important question is what people watch rather than how much they watch?

  A: Yes… maybe…

---

2 Continue the conversations, disagreeing politely with the speakers.

Let's watch the Talent Show tonight.

....

You know I love video games so play with me for a bit now.

....

Chapter 11
Entertainment

Synonyms

1 Underline the words and phrases that mean almost the same the words in bold.

Person A says	Person B replies
1 I need to **investigate** farming techniques in Nigeria for homework.	a) Oh yes, that reminds me I need to research poultry farming techniques for Agricultural Science.
2 The radio gives you **breaking** business news every hour.	b) I agree that it gives you news as it comes in and is certainly the most up to date but …
3 She gave an **award-winning** performance.	d) Yes it was acclaimed all over the country. So many people liked it that she won the prize of Best Actress.
4 I don't know about the **veracity** of what he says. I think he is lying.	e) Me too. I am not sure he is telling the truth.
5 The Nigerian film market **has flourished** for the last 20 years.	f) Yes, it is doing so well that it makes more films than Hollywood.
6 She is an **engaging** speaker.	g) Mmm. She certainly manages to be interesting and keep the audience entertained.
7 The **rise and fall** of pop stars is bound to happen.	h) Oh yes, their popularity goes up and down. Someone very famous this year may not even be talked about next year.
8 I want to **harness** solar energy.	i) It's quite easy to use the power of the sun. You need something that …
9 The Middle East **correspondent** gave us the latest news.	j) The reporter based where the fighting is taking place told us what was happening.

2 Give a word or phrase that means almost the same as the word in bold (a synonym).

1 I always look after my DVDs because they are so **valuable** to me. ....

2 We should wipe the screen with care to avoid **harming** it. ....

3 That was an **interesting** programme. ....

4 The local TV channel is organising a **contest** to encourage children to become TV presenters. ....

5 The organisers will **give** prizes to the ten best competitors. ....

6 In your opinion, which of the television shows is the most **popular**? ....

7 I particularly **like** documentaries. ....

8 The TV show host looked very **elegant** in his suit. ....

9 That sitcom was **not very good**. ....

10 I like watching romantic comedy movies. They are **easy to watch**. ....

Facts about Nollywood

Listen to the listening passage about Nollywood. Complete the gaps using words and phrases you hear to write facts about the Nigerian film industry. In the column on the right, suggest ways in which you could prove (or disprove) the fact

Fact	How can this be proved?
1 Nollywood is the .... film industry in the world.	
2 Nollywood usually makes about .... films	
3 The average movie costs .... to make.	
4 They don't rent .... to make films.	
5 Nollywood makes movies .... , that is on the street or in the countryside.	
6 Most films are shot on .... in just	

Fill in the gaps in the text below using the words from the box on the right.

Making movies is big business in Bollywood. First the producer decides he/she wants to make a film. The **(1)** .... is the person or company who pays for the film and hires everybody.

First the producer asks the writer to give an overview of the **(2)** .... – or what happens in the story. Then the writer writes the **(3)** ...., which is the words of the film. It also shows how many people are in the **(4)** ....

Then the producers hire a director. This person decides who will be his/her **(5)** .... These actors are likely to be famous or at least well known. Maybe they gave a good **(6)** .... in their previous films. The director also decides the "look" of the film. So they decide the type of **(7)** .... the actors will wear. They also decide on the **(8)** .... – whether the action is **(9)** .... an office, in a village, in the market, at home and whether they will **(10)** .... in a film studio or **(11)** ....

The producers often also hire a composer who writes the **(12)** .... to go with the film.

After shooting the film, the editors **(13)** .... to the film to make sure that it is not too long or too short. Sometimes whole **(14)** .... are deleted. The editors also add in the **(15)** .... This is all the music and sounds that happen in the film – not just the songs.

Then the film is distributed to the cinemas. The producers hope that the film is successful. If it gets **(16)** .... from the film critics then it can become a **(17)** .... hit. This means that a lot of people go to see it and it takes a lot of money!

box office

cast

costumes

lead actor

make cuts

musical score

on location

performance

plot

producer

rave reviews

scenes

script

set

set in

shoot the film

soundtrack

Write a film review

Write a review of a favourite film, or your imaginary favourite film, using the questions to guide you.

What happened in the film?

....

....

....

....

What did you like most about the film?

....

....

....

....

What did you like least about the film?

....

....

....

....

Who was your favourite character? And why?

....

....

....

....

Overall opinion:

....

....

....

....

....

....

Tone and style

Match the type of writing to the correct tone and style of document. One tone and style matches two types of writing.

Type of writing
1 A note to your mother telling her you have gone to a friend's house and will be home by 6:00 pm
2 A postcard to your friend with a description of what your holiday destination looks like and all the things you have done
3 An email to your friend
4 A letter to your grandmother and grandfather to thank them for a gift
5 A letter to the head teacher requesting absence from school
6 A posting on your social media site
7 An article for your school newspaper on the reasons why young people should be given the vote at age 16 – the people who read the newspaper are other students and teachers
8 An email to a local business replying to a job advertisement

Correct tone and style
A Formal, handwritten or typed, serious, impersonal tone
B Formal, typed, well thought through, clear paragraphs, impersonal tone
C Formal, typed, well thought through, clear paragraphs, clearly stating your opinion backed up with facts and examples
D Semi-formal, handwritten, friendly with a personal tone
E Informal, personal, typed, cheeky, maybe with slang or idioms
F Informal, personal, handwritten, descriptive
G Informal, friendly, handwritten, short, not in sentences

Blog concept map

Complete the concept map below to summarise the content and tone of a blog you might write.

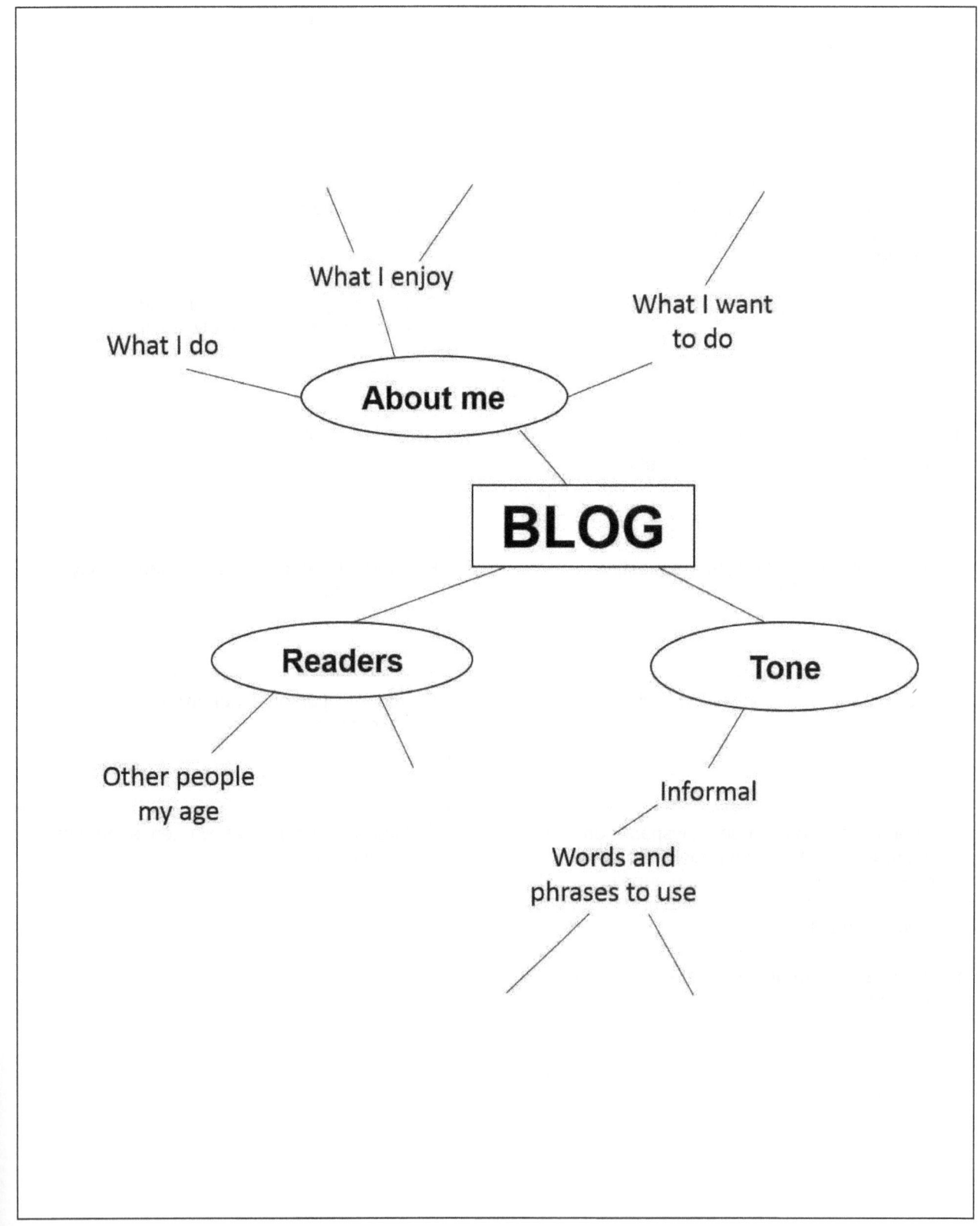

Letter to teacher

Write a letter to your head teacher asking for permission to be absent from school next week. Choose the most appropriate phrase from the options below and, in the box provided, explain the reason for your requested absence.

Jamestown
Friday 4 July

a) Dear Sir or Madam
b) Dear Mrs Lawson
c) Hi Mrs Lawson

a) I am sorry. I can't come to school next week.
b) You'll never guess what??!! I can't make it to school next Wednesday.
c) I am writing to ask permission to be absent from school on Wednesday 9 July.

Give the reason here:

a) I am of course expecting to copy the notes and complete any homework missed.
b) I'll chat to my mates to find out what I missed.
c) My teacher says I don't have to worry about the work missed.

a) Thanking you in advance for your understanding in this matter.
b) Thanks a lot. See you at school tomorrow!
c) Thank you for being the best head teacher.

a) Yours faithfully
b) Yours sincerely
c) Byeee
d) Best wishes

Tallulah White

Use each of the words listed below in a sentence. Use a dictionary to help you.

Word	Sentence
progress	
theory	
established (adjective)	
intention	
dependent on	
crucial	
independent	
carry out tasks	
struggle	
role-play	
skills	
fulfilling	
process	
self-esteem	
identity	
idealistic	
establish (verb)	
look up to	
raise	

Practise an open-response reading question and a multiple matching reading question: sample answers

Use the marking guidance provided by your teacher to mark the sample answers for the practice reading questions below.

Practise an open-response reading question

Answer	Mark	Comment
1. when he opened his boxes last month and found half his 100 million bees missing		
2. it's threatening their livelihoods and many crops		
3. bees look for pollen and nectar		
4. fungus problems		
5. rent them out		
6. fuel costs are higher cost of bees boxes has tripled queen bees have tripled costs more to control bugs		
TOTAL		(out of 8 marks)

Practise a multiple matching reading question

Answer*	Mark	Comment
a) B		
b) C		
c) B		
d) D		
e) A		
f) A		
g) A		
h) C		
i) A		
TOTAL		(out of 9 marks)

Practise an open-response reading question: sample answers marked

Compare your 'Marks' and 'Comments' from **worksheet 13.1** with those below.

Answer	Mark	Comment
1. when he opened his boxes last month and found half his 100 million bees missing	1	*Correct answer but time wasted on unnecessary words.*
2. it's threatening their livelihoods and many crops	1	*Correct answer.*
3. bees look for pollen and nectar	1	*Correct answer, but could be briefer.*
4. fungus problems	0	*Correct answer, but only one of the two answers required has been given.*
5. rent them out	1	*Correct answer.*
6. fuel costs are higher cost of bees boxes has tripled queen bees have tripled costs more to control bugs	3	*The first two and the last one are correct.* *'cost of' has been omitted from the third – it sounds here as if there are three times more queen bees – a wrong answer. This response still scores 3 marks.*
TOTAL	7	**(out of 8 marks)**

Practise a multiple matching reading question: sample answers marked

Compare your 'Marks' and 'Comments' from **worksheet 13.1** with those below.

Answer	Mark	Comment
a) B	1	*Correct answer*
b) B	0	*Incorrect answer. The correct answer is __C__ as his job is* **voluntary**. *We assume that __B__ is paid for her job as she does not have to ask her parents for money.*
c) B	1	*Correct answer*
d) D	1	*Correct answer*
e) A	1	*Correct answer*
f) A	0	*Incorrect answer. __A__ has had 'a few problems' with shopping online.* *The correct answer is __C__ as he doesn't talk about any problems.*
g) A	1	*Correct answer*
h) C	1	*Correct answer*
i) A	1	*Correct answer*
TOTAL	7	**(out of 9 marks)**

The questions, sample answers and marks/comments that appear in this book were written by the author.
In the examination, the way marks would be awarded to answers like these may be different.

Practise a note-taking question: sample answers

Use the marking guidance provided by your teacher to mark the sample answers for the note-taking practice question below.

	Answer	Mark	Comment
How the present way of life for the Inuits is different from the past	They live in many different countries		
	Petrol-driven vehicles		
	Kill animals to eat		
What will not change for many Inuits in the future	The Inuit language		
	Inuit values and ways of life		
	The Arctic Winter Games		

Fill in the gaps: The sample answer received .... marks for the first part and

.... marks for the second part.

Total marks: .... + ... = ... marks out of a possible 7.

The questions, sample answers and marks/comments that appear in this book were written by the author.
In the examination, the way marks would be awarded to answers like these may be different.

Practise a note-taking question: sample answers marked

Compare your 'Marks' and 'Comments' from **worksheet 14.1** with those below.

	Answer	Mark	Comment
How the present way of life for the Inuits is different from the past	They live in many different countries	1	*Correct.*
	Petrol-driven vehicles	1	*Good concise answer.*
	Kill animals to eat	0	*Incorrect They now use guns, however.*
What will not change in the future	The Inuit language	1	*Correct.*
	Inuit values and ways of life	1	*Correct.*
	The Arctic Winter Games	1	*Correct.* *Only 3 answers have been identified out of a possible 4, so 3 out of 4 marks awarded.*

The sample response got ...2... marks for the first part and

....3.... marks for the second part.

Total marks: ....2... + ...3... = ...5... marks out of a possible 7.

Practise multiple-choice reading questions

- Read the text about 'Growing your own fruit and vegetables' below.
- Underline the words and phrases that enable you to answer each question.
- Circle the correct answer for each: A, B or C, noting why you have chosen it.
- Compare your answer with the marking guidance on **worksheet 15.2**.

Growing your own fruit and vegetables

One of my earliest memories was picking strawberries in my grandmother's garden and then sitting at the kitchen table, eating the delicious fruit, but I remember that the best thing was the large helping of cream on top!

The family tradition continues and I now grow fruit and vegetables in my own garden.

At the end of winter, I have to be outside, even though the weather can still be unpredictable, to plant potatoes, beans and cabbage. I won't deny though that the thing that touches me the most and that I most look forward to every year, is noticing the blossom on the apple and plum trees which means that spring is coming.

When my parents want vegetables for a dinner party with friends, like potatoes, beans and tomatoes, they don't have to get in the car to buy them; they just step into the garden and pick what they want for the evening meal. They don't have to spend any money either! The fresh vegetables are cooked and eaten the day they are picked, so they haven't spent days or weeks in storage or on a supermarket shelf. The food that my parents grow is completely organic as they don't use any chemicals.

Sometimes we have too much food, particularly lettuces in summer, so we usually give this surplus food to our neighbours. They have their own vegetable plot so don't need any extra for themselves, but they do sell it at the local market to earn a bit of extra money. This money goes towards a good local charity.

Even if you don't have a garden, you can still grow vegetables and salad in pots on a balcony or on a windowsill and eat healthier while reducing your food costs. Everyone can experience the satisfaction of eating home-grown produce! So why not start today?

---

1 **What was the writer's favourite memory?**
  A picking strawberries
  B eating tasty fruit
  C having cream on their fruit

2 **How does the writer feel about being in the garden after winter?**
  A He loves being outside.
  B He enjoys getting ready to plant new vegetables.
  C He looks forward to the fruit trees flowering the most.

3 **What does 'them' refer to in line 8?**
  A vegetables
  B friends
  C parents

4 **In paragraph 4, the writer talks about his parents to show how…**
  A they appreciate being more environmentally friendly.
  B they like being able to earn a bit of extra money.
  C they love the taste of fresh vegetables.

5 **The writer suggests that people should:**
  A do more to support local charities
  B not spend so much money on food
  C spend more time outdoors

6 **The purpose of the text is to:**
  A offer information about how to grow fruit and vegetables
  B explain the writer's experience of gardening
  C encourage people to grow their own food

The questions, sample answers and marks/comments that appear in this book were written by the author. In the examination, the way marks would be awarded to answers like these may be different.

Practise multiple-choice reading questions

Compare your underlinings, answers and comments from **worksheet 15.1** with these.

Marking guidance

> ### Growing your own fruit and vegetables
>
> One of my earliest memories was picking strawberries in my grandmother's garden and then sitting at the kitchen table, eating the delicious fruit, but I remember that ***the best thing was the large helping of cream on top!*** **(1)**
>
> The family tradition continues and I now grow fruit and vegetables in my own garden.
>
> At the end of winter, I have to be outside, even though the weather can still be unpredictable, to plant potatoes, beans and cabbage. I won't deny though that the thing that ***touches me the most*** and that ***I most look forward to every year, is noticing the blossom on the apple and plum trees which means that spring is coming.*** **(2)**
>
> When my parents want vegetables for a dinner party with friends, like potatoes, beans and tomatoes, they don't have to get in the car to buy ***them*** **(3)**; they just step into the garden and pick what they want for the evening meal. They don't have to spend any money either! The fresh vegetables are cooked and eaten the day they are picked, so they haven't spent days or weeks in storage or on a supermarket shelf. ***The food that my parents grow is completely organic as they don't use any chemicals.*** **(4)**
>
> Sometimes we have too much food, particularly lettuces in summer, so we usually give this surplus food to our neighbours. They have their own vegetable plot so don't need any extra for themselves, but they do sell it at the local market to earn a bit of extra money. This money goes towards a good local charity.
>
> Even if you don't have a garden, ***you can still grow vegetables*** and salad in pots on a balcony or on a windowsill and eat healthier ***while reducing your food costs.*** **(5)** ***Everyone can experience the satisfaction of eating home-grown produce! So why not start today?*** **(6)**

> ### Reasons why answers are correct
>
> **1 = C** This is correct because the phrase in the text 'I remember that the best thing' links to the phrase in the question 'favourite memory'.
>
> **2 = C** This is correct because the phrase 'touches me the most' signals that it is his strongest feeling about being in the garden after winter.
>
> **3 = A** This is correct as 'them' refers to the 'vegetables' whereas 'they' refers to the 'parents'.
>
> **4 = A** This correct as there is no mention of earning money or that the parents love the taste of their vegetables but they don't use chemicals to grow them and so that is environmentally friendly.
>
> **5 = B** This is correct. Answer **A** might seem possible but it refers to the example of the neighbours' actions not what is suggested the reader does in 'you can still grow vegetables… reducing your food costs'.
>
> **6 = C** **C** is correct as it shows the purpose of writing about growing your own vegetables. **A** and **B** summarise the content of text not what its purpose is.

The questions, sample answers and marks/comments that appear in this book were written by the author.
In the examination, the way marks would be awarded to answers like these may be different.

Practise an informal writing question: sample answer

Here is an example question and a sample answer for you to mark and annotate with your own marker's comments. Use the marking guidance provided by your teacher.

> You recently went to an event with your family. There was a problem during the evening.
>
> **Write an email to a friend about the problem.**
>
> In your email you should:
>
> * explain what the event was
> * describe the problem
> * explain how you felt about the situation.
>
> Write about 120–160 words.

Sample answer

Hi Suki

Hope you're well. <u>I just write</u> to tell you what happened when me, mum and dad went to an event in our Town Hall.

It was a dance, with a live band. It was $10 a ticket, which included a meal and the money goes to the Red Cross to help people in <u>crises</u>. I am not <u>keen at</u> dancing but it was for charity!

Anyways we were actually having a good time – my dad really can't dance – it was a scream! Then, around 7.00 the lights suddenly went out and we were in complete darkness. There was a <u>cut of power</u> so we all had to leave – it was scary, we couldn't see anything!

I felt quite sad, but there was nothing <u>nobody</u> could do, there was a <u>mayor</u> problem with the electricity. The <u>organisators</u> say that they will do another event – great, I will get to see more dad-dancing!!

Right, must go – mum's calling.

Cheers, Pedro

The underlined words and phrases indicate language errors. Note down what kind of error has been made, using the following key:

1 error in grammar that reduces level of communication
2 error in grammar that puts the meaning in doubt
3 punctuation missing; sentence not structured clearly with capital letter/full stop
4 spelling error
5 vocabulary error that puts meaning in doubt.

Now give your comments on the content of the email:

Length	....	
Content	**Task fulfilment**:	
	Development of ideas:	
	How many marks would you give this answer?	
Language	**Range and accuracy**:	
	Organisation:	
	How many marks would you give this answer?	

The questions, sample answers and marks/comments that appear in this book were written by the author.
In the examination, the way marks would be awarded to answers like these may be different.

Practise an informal writing question: sample answer marked

Compare your comments from **worksheet 16.1** with those below.

> You recently went to an event with your family. There was a problem during the evening.
>
> **Write an email to a friend about the problem.**
>
> In your email you should:
> - explain what the event was
> - describe the problem
> - explain how you felt about the situation.
>
> Write about 120–160 words.

Sample answer

Hi Suki

Hope you're well. <u>I just write</u> to tell you what happened when me, mum and dad went to an event in our Town Hall.

It was a dance, with a live band. It was $10 a ticket, which included a meal and the money goes to the Red Cross to help people in <u>crises</u>. I am not <u>keen at</u> dancing but it was for charity!

Anyways we were actually having a good time – my dad really can't dance – it was a scream! Then, around 7.00 the lights suddenly went out and we were in complete darkness. There was a <u>cut of power</u> so we all had to leave – it was scary, we couldn't see anything!

I felt quite sad, but there was nothing <u>nobody</u> could do, there was a <u>mayor</u> problem with the electricity. The <u>organisators</u> say that they will do another event – great, I will get to see more dad-dancing!!

Right, must go – mum's calling.

Cheers, Pedro

Length	160 words – the correct length for this answer.
Content	**Task fulfilment**: Task is fulfilled – Content is fully relevant throughout; Consistently appropriate style and register for the text type; Excellent sense of purpose and audience
	Development of ideas: Content is very well developed. All three points are addressed and expanded on well.
	Number of marks: 6 out of a possible 6 marks.
Language	**Range and accuracy**: Uses a wide range of common and less common vocabulary mostly appropriately; Uses a wide range of simple and complex structures; Very good level of accuracy in language use. Occasional errors are present but are restricted to less common vocabulary.
	Errors noted:
	1 errors in grammar that impedes communication – none 'I just write', 'keen at', 'nothing nobody' do not reduce communication.
	2 errors in grammar that puts the meaning in doubt – none
	3 punctuation missing; sentence not structured clearly with capital letter/full stop – could make new sentence at end of paragraph 3 with 'we couldn't see anything!'.
	4 spelling errors: 'crises' and 'organisators' do not impede meaning
	5 vocabulary error that puts meaning in doubt = 'mayor' instead of 'major'
	Organisation: Effectively organised and sequenced; Uses a range of linking words and other cohesive devices appropriately but some over-reliance on commas in places.
	Number of marks: 8 out of a possible 9 marks.
	TOTAL: 14 (out of a possible 15 marks)

The questions, sample answers and marks/comments that appear in this book were written by the author.
In the examination, the way marks would be awarded to answers like these may be different.

Practise a formal writing question: sample answer

Here is an example question and sample for you to mark and annotate with your own marker's comments. Use the marking guidance provided by your teacher.

A recent survey of schools shows that many students do not like learning a new language. Your teacher wants students' opinions and has asked you to write a formal article on the topic for your school magazine. In your article, discuss the advantages and disadvantages of learning languages and give your personal opinion on the subject. Here are some comments from students:

It takes a long time to become good at another language.	Other subjects are more important than languages.	Learning a language increases the range of jobs you can do.	It is fun to be able to speak another language on holiday.

These comments may give you ideas for your 120–160 word article.

Sample answer

Learning another language

I suppose a lot of people are talking about learn languages and I talked to my friends at school about the subject. Most of them said that they don't like to learn another language because it is boring. Other people said that to learn another language well takes a long time and we have other things more important to do.

There were other people in my class who said it is a good idea, they love learning languages because then they can communicate with more people, like people when we are on holiday and other classmates said that it gives you more job opportunities when you speak another language, like traductor, for example.

Anyways, different people think different things so I think there is no conclusion to the question.

The underlined words and phrases indicate language errors. Note down what kind of error has been made, using the following key:

1 error in grammar that reduces level of communication
2 error in grammar that puts the meaning in doubt
3 punctuation missing; sentence not structured clearly with capital letter/full stop
4 spelling error
5 vocabulary error that puts meaning in doubt

Now give your comments on the content of the answer.

Length	....
Content	Task fulfilment: ....
	Development of ideas: ....
	How many marks would you give this answer? ....
Language	Range and accuracy: ....
	....
	Organisation: ....
	How many marks would you give this answer? ....

The questions, sample answers and marks/comments that appear in this book were written by the author. In the examination, the way marks would be awarded to answers like these may be different.

Compare your comments from **worksheet 17.1** with those below.

Sample answer marked

Learning another language

I suppose a lot of people are talking about learn languages and I talked to my friends at school about the subject. Most of them said that they don't like to learn another language because it is boring. Other people said that to learn another language well takes a long time and we have other things more important to do.

There were other people in my class who said it is a good idea, they love learning languages because then they can communicate with more people, like people when we are on holiday and other classmates said that it gives you more job opportunities when you speak another language, like traductor, for example.

Anyways, different people think different things so I think there is no conclusion to the question.

Length	132 words – the correct length for this answer. They could have used up to 160 words.
Content	**Task fulfilment**: All content is relevant. The writer uses the opinions raised by other students in their class.
	Style and register: generally good sense of reader – neutral – formal tone mostly used, although some informal language choices
	Development of ideas: content is appropriate but with little development: writer does not add further ideas to the ones given in the speech bubbles by the other students or include any detail; they do not clearly express their own opinion at the end.
	Errors noted:
	1 – use of 'I suppose' and 'anyways' is too informal for purpose, reader and form.
	Number of marks: 4 out of a possible 6 marks
Language	**Range and accuracy**: Uses a range of common vocabulary appropriately, and attempts to use some less common vocabulary ('stressful') however this is not always successful; uses a range of simple structures accurately although with some repetition. They succeed in using some more complex structures ('they love learning languages') but are not always successful.
	There is some reliance on words used in the task wording when own words should be used.
	Organisation: It is generally well organised, with effective paragraphs. Simple linking words are included ('because/and/so') and pronouns ('it').
	Errors noted:
	1 errors in grammar that impedes communication – none 'About learn languages' incorrect but does not reduce communication.
	2 errors in grammar that puts the meaning in doubt – none ' they like to learn' would be more correct if gerund 'learning' was used'; awkward phrasing – 'other things more important to do'.
	3 punctuation missing; overly long sentence in second para – better to start new sentence with 'For example' after 'with more people or after the word 'on holiday'.'.
	4 spelling/vocabulary error – 'traductors' do not impede meaning.
	Number of marks: 5 out of a possible 9 marks
	TOTAL: 9 out of a possible 15 marks

Practise a multiple choice listening with visuals question: sample answers

Here is a sample for you to mark and add your own comments, referring to details from the recording. Use the marking guidance provided for you by your teacher. Fill in the 'Mark' and 'Comments' columns.

Answer	Mark	Comments
1 What birthday present is the girl going to give to her mother? **D** [1]		
2 Which museum do the boy and girl decide to visit first? **B** [1]		
3 Where does the family decide to go camping? **C** [1]		
4 Where did the girl leave her library book? **A** [1]		
5 Why can't Alan and Paula go out together in the afternoon? **B** [1]		
6 What will the second performance of the evening be? **A** [1]		
Total	**[6]**	

The questions, sample answers and marks/comments that appear in this book were written by the author.
In the examination, the way marks would be awarded to answers like these may be different.

Compare your 'Marks' and 'Comments' from **worksheet 18.1** with those below.

Answer	Mark	Comments
1 What birthday present is the girl going to give to her mother? **D** [1]	0	*Incorrect.* ***Correct answer is B*** *- a necklace. She was going to get gold earrings but remembered her mum doesn't like gold.*
2 Which museum do the boy and girl decide to visit first? **B** [1]	1	*Correct answer. They will go there in the morning and to the others in the afternoon.*
3 Where does the family decide to go camping? **C** [1]	1	*Correct answer. The forest was their parents' first idea.*
4 Where did the girl leave her library book? **A** [1]	1	*Correct answer. It fell out of her bag when she had a sandwich in the cafeteria.*
5 Why can't Alan and Paula go out together in the afternoon? **B** [1]	1	*It is not that he has to do the shopping as that was only decided because the car was not yet fixed.*
6 What will the second performance of the evening be? **A** [1]	0	*Incorrect as the singers close the concert and so are last.* ***Correct answer is B*** *– the musical trio are second as a replacement for the pianist.*
Total (out of a possible 6 marks)	**4 marks**	

The questions, sample answers and marks/comments that appear in this book were written by the author.
In the examination, the way marks would be awarded to answers like these may be different.

Practise a gap-fill listening question: sample answers

Here is a sample answer for you to mark and add your own comments.
Use the marking guidance provided for you by your teacher.
Fill in the 'Mark' and 'Comments' columns.

Answer		Mark	Comments
1 Josh has been a National Champion .... times. **B** 21 times	[1]		
2 Josh first became interested in chess when he was .... **B** in a playground	[1]		
3 Josh became an International Master at the age of .... **A** 16	[1]		
4 *How to Win at Chess* was Josh's .... book. **C** first	[1]		
5 The writer recommends that .... read *I am a Player not a Piece*. **C** people in general	[1]		
6 Chess master is the second in a series of .... **B** instructional videos	[1]		
7 Josh is .... teaching chess because he wants to make his ideas available to everyone. **C** dedicated to	[1]		
8 Josh was attracted to Tai Chi Chuan because of his interest in .... philosophy. **B** eastern	[1]		
9 Josh travels the world ....methods of learning, mental attitude and the psychology of competition. **B** giving lectures on	[1]		
10 Josh believes that people have to be prepared to ....in order to be successful. **A** face new challenges	[1]		
Total (out of a possible 10 marks)			

The questions, sample answers and marks/comments that appear in this book were written by the author.
In the examination, the way marks would be awarded to answers like these may be different.

Compare your 'Marks' and 'Comments' from **worksheet 18.3** with those below.

Answer	Mark	Comments
1 Josh has been a National Champion .... times. [1] **B** 21 times	1	*21 times*
2 Josh first became interested in chess when he was .... [1] **B** in a playground	0	*Incorrect. He was on the way to the playground but not there yet so he was walking in the park with his mother.* **Correct answer is A.**
3 Josh became an International Master at the age of .... [1] **A** 16	1	*At 13 he was Grand Master and 3 years later International Master = 16.*
4 *How to Win at Chess* was Josh's .... book. [1] **C** first	0	*Incorrect. It was not his first book. It sold fewer copies than his first book and his third book sold best.* **Correct answer is A.**
5 The writer recommends that .... read *I am a Player not a Piece*. [1] **C** people in general	1	*'I would totally recommend it to anyone.*
6 Chess master is the second in a series of .... [1] **B** instructional videos	1	*Although in the text it uses DVDs not videos, this is the only answer that fits and we can accept that DVD and Video mean the same thing.*
7 Josh is .... teaching chess because he wants to make his ideas available to everyone. [1] **C** dedicated to	1	*The other two adjectives are used but not in connection with teaching.*
8 Josh was attracted to Tai Chi Chuan because of his interest in .... philosophy. [1] **B** eastern	1	*The other two are mentioned but not connected to how he became interested in Tai Chi Chuan.*
9 Josh travels the world ....methods of learning, mental attitude and the psychology of competition. [1] **B** giving lectures on	1	*Correct – 'giving lectures on'. He does teach but not in the context of travelling around the world.*
10 Josh believes that people have to be prepared to ....in order to be successful. [1] **A** face new challenges	1	*Correct answer*
Total (out of a possible 10 marks)	8 marks	

The questions, sample answers and marks/comments that appear in this book were written by the author.
In the examination, the way marks would be awarded to answers like these may be different.

Practise a listening question on longer interviews: sample answers

Here is a sample answer for you to mark and add your own comments.
Use the marking guidance provided for you by your teacher.
Fill in the 'Mark' and 'Comments' columns.

Answer	Mark	Comments
1 How can we tell that pearl divers have been at work for at least 2000 years? [1] **B** There is a 2000-year-old book that describes pearl diving.		
2 What quantity of shellfish do you need to give you about four good pearls? [1] C 1 tonne		
3 Why were people prepared to face death by diving down so deep? [1] **C** They knew the pearls were valuable.		
4 In Japan, why are women thought to be better than men at diving for pearls? [1] **A** Their bodies are able to keep warm better.		
5 How does Ms Sakai feel now about her life as a pearl diver in the old days? [1] **A** sad		
6 What did the divers use to help them dive down as quickly as possible? [1] **C** a big stone		
7 Why do the women pearl divers in Toba dive nowadays? [1] **A** to find pearls to sell to tourists		
8 In the last hundred years, the number of pearl divers in Toba has [1] **A** gone down		
TOTAL (out of 8 marks)		

The questions, sample answers and marks/comments that appear in this book were written by the author.
In the examination, the way marks would be awarded to answers like these may be different.

Compare your 'Marks' and 'Comments' from **worksheet 18.5** with those below.

Answer	Mark	Comments
1 How can we tell that pearl divers have been at work for at least 2000 years? [1] **B** There is a 2000-year-old book that describes pearl diving.	1	*Correct answer*
2 What quantity of shellfish do you need to give you about four good pearls? [1] **C** 1 tonne	1	*Correct answer*
3 Why were people prepared to face death by diving down so deep? [1] **C** They knew the pearls were valuable.	1	*Correct answer*
4 In Japan, why are women thought to be better than men at diving for pearls? [1] **A** Their bodies are able to keep warm better.	1	*Correct answer*
5 How does Ms Sakai feel now about her life as a pearl diver in the old days? [1] **A** sad	0	*Incorrect. There is no evidence or implication that she feels either sad or angry. It is implied that she is 'proud' so the **correct Answer is C**.*
6 What did the divers use to help them dive down as quickly as possible? [1] **C** a big stone	1	*Correct answer*
7 Why do the women pearl divers in Toba dive nowadays? [1] **A** to find pearls to sell to tourists	0	*Incorrect. There is no mention of finding pearls. **The correct answer is B** 'to give tourists an idea of the past'.*
8 In the last hundred years, the number of pearl divers in Toba has [1] **A** gone down	1	*Correct answer*
TOTAL (out of 8 marks)	6 marks	

The questions, sample answers and marks/comments that appear in this book were written by the author.
In the examination, the way marks would be awarded to answers like these may be different.

Chapter 18
Responding to listening questions

Understanding Speaking Cards

1 Look at the speaking card about 'Daily Life in the Future' in the Student's Book.

2 Look at each point in the following checklist and tick them when you have completed each check. Once this is done, you can be sure that you fully understand the card and the requirements of the task.

Card comprehension check-list	✓
a) Underline the key words or phrases in the question.	
b) Identify if there are any words or phrases that you do not understand and find out what they mean.	
c) Think about what your personal attitude or opinion is towards the subject.	
d) Think about what you could include in your response. Remember that you will be discussing the advantages and disadvantages?	
e) Think about the topic-based vocabulary that you could use	

3 Compare your answers with a partner to see if you have similar thoughts.

Daily Life in the Future	
With your partner, write three possible advantages and disadvantages for each option in the list below.	
• updating the school's computers and technological equipment.	Advantages
	Disadvantages
• buying more books and other paper resources for the library.	Advantages
	Disadvantages

4 For a challenge, imagine you are going to write a topic card together for people in your class. Choose a subject that you think many of them would be interested in.

Now write a topic card for the topic. Provide two options to discuss.

Try to make it look as realistic as possible.

Your teacher might decide to use some of the cards for class practice.

Short talk

Working with a partner, look at the practice interview 'Daily Life in the Future' again. Make notes to plan the structure and content of your talk. Remember for this practice interview that you will have to talk for 3–4 minutes.

Think about the structure:

A Will you discuss the advantages and disadvantages of one option then move on to do the same for the second option?

OR **B** Will you compare and contrast the advantages of both options followed by the disadvantages?

Once you have decided on this:

Think about a suitable opening sentence or phrase to begin your talk to explain which of the above two structure options you have decided on.

....

....

Write appropriate estimated timings for each part of the talk so that your ideas are balanced and you have enough to say but not too much.

....

....

....

Write down some alternative language for 'advantages and disadvantages' so that you do not repeat those words too often in your talk.

....

....

....

Write down some appropriate phrases to give your opinion, to avoid repeating 'in my opinion'.

....

....

....

Decide whether you can bring in personal experiences, to make your talk more engaging for the listener and also give you more to say on each point.

Think about a suitable closing sentence or phrase to summarise your talk and give your own personal preference, explaining why this would be your choice.

....

....

....

Practise this type of planning at home to give a talk and record yourself. When you finish, play it back to assess your own speaking.

Developing a conversation and improving fluency

In order to develop a conversation and speak fluently, you need to be able to respond to the other speaker quickly if they challenge your opinion, or ask you to think about another aspect of the topic of conversation, maybe something you hadn't thought of yourself. You have to think quickly.

You still have to think of the conversation as a game of football. But now it is at a higher level. If the ball is passed to you from an unexpected direction, you have to be able to get possession of the ball and pass it forwards.

Look again at the following extract, which continues from the effective response given in STEP 2.1 in Chapter 19 of the Student's Book on the topic of how having more money might help you in your daily life. Notice how the speaker has developed the conversation in a different direction and answer the questions below:

Speaker 1	So do you think society could function if we didn't have any money at all in the world?
Speaker 2	That sounds like a very good idea... er... it would be nice... but I think it's proven that it doesn't work... and I think people wouldn't work... they wouldn't... people need to have something back for their hard work.

Identify the phrase where you can tell that Speaker 2 is thinking about this new idea, this change in direction:

....

Identify the word that Speaker 2 uses to show that she does not agree with this new suggestion:

....

Identify two reasons that Speaker 2 gives for their opinion.

1 ....

....

2 ....

....

Now, in pairs, practise responding to a change of direction through role-play.

Take the question from the last exercise and have a conversation together.

- **Instruction for the role-play Speaker 1** – Offer a different view during the conversation. You could introduce it with: 'I see what you mean, but other people might think that...'

  Use the second table in **worksheet 19.1** to help you get some ideas.

- **Instruction for the role-play Speaker 2** – You will then have two choices:
  - either agree, and say: 'I can see that is possible, because...'
  - or disagree and say: 'I disagree with that point of view because...'

  You must try to use your own words and phrases to do this – just use these examples to get you started and used to the idea. But remember to include at least one reason for your opinion.

Practice speaking question: reviewing Answer 3

Listen to the recording of Answer 3 discussing the topic card 'Daily life in the future'.

Assess the conversation using the table below, deciding on marks for 'Grammar', 'Vocabulary', 'Development' and 'Pronunciation'. Make a few notes in the 'Comments' column, perhaps jotting down some examples of words or phrases used by the speaker in Answer 3.

Speaking questions	Mark	Comments
Grammar	(out of 10)	
Vocabulary	(out of 10)	
Development	(out of 10)	
Pronunciation	(out of 10)	
Total: out of 40 marks		

Speaking skills: Advice and guidance for teachers

The teaching of speaking skills can sometimes be challenging, but it's important to encourage students to become confident communicators so this section has been designed to support you with advice to give students as well guidance for teachers on giving exam-style speaking tests. It comprises two sections:

1 **Advice to students** –how to help students improve their speaking skills.

2 **Speaking tests** – practical tips on setting up a speaking test in an exam-style format as well as guidance on how to run the speaking test.

1 Advice to students

It's a good idea to reiterate and reinforce these points regularly throughout the course.

Listen to English:

* Advise students on the benefits of listening to as much English as possible.

* Give them information on how to access English-language films, English language TV programmes and series, podcasts, blogs and radio programmes.

* Remind students that it is preferable to watch English language TV and films in their original version, rather than dubbed, as this will help them to improve their pronunciation and intonation, as well as their vocabulary and use of collocations and structures.

* Create worksheets for the students to use when they are watching or listening to English; these could be general comprehension questions, summary-writing activities, vocabulary-building exercises, argumentative or discursive essays or even story or narrative-writing on topics raised in the film/programme. The students' individual work can then be used communicatively for further discussion and debate in class in pairs or small and open groups.

* Encourage students to listen to music in English as this is an enjoyable way for many young people to improve their English. If you plan to use any authentic materials in class with your students, make sure that the type and genre of music, as well as the lyrics and topics are culturally appropriate.

Make friends:

* Give students information on how to find a pen-pal (or e-pal) in an English-speaking country so that they can connect with people of their own age, share letters and practise their skills in a safe and fun environment. This will, in turn, help them to build up their confidence when using English, as well as possibly leading to future online or face-to-face meetings with the other person. There's a very useful web page on the Cambridge Assessment English website which can be found by searching 'penfriends Cambridge English' on a search engine – this would be a good one to recommend as, to date, it has helped students in over 20 000 schools, in more than 180 countries, to connect and enjoy communicating with each other.

Be confident when talking about yourself:

* Prepare students to be able to talk confidently about themselves, by having information-exchange classes in which they ask and answer questions of a more personal nature on a variety of different subjects. Suitable topics would be their family, friends, hobbies and interests, the place where they live and their country, their past and future holidays and their hopes and dreams for the future, both personally and professionally. Remind students that they only need to talk about

personal details that they're comfortable to share, and that the main point of this is to practise talking on a variety of subjects.

Be confident when talking about other subjects:

- Make sure that students have the appropriate vocabulary to be able to discuss a variety of more abstract subjects about the wider world, as this can often prove to be difficult for them. Give them lots of topic-based vocabulary-building exercises followed by opportunities to use the vocabulary in discussions. Suitable topics:

– the environment	– food and drink	– travel and tourism
– health and fitness	– books and films	– the arts
– computers and technology	– clothes and fashion	– traditions
– town and country	– jobs and careers	– science

Many of these are covered in the Student's Book; encourage students to build up their own vocabulary banks for each topic.

- Bear in mind that there are topics that may not be appropriate for discussion at this level and for this age-group, nor for the cultural background of the students that you are teaching, so make sure that you know which of these sensitive areas to avoid. Examples of these may include: politics, conflict, religion, country leaders, magic or witchcraft, dangerous or life-threatening situations, controversial topics, ethical topics, race, ethnicity and gender-specific questions or matters concerning certain cultural customs and traditions. Know your students and your and their boundaries!

- Make sure that students have the appropriate functional exponents to be able to discuss a variety of more abstract subjects. Give them lots of language-building exercises followed by opportunities to use these exponents in discussions. See the accompanying Workbook Section 5 on Speaking for appropriate functional exponents to practise with your students. Areas to cover include: giving and asking for opinions, agreeing and disagreeing, evaluating options, pros and cons, advantages and disadvantages, explaining cause and effect, making suggestions and recommendations, speculating and hypothesising.

Learn how to trouble-shoot:

- Give students the language to be able to deal with communicative problems. For example, they need to be able to clarify and check meaning when they don't understand what somebody says, and they also need to be able check whether the person they're speaking to understands them. Refer to the Collins Cambridge IGCSE English as a Second Language Workbook Section 5, Speaking, which provides practice activities for clarifying and checking language. For example: *Can you speak slower please? Can you repeat the question please? Can you explain what that word means please? Do you see what I mean? Do you follow me?*

- Advise the students on ways in which to feel calmer when they are speaking English and how to deal with moments of uncertainty, such as breathing, visualisation, mindfulness exercises. Introduce fillers such as '*Um*', '*Er*', etc. to give students time to think.

Do not seek perfection:

- Bear in mind that students often worry about their English-speaking skills so reassure them that whilst their pronunciation should be clear and appropriate, they do not have to sound exactly like a native English speaker. It is fine to make a mistake but they should not be afraid of realising the mistake and correcting it if they can. Point out that it is better to say something than nothing, so they should try to avoid complete silence and instead say something to keep the conversation going, even if they are not sure it is absolutely correct.

- Reassure the students that if they do not understand, it is perfectly acceptable to ask for explanation or clarification.

- Remind students that language is all about communication so they should try to enjoy the conversations!

Speaking skills

2 Speaking tests

Setting up a speaking test:

- Make sure the students know that they are going to be taking a speaking assessment so that they feel prepared for this and have had a chance to practise beforehand.

- Bear in mind how many students are going to be doing the test and ensure that there are enough teachers to conduct the assessments.

- Remember the importance of finding a quiet room at school where there won't be any disturbing background noise and which is clear of any materials that may inadvertently assist the students during their assessment, such as vocabulary or grammar charts.

- Make sure that students have no access to technology such as mobile phones or iPads during the assessments and that you and other teachers are not likely to be interrupted by non-assessment-related matters on mobile phones.

- Bear in mind that assessments are usually timed, so make sure that you and other teachers have an appropriate means of timing the overall assessment or the various parts to the assessment. Ensure that the timing is the same for each student.

- Bear in mind the fact that it is extremely important that you and other teachers know exactly how the assessment should be conducted and that you all follow the same criteria for every student. Remember that the validity and reliability of each assessment should be the same for each student, to ensure fair results across the full candidature.

Running a speaking test:

- Make sure that you understand and follow your required role during each part of the assessment. For example, are you interviewing, prompting, facilitating, just listening, etc.?

- Bear in mind that it is your role to ensure that the student is able to demonstrate their speaking skills to the best of their ability. The following points will all help with this.

- Ask precise and unambiguous questions. Long and complex questions are not appropriate and may confuse the student so that they either cannot answer the question or that they do so vaguely or inappropriately.

- Be aware of how you are asking the student questions. Remember that if you ask a closed question, the student can only answer in single words, so allow them to provide a longer answer by asking open questions. For example, rather than asking 'Do you like fast-food?' it would be better to ask 'What type of fast-food do you enjoy eating?'

- Ensure that you as the interviewer do not speak too much.

- Ensure that you do not, at any point, make the student feel uncomfortable about what they are saying, feel disapproved of, or feel that you disagree with them. The students should be allowed to speak without feeling any pressure of having to provide right or wrong or acceptable or unacceptable answers.

- Bear in mind that there are many cultures in which the students show extreme respect and courtesy towards their teachers, which could make them nervous and mean that they don't perform to the best of their ability during a speaking assessment.

- On the other hand, ensure that students do not treat the situation too informally. If they are very familiar with the teacher conducting the interview, they may be tempted to use inappropriately informal language or engage in inappropriately informal conversation. Remind them that this is a formal exam-style assessment.

- Bear in mind at all times that this should be a neutral, impartial environment and conducted as if it were in exam conditions. As such, avoid any comments on the student's answers or performance that could be construed as praise – this includes any comments along the lines of 'good', 'well said', 'you've done very well', don't worry you're doing great', 'I think that's a brilliant answer', etc.

Speaking skills

Reading and Writing practice test

Part 1

Read the article about a young person who has raised a lot of money for charity and then answer the questions.

Around the World in 80 Dishes

I recently had the pleasure of interviewing Binita Devi, who makes money for charity by selling her very own cookery book of recipes from around the world. I asked her how it had all started.

Binita said that she really enjoyed her English course at college because the teachers were very kind and made the classes fun. When asked what she liked the most though, her answer was rather surprising. 'The coffee breaks,' she said, with a big smile on her face. 'I got to mix with students from all sorts of other cultures that I had previously only read about in novels – my library back home was so tiny that it didn't even have non-fiction books or even magazines. Some students liked talking about films and others about music and I didn't mind that, but I preferred chatting about everyone's favourite dishes from their own countries. Their descriptions really made the dishes come to life, so I could almost smell the sweet spices and taste the fresh fruit. I especially liked having discussions about food I'd never even heard of before, like cowberries and dragon tongue beans!'

One day, her English class had been about the work of international charities, and she was upset to hear about the millions of people around the world who struggle to feed themselves and their families. Suddenly, she was hit by an idea. Why didn't she collect all the fantastic recipes that she had heard about in one single book, which she would then encourage people to buy. All the money that she raised could go to a charity that sends food to countries in need.

Well, there was no stopping her then. She continued to chat to her classmates to get more ideas – in the coffee breaks of course – and decided that each chapter should focus on a different country's dishes, accompanied by colourful photos. 'I did not want it to be just a recipe book, though,' she insisted. 'I also wanted to add explanations from the students about why a particular dish was special to them.

'The next task was the most challenging,' she sighed. 'I had to decide exactly what to include in my book, but how do you choose from Spanish tapas, Indonesian street food, Italian antipasti or Thai curries? And they were just a handful of the ideas. The other problem was that I woke up every morning feeling hungry because I had been dreaming about food all night!'

It would also be expensive to produce the book, but luckily, when her English teachers heard about the idea, they begged the college principal to ask the college to print it for free. Binita says she will never forget the moment when saw the first printed copy. 'It was a beautiful and deeply moving collection of stories, thoughts and feelings, thanks to everyone who had contributed their personal memories.'

The next step was for Binita to sell a copy to absolutely everybody she knew. 'I didn't give them any choice,' she joked. When a friend suggested publishing it online, she did that too, and within the first fortnight she'd sold 500 copies. 'Many of those sales were from paper copies,' she explained, 'but it was selling online that proved to be most profitable, and before I knew it, I'd sold over 3000 books!'

Binita says it is hard to describe how she feels about managing to make so much money for charity – she is not at all arrogant about her efforts. But having read her book and met her in person, I have only two words to describe her and her achievement, and that is *'totally awesome'.*

1 How did Binita find out about other cultures before she joined the college English course?

.... [1]

2 What did she most enjoy talking to other students about, outside of class time?

.... [1]

3 What made her cookbook more personal than other recipe books?

.... [1]

4 What was the biggest problem that she had when creating her cookbook?

.... [1]

5 How did she make the most money from her book?

.... [1]

6 How were other people helpful to Binita while she was creating and selling her cookbook?
Give **three** details.

....

....

....

.... [3]

[Total: 8]

Reading & Writing
Practice test

Part 2

Read the review of four online photography courses (**A–D**). Then answer Question **7** (a)–(i)

A 'Images R Us'

It's hard to stand out from the crowd these days. Everyone is out there posting photos and videos of anything and everything from smiling babies to dancing dads. Well, if that makes you want to develop your social media presence, then this is the workshop for you and all you need is your computer and phone! A qualified tutor, who is also a professional photographer, will take you through everything you need to know to improve your online photos. You'll start by looking at what to share and where and then move on to tips for creating great pictures on your phone. The final session will be on editing your photos so the end result is as perfect as it can be. This online 12-hour course, complete with videos and tutorials can be taken at your convenience and is great value for money. Highly recommended.

B 'Super Shots'

So, you've been taking photos for years, first with the camera you got for your 13th birthday and more recently with your smartphone and now you know everything there is to know about taking great pictures. 'What next?' you find yourself thinking. Well think no longer. You can learn how to take your photography to another level to start to make money from all that knowledge, with this two-day online course. Sell your prints online or to magazines, make personalised cards and calendars, sell to photography sites, companies or businesses, start a blog, become a teacher – and those are only a few ideas. Who knew there were so many opportunities for you to benefit financially from your little hobby! You have to be available on certain days and the course is a little overpriced for what you get out of it, but don't worry, you'll soon be making a fortune!

C 'Fabulous Photos'

Have you ever found yourself looking at other award-winning pictures of pets, people and places and thinking that you could do better? Well perhaps you could and there are actually loads of photography competitions with prizes ranging from cash to holidays. Before you start entering every competition that you can find, however, you might find it useful to enrol on this inexpensive course. It is basically a two-hour interactive video presentation, which gives you details of what competitions exist and what you have to do to enter. It is extremely honest and does not hold back from telling you exactly what your chances are of winning a competition with thousands of entrants! If you have the time, it is well worth doing, if only to see what the possibilities are. This workshop is all about facts, not false promises.

D 'Perfect Pictures'

Do you ever remember seeing an incredible sunset, or catching a rare sight of a shy, red deer between the trees of a forest? Have you ever passed through snow-covered mountains and been amazed by the beauty of nature? If this sounds familiar, then why don't you consider learning how to make those memories permanent, with stunning photographs. This online course is not for those who already know how to use a camera, nor indeed for fans of smartphones or people portraits. It is for anyone who has never explored the field of nature and wildlife photography but would like to learn. It requires more of your time than most other courses – six weeks in total – and you have to put in lots of hours of study. You also need to have the money to invest in good camera equipment. If you have the time and money available, it is well worth it. Make your memories come to life with this interesting and educational course.

For each statement, write the correct letter A, B, C or D on the line.

7 Which review gives the following information?

(a) an understanding that you can do the course whenever you want .... [1]

(b) the idea that the course will take longer to complete than others .... [1]

(c) the suggestion that you could turn professional with your photography .... [1]

(d) the suggestion that you could improve your photographic skills in less than a day .... [1]

(e) the idea that the course is more expensive than it should be .... [1]

(f) the understanding that you should be realistic about your photography .... [1]

(g) the idea that you could improve your profile online .... [1]

(h) a description of the person who will be teaching you .... [1]

(i) the understanding that there will not be any information about people photography .... [1]

[Total: 9]

Reading & Writing
Practice test

Part 3

Read the article about a man who took up a new hobby, and then complete the notes.

Learning to snowboard

Strange though it may seem, Joni Kumar never saw real snow until he was 11 years old, when he fell in love with it, whilst on holiday in Austria. Perhaps it won't be so surprising though, when you know that he is actually from Fiji, and one thing that Fiji is definitely not known for is snow.

Imagine then his horror when, some years later, he found himself looking at a very different Austria on the internet. That same landscape now seemed to be mostly green, with just a few small patches of thin, white powder here and there. This was Joni's first encounter with the devastating results of climate change and he decided there and then that he would do something to really appreciate snow, while he still could. And that's why he decided to learn how to snowboard!

He booked himself onto a three-week course with a professional tutor, at a ski-school in Switzerland, and invested in his own snowboard when he arrived, although it was a whole day before he could even successfully strap this to his feet on his own!

From the very first moment, what he most loved about learning to snowboard was the incredible scenery that he was surrounded by every day. He never tired of the crisp, clean, beauty of mountains covered in a thick blanket of white. It would be true to say, however, that his first week was not an easy one. He found that he was seldom on his feet because he had trouble keeping his balance, and went to bed every evening tired and covered in bruises. He did notice, though, that he no longer minded using the chair lift to go up to the top of the slope. When he first had the idea of learning to snowboard, he hadn't thought about this and it did take him some time to get over his fear of heights.

By the end of the third week, Joni was no expert, of course, but he had moved onto more difficult slopes. Not only that, but he had also managed to complete several fairly simple jumps, much to his instructor's delight. When he finally managed to do his first jump, the feeling of freedom that it gave him to fly through the air – even for a short distance – was fantastic.

On Joni's last evening in Switzerland, he and his instructor talked about the highs and lows that Joni had gone through in his determination to learn how to snowboard. Joni had to laugh as he recalled being told for the hundredth time not to lean on his back foot when turning. This was something that he had instinctively done every time, and learning to put all his weight on his front foot to make a turn, was, for him, the most challenging thing about snowboarding.

As Joni was flying back to Fiji, he cheered himself up by thinking that another good reason for loving his new hobby was that he would be the only Fijian he knew who could do it, and that made him feel very special!

© HarperCollins*Publishers* 2022

Reading & Writing
Practice test

Imagine you are going to give a talk about Joni's story at school.
Prepare some notes to use as the basis for your talk.

Make short notes under each heading.

8 What he enjoyed about learning to snowboard:

....

....

.... [4]

9 Things that he found difficult about learning to snowboard:

....

....

....

....[3]

[Total: 7]

Part 4

Read the blog written by someone who has just returned from a year of volunteering abroad, and then answer the questions.

'Make a difference'

By Anika Johnson

For as long as I can remember I have wanted to do something to make a difference, not just to my life but to the lives of other people. I am pleased to say that in the past year I had the opportunity to do just that. So how did I do it? Well, I finished my school exams aged 17 and like many people at that age, knew I wanted to go to university, something which would also please my parents. I have to admit, though, that I was tired of all the learning as well as the endless revision of facts and figures in the weeks before an exam. So instead of applying for degree courses, I decided, much to my parents' initial concern, to take a 'gap year'. Fortunately, Mum and Dad eventually came round to the idea, as, at the end of the day, they were happy if I was happy!

When I made the decision, all I knew was that I would be taking a gap, or break, from studying, to do something different for up to a year. The problem was that there were so many possibilities out there of what to do, from travelling to working, even volunteering, and in so many countries! So the first thing I did was make a list of my likes and interests, followed by another list of things that I was good at and what I was interested in learning or achieving. It was clear that I enjoyed physical activities and learning practical skills and also wanted to improve my knowledge of other cultures and languages. In addition, I was thinking about studying education at university before seeking a career in teaching.

The next step was to go on to the internet to start researching organisations that could offer me something appropriate and, believe it or not, I found the perfect advertisement almost straight away. **'Make A Difference' – Join us and volunteer your help with the development of 3 schools for children in a semi-rural community – Belize'**. Well, I had always wanted to travel to that part of the world so it seemed the perfect option. By the way, if you don't know where Belize is, it is a Caribbean country, near Mexico and Guatemala.

It was then a fairly simple process of applying online, having a telephone interview, receiving an offer, confirming my acceptance and finally making the required payment. Before I knew it, I was on the plane heading for the most thrilling period of my life! Every day in Belize was a fantastic learning experience for me and that's what gave me the most satisfaction. One day I could be working on the external construction of a building, helping to install toilets, or painting the interior walls of a room. The next day I could be having a laugh, teaching silly songs in English to children from the local area. Additionally, I was warmly welcomed by everyone working on the project, either locals or volunteers from abroad like me. The worst part of the whole experience was when the day came for me to say goodbye.

As a result of volunteering for **'Make a Difference'**, I have developed a range of new skills and abilities. I also appreciate much more how other cultures live and what support they can be given to improve the quality of their lives. I also realise how important it is to appreciate what I have, but the main thing is that I now feel ready to move on to the next period of my life with excitement and motivation – university here I come!

10 How did Anika's parents first react when she told them that she was going to take a gap year?

A   They were worried.

B   They agreed that she shouldn't have to do any more exams.

C   They wanted her to do something that would make a difference to her life.   [1]

11 Why did Aneka find it difficult at first to know what to do on her gap year?

A   She didn't know what career she wanted to do afterwards.

B   She didn't want to have to go abroad.

C   There was too much choice.   [1]

12 What does 'it' refer to in line 23?

A   doing research on the internet

B   finding the ideal gap year experience very quickly

C   having the opportunity to travel to a country she had always wanted to visit   [1]

13 What was the best part of the volunteering experience for Anika?

A   the fact that she worked with children

B   the time that she spent with her colleagues on the project

C   the fact that she acquired new knowledge on a daily basis   [1]

14 Anika suggests that biggest benefit for her of having taken the gap year is

A   she now understands more about other cultures and their way of life.

B   she now knows how to do things that she had never done before.

C   she now feels more confident about and prepared to go on to further education.   [1]

15 What was Anika's main reason for writing this blog?

A   to provide a record of her gap year experience

B   to explain to people what a gap year is

C   to persuade people not to go to university straight after finishing school   [1]

[Total 6]

Reading & Writing
Practice test

Part 5

16 You recently had a problem when you went out with some friends for the day.

Write an email to a friend explaining what happened.

In your email, you should:

*   explain where you went and what happened

*   describe what your friends did to help

*   say how you felt about what happened.

Write about 120-160 words.

You will receive up to 6 marks for the content of your email, and up to 9 marks for the language used.

[15]

[Total: 15]

Part 6

17 Your class is planning to start a reading club. Your teacher wants students' opinions about reading books, and you have been asked to write an article for the school magazine.

In your article, say the benefits and disadvantages of reading books.

Here are some comments from students in your class:

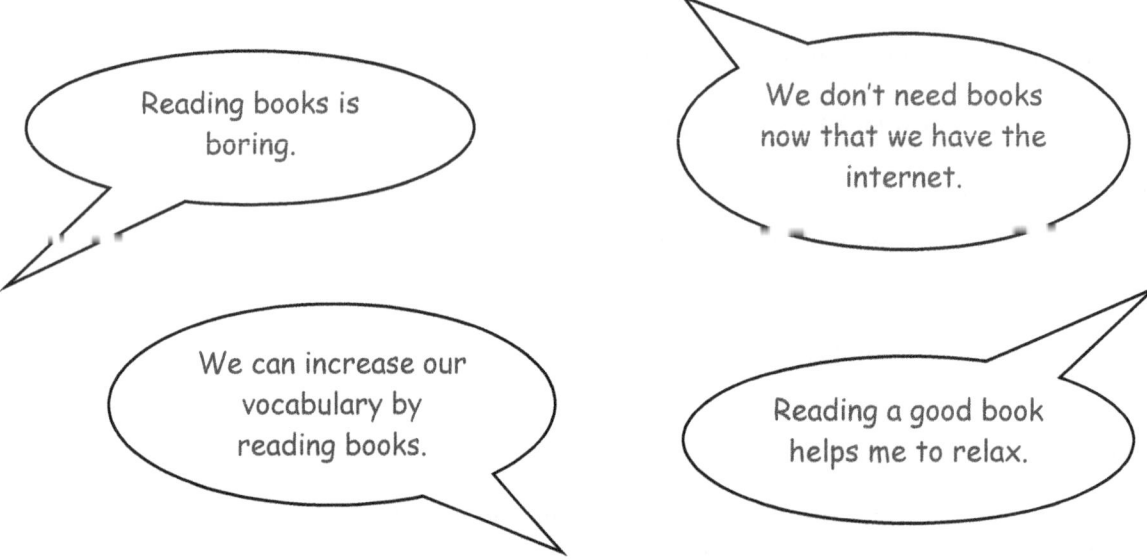

Reading books is boring.

We don't need books now that we have the internet.

We can increase our vocabulary by reading books.

Reading a good book helps me to relax.

Now write an article for your teacher, giving your views.

The comments above may give you some ideas, and you can also use some ideas of your own.

Write about 120 to 160 words.

You will receive up to 6 marks for the content of your report and up to 9 marks for the language used.

[15]

[Total: 15]

Reading and Writing answers

Part 1

Question	Answer	Mark	Comment
1	she had previously only read about them in novels / she had read about them in novels / by reading about them in novels	1	'from non-fiction books' – incorrect. 'from newspapers' – incorrect. 'from magazines' – incorrect. 'from reading' – incorrect (not specific enough). 'I' or 'She' – correct for all answers.
2	food (she) had never heard about before	1	'her favourite subject' – incorrect (not specific enough). 'films' – incorrect. 'music' – incorrect. 'fruit' / 'spices' /'cowberries' / dragon tongue beans' / – incorrect. The words 'especially liked' best convey the idea of 'most enjoy' from the question.
3	she wanted to add explanations from the students about why a particular dish was special to them	1	'she was particularly upset to hear about the millions of people who struggle to feed themselves and their families' – incorrect (not specific enough) Anything to do with 'fantastic recipes' – incorrect.
4	she had to decide/having to decide/ deciding what to include in her book choosing from so many ideas	1	'she had to choose/choosing from Spanish tapas, Indonesian street food, Italian antipasti or Thai curries' – not accepted – as these were just a selection of what she received and her problem was to choose from everything that she had received. 'I/she woke up every morning feeling hungry' – incorrect. 'she had been dreaming / was dreaming / dreamt about about food all night!' – incorrect. 'expensive to produce the book' – incorrect something like 'deciding from so much choice (about) what to include' would be acceptable/correct.
5	selling online/by selling it online/from online sales	1	'publishing it online' – incorrect. Must be an idea of 'selling' / 'sales' 'selling it to everyone she knew' – incorrect, not specific enough.
6	students/classmates gave her ideas/recipes for the book her English teachers begged/ asked for help from college principal the college principal allowed her to print it for free at the college people/staff at college helped print the book/printed the book everyone she knew bought a copy a friend suggested that she publish it online	3	Three of the points from any of the options provided – correct. The person (i.e. classmates, English teachers, etc.) should be mentioned as well as the way they helped, for the answers to make full sense and to be awarded full marks.

The questions, sample answers and marks/comments that appear in this book were written by the author.
In the examination, the way marks would be awarded to answers like these may be different.

Part 2

Question 7	Answer *The relevant part of the text is given below the answer for reference.*	Marks	Comments
(a)	**A** This online 12-hour course, complete with videos and tutorials can be taken at your convenience.	1	B – does not specify C – does not specify D – does not specify
(b)	**D** It is a long course – six weeks in total.	1	A – 12 hours B – 2 days C – 2 hours
(c)	**B** You can learn how to take your photography to another level and start to make money from all that experience and knowledge.	1	A, C, D – not mentioned. B is the only one that focuses on you turning from amateur to professional.
(d)	**C** It is basically a two-hour interactive video presentation.	1	Students will have to use scanning skills to find the answer.
(e)	**B** the course is a little overpriced for what you get out of it.	1	A – good value for money C – inexpensive D – 'you need to have the money to invest in good cameral equipment' refers to the equipment being expensive, not the course
(f)	**C** It is extremely honest and does not hold back from telling you exactly what your chances are of winning a competition with thousands of entrants.	1	A – not specified B – not specified D – not specified
(g)	**A** if that makes you want to develop your social media presence.	1	B – not specified C – different focus D – different focus
(h)	**A** A qualified teacher who is also a professional photographer.	1	B, C, D – no mention
(i)	**D** This online workshop is not for those who already know how to use a camera, nor indeed for fans of smartphones and people portraits.	1	A – focuses on people pictures B – no mention C – mentions taking pics of people

Part 3

Correct answer	Mark	Comment
Question 8 the feeling of freedom that it gave him to fly through the air – even for a short distance – (was fantastic) incredible scenery that he was surrounded by every day/ He never tired of the crisp, clean, beauty of mountains covered in a thick blanket of white that he would be the only person in Fiji who knew how to to do it, (and that made him feel very special!)	4	'using the chair lift to go up to the top of the slope' – incorrect. He didn't mind it in the end, but did not enjoy it. 'moved onto more difficult slopes' – incorrect (no idea of enjoyment) 'complete several fairly simple jumps' – incorrect (no sense of enjoyment for him, but rather for his instructor). 'feeling special' – not enough, incorrect.
Question 9 strapping on his snowboard (to his feet) on his own staying on his feet/finding his balance/keeping his balance getting over his fear of heights not leaning on his back foot when turning / learning to put all his weight on his front foot to make a turn	3	'Strapping on his snowboard' must include 'on his own' for 1 mark.

Part 4

Question	Answer *The relevant part of the text is given below the answer for reference.*	Marks	Comments
10	**A** 'much to my parents' initial concern'	1	'pleased/happy' – incorrect
11	**C** The problem was that there were so many possibilities out there of what to do,	1	'knowing her likes and dislikes, what she was good at', etc. – incorrect
12	**B** 'believe it or not I found the perfect advertisement almost straight away'	1	'researching organisations/internet' – incorrect
13	**C** Every day in Belize was a fantastic learning experience for me and that's what gave me the most satisfaction.	1	'building, painting, having a laugh, silly songs', etc. – incorrect
14	**C** the main thing is that I now feel ready to move on to the next period of my life with excitement and motivation – university here I come!	1	'develop new skills and abilities, understand other cultures' – incorrect
15	**A**	1	

The questions, sample answers and marks/comments that appear in this book were written by the author.
In the examination, the way marks would be awarded to answers like these may be different.

Part 5

Sample response 1

Hi Allie,

I wish you well and hello to your family. We go to our house at the beach next week because of now we have holiday, so I am writing to you about when I went for pizza with friends last week for celebrate my birthday.

We went to a restaurant that we been before and we were lucky because was full but we got a table. We choose pizzas and had good time eating and loughing.

 I said I wanted pay the meal so I picked up my bag from the floor but when I looked in my bag, no purse. Somebody steal my purse. I was really sad but my friends said don't worry, they will pay.

At the end the manager said sorry but nothing he can do because of the restaurant was crowded. In conclusion we will not go this restaurant again.

I will finish now because I need do homework.

Yours sincerely

Becca

Comments on Sample response 1

Total marks = 10

Comments on content (Mark = 4)

- **Relevance:** All three prompts are covered. There is some irrelevance.

- **Style and register:** generally good sense of reader – informal tone used, appropriate for a friend, for example, 'I wish you well and hello to your family' / I hope see you soon'. The close, however, is rather formal ('yours sincerely') as is the use of the phrases 'I am writing to you' and 'in conclusion'.

- **Development:** the content is generally developed but lacks detail on each prompt. The response is of appropriate length.

Comments on language (Mark = 6)

- **Range and accuracy:** Uses a range of common vocabulary appropriately, and attempts to use some we less common vocabulary ('purse' / 'crowded' / 'picked up'). Uses a range of simple structures, and attempts to use some complex structures ('been' / 'a good time eating'). Generally good level of accuracy and meaning is always clear despite the errors when more complex language is attempted ('choose' / 'loughing' /'steal').

- **Organisation:** It is generally well organised, with effective paragraphs. Simple linking words and cohesive devices are used ('and' / 'after' / 'and so' / 'but' / 'when I looked...'), but they are not always accurate ('because of') and there is inappropriate use of the phrases 'at the end' and 'in conclusion'.

Sample response 2

> Hey Marc,
>
> Sorry I haven't written for ages – my bad – life's been crazy. How're you doing? Just thought I'd drop you a line, to give you a laugh.
>
> I went out recently with my BF's James and Ling – remember them – and it was awesome catching up on all the goss. Anyway, as we were leaving I saw girl, who I recognised, so I went and tapped her on the shoulder, saying, 'Hey Bex, long time, no see!' Well, when she turned round, I went as red as a tomato, because it wasn't Becca at all!! I muttered sorry and walked off, feeling like a right idiot!
>
> So embarrassing – can you imagine? My friends were sympathetic, saying that it could happen to anyone but then James shot a smile at Ling and before we knew it, we were all laughing til we were crying! Thanks to them, it all turned into a bit of joke and I started to feel a bit better about the mistake I'd made!
>
> Anyway, must go – Mum's calling. Can't wait to see you soon.
>
> Hugs,
>
> Your mate Timmo

Comments on Sample response 2

Total marks = 15

Comments on content (Mark = 6)

- **Relevance:** All three prompts are covered and the content is fully relevant throughout.

- **Style and register:** there is an excellent sense of the reader – informal, friendly tone used throughout, with direct address to the reader ('how are you doing' / 'remember them' / 'can you imagine' / 'can't wait to see you' / 'hugs').

- **Development:** the content is very well developed for each prompt. The response is 185 words which is slightly longer than required but this is acceptable in this case because it is all relevant.

Comments on language (Mark = 9)

- **Range and accuracy:** there is a wide range of common vocabulary used appropriately but the candidate also demonstrates a range of less common words or phrases ('drop you a line' / 'crazy' / 'give you a laugh' / 'tapped her shoulder' / 'as red as a tomato' / 'muttered').

  There is a high level of accuracy of language throughout and simple and more complex tenses and structures are used confidently ('saying' / ''feeling like' /'James shot a smile at' / 'the mistake I'd made'). There were two errors with the indefinite article, but these do not impede communication.

- **Organisation:** It is very well organised, with effective paragraphs and uses a wide range of appropriate linking words and more complex cohesive devices such as pronouns and discourse markers and connectives.

Summary

The candidate wrote about the three bullet points with a good amount of development for each one. The overall tone and register was appropriately informal and friendly. The candidate wrote an interesting story line which would engage the reader. The task was fulfilled and ambitious,

Reading & Writing
Answers

with a very natural style throughout. The meaning was consistently clear and there was frequent evidence of complex structures and less common vocabulary. There are only two grammatical slips and the email is effectively paragraphed, with good use of cohesive devices and linking words. It is a detailed, comprehensive and cohesive answer, that has achieved full marks.

Part 6

Sample response 1

Reading books

I guess it is a common subject at the moment to debat about reading books and I talked to the other students in my class about the topic. Most of them said that they hate reading books because it is boring. Other people said that reading books are not necessary today because we have everything that we need on the internet.

There were some other students in my class who said that they love reading books because it helps them learn new vocabulary and grammar and other more people who said that it is good reading a book as it is good for relax if they feel stress.

Anyways, there are no people who agree on if it is good reading books or not, so it will continue be a subject that everyone will debat about.

Comments on Sample response 1

Total marks = 9

Comments on content (Mark = 4)

- **Relevance:** All content is relevant. The writer uses the opinions raised by other people in their class.

- **Style and register:** generally good sense of reader – neutral – formal tone mostly used, although the use of 'I guess' and 'anyways' is rather informal.

- **Development:** the content is appropriate but the opinions lack development. The writer does not add any further arguments to those that were expressed by the other students and neither do they include their own opinion. The response is of appropriate length.

Comments on language (Mark = 5)

- **Range and accuracy**: Uses a range of common vocabulary appropriately, and attempts to use some less common vocabulary ('stress') however this is not always successful ('debat' – spelling slip but non-impeding). Uses a range of simple structures accurately although with some repetition. There is an attempt to use more complex structures ('it is good reading'), which are not always successful ('it will continue be').

There is some reliance on words used in the input/task.

- **Organisation:** It is generally well organised, with effective paragraphs. Simple linking words ('as' / 'so') and pronouns ('it') are used but there is an over-reliance on 'because'.

Sample response 2

> Books, do we need them?
>
> Will people be reading books 20 years from now? Perhaps it's time to consider whether these time-old sources of fact and fiction are still relevant to today's society.
>
> Nowadays everything we want to know, is there at the click of a button. Using the internet to find what you need, can certainly be much quicker than trying to find it in a book.
>
> Other people say that books are just not interesting and in addition, there is the inconvenience. If you need information late at night, you can't just visit your local library.
>
> On the other hand, there is no doubt that if you lose yourself in a book, it is a fabulous way to switch off from everyday stress. Also, as a student of English, I find that another advantage is that they help with my language skills.
>
> I think books are incredible. I love the way they feel and smell and will never stop reading them and I wouldn't hesitate to urge everyone to go and immerse themselves in a good book immediately.

Comments on Sample response 2

Total marks = 15

Comments on content (Mark = 6)

- **Relevance:** All content is fully relevant throughout. The writer uses the opinions of the other students and also effectively brings in their own arguments.

- **Style and register:** there is an excellent sense of the reader – a formal but engaging tone is used throughout, from the first metaphorical question, to the final personal recommendation.

- **Development:** the content is very well developed. The advantages and disadvantages are clearly discussed and the article ends with the writer's personal opinion.

  The response is 175 words (minus the title) which is slightly longer than required but this is acceptable in this case as it is relevant.

Comments on language (Mark = 9)

- **Range and accuracy:** there is a wide range of common vocabulary used appropriately but the candidate also demonstrates a range of less common words or phrases ('time-old sources' and 'fact and fiction' / 'switch off' / 'immerse' / 'regret' / 'urge').

  There is a high level of accuracy of language throughout and simple and more complex tenses and structures are used confidently ('will people be reading' / 'using the internet' / 'quicker than trying to find' / 'if you need….you won't…' / 'will never stop reading' / 'go and immerse yourself'). There are no errors.

- **Organisation:** It is very well organised, with effective paragraphs and good use of a wide range of appropriate linking words and cohesive devices ('also' / 'in addition' / 'on the other hand' / pronouns).

Reading & Writing Answers

Listening practice test

Part 1

You will hear eight short recordings. For each question, circle the correct answer, **A**, **B**, **C** or **D**.
You will hear each recording twice.

1 Which house do the couple decide to go and look at first?

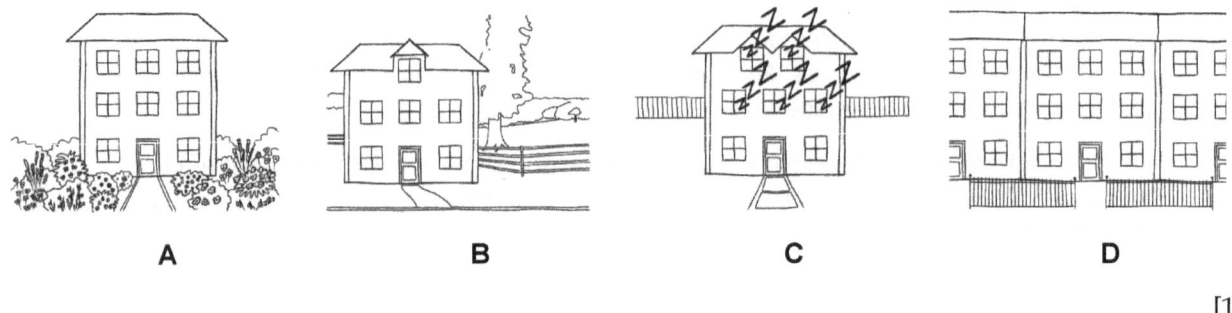

A   B   C   D

[1]

2 Which of the children's holiday suggestions do the parents choose?

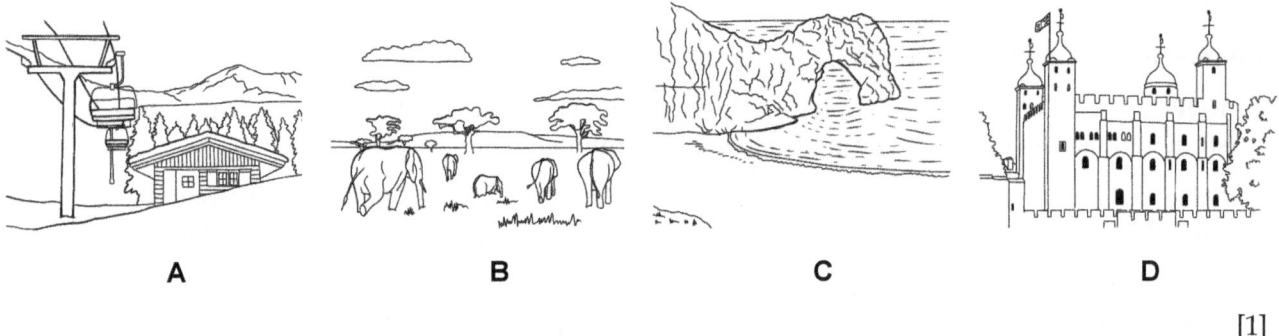

A   B   C   D

[1]

3 What type of student work has never been shown in Arts Week before?

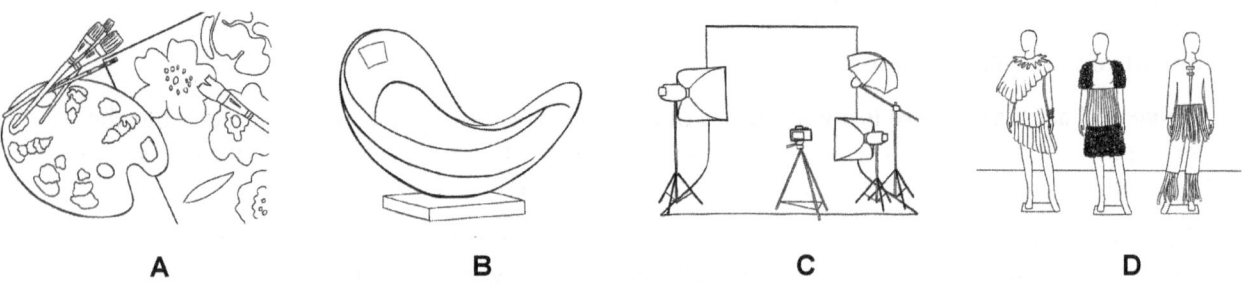

A   B   C   D

4 What have the girls forgotten for the party?

A   B   C   D

[1]

The questions, sample answers and marks/comments that appear in this book were written by the author.
In the examination, the way marks would be awarded to answers like these may be different.

© HarperCollins*Publishers* 2022

5 Why can't the boy go to the barbecue?

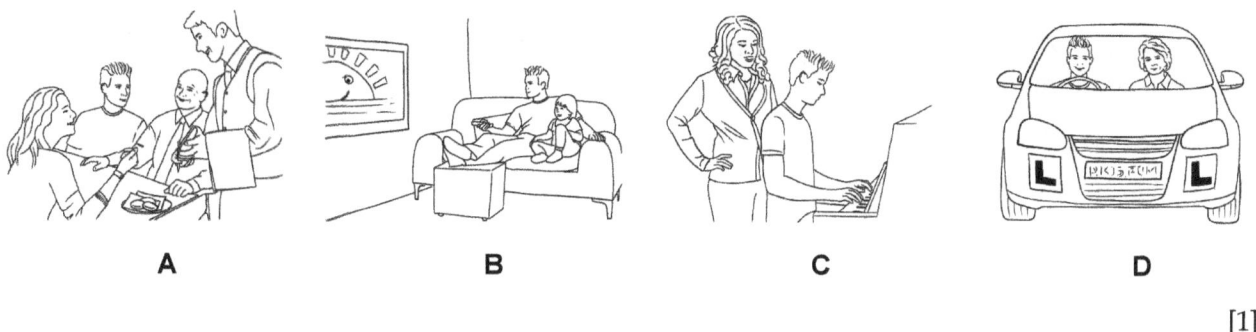

A   B   C   D

[1]

6 Which film are the friends going to see at the cinema?

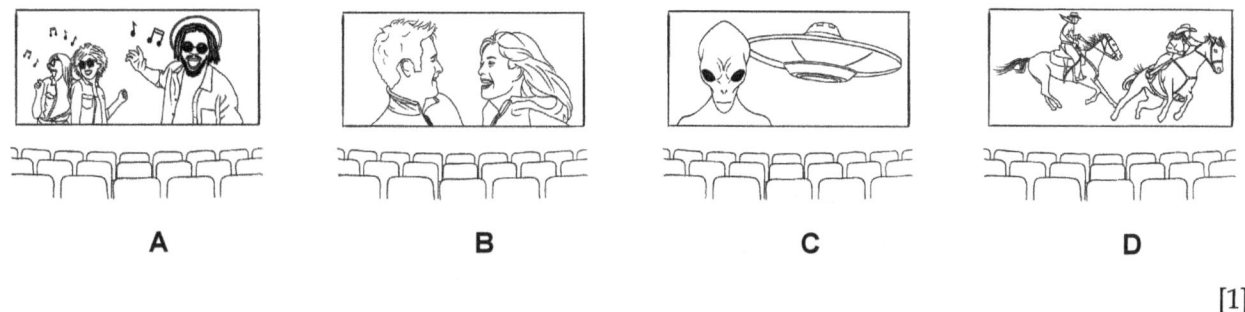

A   B   C   D

[1]

7 What will the parents be doing during the daytime on their holiday?

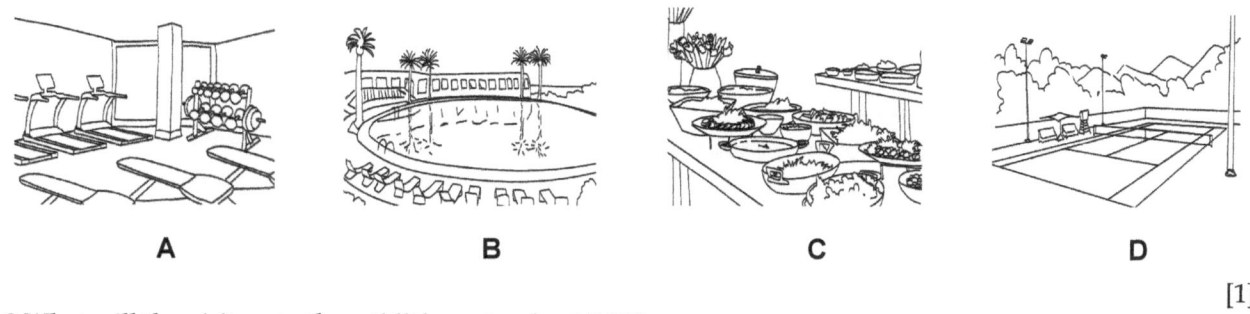

A   B   C   D

[1]

8 What will the visitors to the wildlife centre do at 3.00?

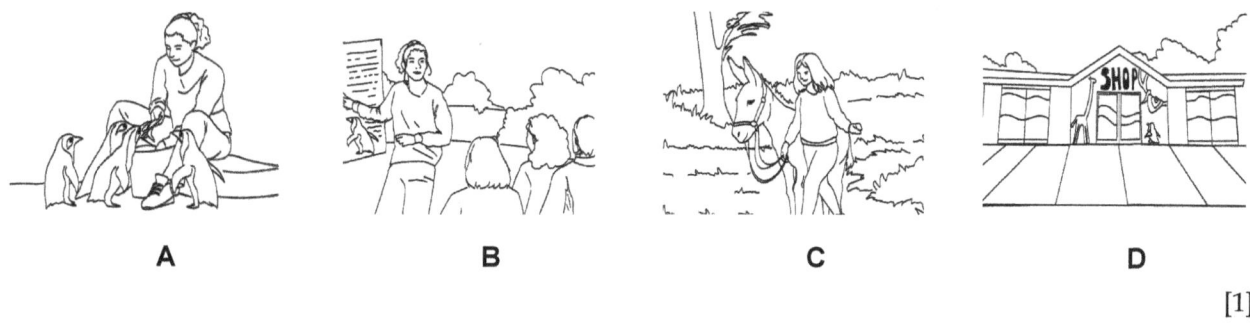

A   B   C   D

[1]

[Total: 8]

The questions, sample answers and marks/comments that appear in this book were written by the author.
In the examination, the way marks would be awarded to answers like these may be different.

Part 2

You will hear five short recordings. There are two questions for each recording. For each question, circle the correct answer, **A**, **B**, or **C**.

You will hear each recording twice.

You will hear a girl talking to a shop assistant.

1 Why does the girl want to return the shirt?

    A   She does not like the colour.

    B   It is not the right size.

    C   There is something wrong with it.   [1]

2 Why can't the assistant give a refund?

    A   There is a hole in the shirt.

    B   The girl does not have the receipt.

    C   The girl has already worn the shirt.   [1]

You will hear a radio presenter talking about a listener's email.

3 How did Barbara feel about John when they first met?

    A   She didn't like his voice.

    B   She thought he was rude.

    C   She didn't immediately fall in love with him.   [1]

4 How would John like to celebrate the couple's anniversary?

    A   He would like to go on a skiing holiday.

    B   He would like to have a huge party with friends and family.

    C   He would like to go away somewhere warm.   [1]

You will hear a teacher giving some information about his students' practice interviews.

5 Where will the interviews be held?

    A   in the classroom

    B   we don't know

    C   in the library   [1]

6 What would their teacher prefer them to wear?

    A   a smart suit

    B   whatever they decide

    C   a school uniform   [1]

The questions, sample answers and marks/comments that appear in this book were written by the author.
In the examination, the way marks would be awarded to answers like these may be different.

You will hear two friends talking about some school clubs.

7   When will the drama club start?

    A   a week later than planned

    B   the following Tuesday

    C   in a few weeks   **[1]**

8   Why won't Ravi be able to join the drama club?

    A   because the drama teacher is off-sick

    B   because it will be on the same week day as football practice

    C   because it will be on Tuesdays, not Wednesdays   **[1]**

You will hear a young boy being asked some questions about his hometown.

9   What does the boy think of the places where young people can go to eat and drink?

    A   There are enough of them but they are too expensive.

    B   They are cheap but there are not enough of them.

    C   They are easy to get to because they are in the centre of the town.   **[1]**

10   What is the boy's opinion of what is available for young people to do in the evening?

    A   He enjoys being able to play games and learn new crafts.

    B   He wishes the community centre hadn't closed.

    C   He thinks it is good that there is a cinema.   **[1]**

[Total: 10]

Listening
Practice test

Part 3

You will hear a man called Roger Darcy giving a talk about assistance dogs. For each question circle the correct answer, **A**, **B** or **C**. You will hear the talk twice.

Now look at questions 1–8.

Dogs with jobs

1 Roger says that people first started using assistance dogs in

    A   the eighteenth century.

    B   the 1900s.

    C   the twenty-first century.

2 Roger thinks that many people would say that an assistance dog's most vital role is to

    A   help people out with practical things.

    B   give people more confidence when doing daily activities.

    C   provide friendship to a person.

3 Roger explains that guide dogs alert a blind person of potential danger when out walking, by

    A   making a certain noise.

    B   stopping.

    C   touching the person on the leg.

4 Assistance dogs that usually wear a purple coat are ………….., according to Roger.

    A   hearing dogs

    B   guide dogs

    C   medical alert dogs

Listening Practice test

5 Roger explains that a hearing dog could actually save someone's life, because they can

- **A**   smell a potential fire in the person's house.
- **B**   protect the person if they hear someone breaking into their house.
- **C**   prevent the person from crossing busy, dangerous roads.

6 The type of dog that mostly uses its sense of smell to help someone is the

- **A**   guide dog.
- **B**   hearing dog.
- **C**   medical alert dog.

7 According to Roger, he has to finish his talk because

- **A**   he has run out of things to say.
- **B**   Toby is hungry.
- **C**   it is time for the audience to go into lessons.

8 Roger says that he will ………….. to help the children find out how to get involved with assistance dogs.

- **A**   leave some information behind for them
- **B**   write to their teacher Mrs Matthews with more details
- **C**   ask different organisations to contact them with more details

[Total: 8]

Listening
Practice test

Part 4

You will hear six young people talking about their part-time jobs. Match the ideas (A-H) to the speakers(1-6). Use each letter only once. There are two extra letters which you do not need to use. You will hear the recordings twice. Now look at the ideas **A–H**.

Ideas

A	I never feel like I am really working.

B	The only good thing about my part-time job is that I am saving money for the future.

C	The best thing about my job is it gives me the opportunity to do things I can't do in my normal everyday life.

D	My part-time job gives me the chance to spend more time enjoying my hobby.

E	I only did a part-time job for academic reasons.

F	I love my part-time job because I get some physical exercise.

G	I am glad that I am doing something that will be useful for my future work.

H	I am saving up for a new apartment where I can have pets.

Speaker 1 .... [1]

Speaker 2 .... [1]

Speaker 3 .... [1]

Speaker 4 .... [1]

Speaker 5 .... [1]

Speaker 6 .... [1]

[Total: 6]

Listening
Practice test

Part 5

You will hear an interview with a student called Jasmine who organised a project to clean up a public space in her town. For each question circle the correct answer, **A**, **B** or **C**. You will hear the interview twice. Now look at questions 1-8.

1 What depressed Jasmine the most when she first saw Pleasant Fields?

    A   the fact that nobody had looked after the plants

    B   seeing how unattractive the place was

    C   people's behaviour towards the place   [1]

2 Why did people stop using the building that was originally on the site?

    A   the council didn't let them use it

    B   they didn't need it any more

    C   because it was in a terrible state   [1]

3 What did Jasmine and Sasha think the biggest benefit of 'Clean up if you care' would be?

    A   All the rubbish would be taken away.

    B   It would be a great place for children to play.

    C   It would have a positive influence on people's mood.   [1]

4 The most successful way of getting volunteers for 'Clean up if you care' was

    A   putting up posters.

    B   telling everyone at school about it.

    C   using social media.   [1]

5 Who offered Jasmine the most money to support the project?

    A   Jasmine didn't know who it was

    B   people who gave them money for a sponsored event

    C   people who bought things that they had made   [1]

6 The most surprising part of the first day of 'Clean up if you care' project was

    A   the weather was good.

    B   there were a lot of volunteers.

    C   the food and drink that people she knew had brought for everyone.   [1]

7 Jasmine said that the biggest lesson she learned from doing the 'Clean-up if you care' project was

    A   how to dispose of rubbish safely.

    B   the fact that people can be so generous.

    C   how quickly this type of clean-up can be done.   [1]

8 What's next for Pleasant Fields?

    A   Jasmine will take six months to decide what to do next

    B   Jasmine wants to get more money before she can continue with the project

    C   Jasmine wants to continue making it an attractive, useful space.   [1]

[Total: 8]

Listening Practice test

Listening answers

Part 1

Question	Answer	Mark
1	A	1
2	C	1
3	A	1
4	A	1
5	D	1
6	B	1
7	D	1
8	A	1

Part 2

Recording	Question	Answer	Mark	Comment
Girl in shop	1	C	1	It's not her usual colour or normal size, but neither factor is a problem. The problem is there is something wrong with it – i.e. it has a hole.
	2	B	1	The assistant could change the shirt if there was a receipt as it has not been worn and the hole is not an issue.
Radio presenter	3	C	1	'It wasn't love at first sight'. She didn't mind his voice and thought he had good manners.
	4	A	1	It is Barbara who wants the big party and is not bothered about going away, even somewhere warm.
Teacher to students	5	B	1	We don't know where the interviews will be held. They should have been in the library but there's a book sale there and they are meeting in the classroom before the interviews so that is the first not the second room.
	6	A	1	He would prefer them to wear a smart suit, but if they don't have one, they can either decide on something themselves or wear their uniform.
Two school friends	7	A	1	It will start a week later than planned – other days, and reasons are distractors.
	8	B	1	Now it will be the same day as football practice, i.e. Wednesdays not Tuesdays.
A boy being interviewed	9	A	1	'plenty of them but they could be cheaper'
	10	B	1	'used to be a fantastic community centre … I was upset when it closed'

Part 3

Question	Answer	Mark	Comment
1	A	1	Not a 21st-century concept and became common in 20th century, but first records are from the 18th century.
2	C	1	Be a best friend
3	A	1	You might think they bark or touch the person but they actually stop.
4	A	1	Hearing dogs wear burgundy coats – not necessary to understand 'burgundy' with a process of elimination, i.e. guide dogs wear white and yellow and medical alert dogs wear red.
5	C	1	They inform people of visitors not warn if they hear someone breaking into the house. They can hear the traffic, and therefore prevent the person from crossing a busy, dangerous road. The answer option A is a distractor in that the dogs don't smell a fire, but instead can hear the smoke alarm, i.e. warning of a possible fire.
6	C	1	'they can detect changes in a person's scent'
7	C	1	'I had strict instructions from your teacher not to make you late for class'
8	A	1	Leaflets left behind

Part 4

Question	Answer		Mark	Comments F and H are the letters they do not need.
Speaker 1	G	I am glad that I am doing something that will be useful for my future work.	1	'I just wanted to gain real experience of working in a busy hotel so it won't come as such a shock when I actually start doing it for a living'
Speaker 2	B	The only good thing… I am saving money for the future.	1	'I just try to remember that every pay cheque goes towards that extra bit of pocket money when I'm at university'
Speaker 3	D	…spend more time enjoying my favourite hobby.	1	'it is basically a way of continuing to do something that I love… always enjoyed singing although… not going to be my future work'
Speaker 4	C	…it gives me the opportunity to do things I can't do in my normal everyday life.	1	'we live in an apartment… we are not allowed pets'
Speaker 5	A	I never feel like I am really working.	1	'helping my family out just doesn't feel like a job'
Speaker 6	E	I only did it for academic reasons.	1	'it was about the advantages and disadvantages of doing a part-time job while studying and I just didn't have any ideas on the subject.

The questions, sample answers and marks/comments that appear in this book were written by the author.
In the examination, the way marks would be awarded to answers like these may be different.

Listening
Answers

Part 5

Question	Answer	Mark	Comments
1	**C** – people's behaviour towards the place	1	'what made me even more miserable was knowing that people could just throw their rubbish away in this space'
2	**B** – they didn't need it any more	1	'the school was closed when a bigger, more modern one was built'
3	**C** – it would have a positive influence on people's mood	1	'best of all, just make people feel happier and less stressed by being outside, surrounded by nature'
4	**C** – using social media	1	'social media would probably be the best way… as in fact was the case'
5	**A** – she didn't know who it was	1	(Raised some funds with sales and swim) 'the biggest and best surprise … a huge and unexpected donation from someone … they hadn't wanted to give their name…'
6	**C** – the food and drink brought by people she knew	1	'the most unexpected thing for me was that our friends … brought us tea and coffee … sandwiches…'
7	**B** – the fact people can be so generous	1	'the most important thing that this whole experience has taught me is that people … generous'
8	**C** – continue to make it an attractive, useful space	1	'benches, picnic table, play equipment … planting…'

A – Family holiday

Your family are planning to go on holiday together soon. You are considering the best way to make it enjoyable for the whole family. You can either:

- go on holiday in your own country
- go on holiday abroad

Discuss the advantages and disadvantages of each option. Say which option you would prefer, and why.

A – Family holiday

Your family are planning to go on holiday together soon. You are considering the best way to make it enjoyable for the whole family. You can either:

- go on holiday in your own country
- go on holiday abroad

Discuss the advantages and disadvantages of each option. Say which option you would prefer, and why.

A – Family holiday

Your family are planning to go on holiday together soon. You are considering the best way to make it enjoyable for the whole family. You can either:

- go on holiday in your own country
- go on holiday abroad

Discuss the advantages and disadvantages of each option. Say which option you would prefer, and why.

The questions, sample answers and marks/comments that appear in this book were written by the author.
In the examination, the way marks would be awarded to answers like these may be different.

Speaking questions - teacher notes

Speaking questions are covered in Chapter 19 of the Student's Book, with explanations and practice exercises for students, while accompanying explanations and notes for teachers are provided in Chapter 19 of this Teacher's Guide. This separate **Speaking** section provides a teacher's script and a student topic card so that you can conduct a formal exam-style practice test with your students. Step-by-step guidance is given below and an example topic card is provided on the opposite page for you to photocopy and use at part 2.

Introduction (approximately 1 minute)

Start the recording, give the student's name and welcome the student. Then read the following to the student.

Teacher script: First, we will start with a short warm-up where I will ask you some questions to find out a bit more about you. This part isn't assessed. After the warm-up there are three assessed parts to the practice test: an interview, a short talk and a discussion.

Then start the practice test.

Warm-up (1–2 minutes)

Use the following questions to find out more about the student.

- Where do you live?
- Can you tell me something about your family?
- What would you like to do when you finish school?

Part 1 Interview (2–3 minutes)

Read the following script to the student and ask the questions listed below in the order given. Allow students to respond to each question as fully as they can before you move on to the next one.

Teacher script: The first assessed part of the practice test is an interview. I am going to ask you some questions about <u>your holidays.</u> Try to say as much as you can for each question. Before we start, do you have any questions?

Your holidays

Can you tell me what you and your friends enjoy doing in your school holidays?

Can you tell me about a family holiday that you enjoyed, and why?

Do you think it is better to spend holidays relaxing or being active? Why? Why not?

Part 2 Short talk (3–4 minutes)

Read out the following script and then give the student the topic card: A Family Holiday.

Teacher script: The second assessed part of the practice test is a short talk. I will give you a card and you will have one minute to read it and think about what you want to say. You should talk about the points on the card. You can't make any written notes, but you can ask me if there is anything you do not understand. You may keep the card until the end of the short talk.

Before you start, do you have any questions?

Here is your card.

Give the student a copy of the topic card. It is also printed here for your reference.

> A – Family holiday
>
> Your family are planning to go on holiday together soon. You are considering the best way to make it enjoyable for the whole family. You can either:
>
> - go on holiday in your own country
> - go on holiday abroad
>
> Discuss the advantages and disadvantages of each option. Say which option you would prefer, and why.

Allow one minute for preparation and then ask the student to start the short talk.

Teacher script: You now have up to two minutes to talk about the topic: I will stop you after two minutes and do not worry if you have not finished your talk. Would you like to start?

After two minutes, thank the student and collect the card. Then move on to Part 3 of the practice test.

Teacher script: Thank you. Can I have the card back please? Now let's move on to Part 3 of the practice test.

Part 3 Discussion (3–4 minutes)

Select questions as appropriate to further develop the discussion. Avoid asking students questions on aspects they have already covered in Part 2. Where students have responded at length, it may not be necessary to use all the questions.

Teacher script: Now I am going to ask you a few questions on the topic you have just talked about. This part of the practice test will last approximately three minutes. Before we start, do you have any questions?

> Do you think that young people should have to study and do homework in their holidays?
>
> There is an opinion that young people can benefit from getting a job in their holidays. What do you think?
>
> Many cultures have their own national holidays or celebrations. Do you think they are important?
>
> Many people think that in the future we will all be able to have holidays in space. What do you think?

Teacher script: Thank you. This is the end of the practice test. End of recording.

Speaking
Teacher notes

Speaking - sample responses

Below are some sample responses to the practice test. Any inaccuracies or errors have been highlighted, as well as words that may cause problems for some students, so that you can see where further practice may be needed. If you thought it was helpful for your students, you could go through these with your class and discuss how the answers could be improved.

Warm-up

Teacher: So Carlos, where do you live?

Erm, well I live here in the province of Sevilla, which is in Andalucia, in the Southern Spain. Well, to be more exact, my home is actually a very beautiful little village, just a short drive from the city, called San Juan de Aznalfarache. I was born there and I have lived in that village all my life although during term time I live here in the city, because I go to the university.

Teacher: Thank you. And now can you tell me something about your family?

Er, well I have quite a large family. We are two brothers, including myself, and one sister and my mum and dad. We are enough lucky to have a big house, so my grandmother also lives with us. Oh and I don't have to forget our two rabbits, and one very lazy cat, called Pere – this is short for 'perezosa' which is Spanish for 'lazy'. My mum is a teacher for very young children and my father is a doctor, he specialises in cardiology. My mum is actually Canadian by birth, although she has lived here now for a long time, so I grew up speaking English with her family, which is a big advantage to me.

Teacher: Thank you. Now, one last question. What would you like to do when you finish school?

Well I am going to be the first person in the family to not study medicine or teaching, because I actually want to be a journalist, like a travel writer. I have always enjoyed writing since I was very little. Last year I did some work experience for a local newspaper and I loved every minute of it. Although, I love Spain, I want to have the opportunity to travel to and write about other countries.

Teacher: Which countries?

Well, I am especially interested in Japan and Japanese culture.

Interview

Teacher: Can you tell me what you and your friends enjoy doing in your school holidays?

Well, my friends back home in the village, we all enjoy going for walking because the countryside is very pretty. Here in Andalucia, the weather is boiling for most of the year and some of my village friends have pools so we love just chilling in the water and then maybe have a barbecue. In the city, of course we all love going to eat out in bars. I belong to a volleyball club also so we often have team practice or matches at the weekend.

Teacher: And do you often win your matches?

To be honest, no. We are not very good! But it's funny!

Teacher: And now can you tell me about a family holiday that you enjoyed, and why?

Erm, well we have had a lot of great holidays together but I think the best one for me, was a few years ago. It was actually our last family holiday when we all still lived at home. We all went for two weeks to a wonderful island called Crete. Do you know it?

Teacher: I know of it but I haven't been there. Tell me about it and why you enjoyed the holiday.

So, Crete is, I believe, the largest of all the Greek islands. We decided to go there because some friends of ours, went to live there a while back and they have been inviting us to go and visit them since then. It was an incredible holiday because the place is absolutely gorgeous. The climate is similar to Spain, but the history is very unique to Greece and the landscape are spectacular. We had a fantastic time going sightseeing. Then on other days we just relaxed by the pool or wandered around the shops. At night, we all got dressed up, to go out in one of the bars or restaurants in the old harbour. I will always remember that holiday.

Teacher: Its sounds wonderful! So do you think it is better to spend holidays relaxing or being active? Why? Why not?

In my opinion it is important to do a mixture of both. If you do too many things and are always on the go then you may get tired and that is not the point of a holiday. However, if you just chill out and never do nothing every day, then you are wasting your time and not taking advantage of being somewhere different. It's important when you go on holiday, to experience new places and customs. The holiday in Crete that I was saying you about was the best for me because as I said, we had a lot of new experiences but also had time to just sit together and relax and chat. So, I think doing both is the best option.

Short talk

So I am going to talk about family holidays and the best way to make them enjoyable for the whole family. I will divide my talk into two sections: I will begin with the advantages and disadvantages of going on holiday in our own countries and then move on to the pros and cons of going on holiday abroad. I will then finish with my own personal preference and explain you why.

Well, I think that there are a lot of benefits to going on holiday in one's own country. Obviously the first thing that comes to mind is the language. You don't have to worry about not understanding people when they speak, or road signs, for example. And more important, you don't have to wonder what you have actually ordered to eat from a menu of incomprehensible dishes. In addition to that, another advantage is that you understand the culture and the customs. You know the simple things like when the shops are open and they close, but you also understand people so you know how not to offend them by doing or saying the wrong thing. As well as all that, you can learn things about your own country that you did not know before.

On the other hand, there are definitely disadvantages of a holiday in your own country and the main one is that you don't get the chance to explore a culture that is different to your own. It can be boring to spend time in cities that you know about and eat the same food as you do all the time. If you live in a cold or rainy country then it may be that the weather is a disadvantage too. It might stop you from doing what you want to do and there is nothing fun about sitting on a beach when it's pouring with rain.

Now, moving on to the pros of going on holiday abroad. Well I have already mentioned a couple of them, but there are more, like the fact that it can be cheaper. I know a lot of

Speaking
Sample responses

English people enjoy coming to Spain for example because it is generally cheaper to stay here – hotels, food and other things often do not cost as much as in the UK. I really think it can be more of an adventure to go abroad and you will create fantastic memories and have experiences that will help you to grow as a person. There is nothing like travel to broaden your horizons and give you new ideas about the world and this can also help us to get rid of prejudices and stereotypes.

There are again little things that can be a disadvantage when you go on holiday abroad. I talked about the food problem but there can be other things. I remember when my family took us to London when I was very little and I was so terrified of the traffic because I didn't understand why the cars were on the other side of the road. The other issue is also connected to traffic but in my opinion much more significant today and that is that our carbon footprint is bigger when we go abroad. Just catching a plane to go somewhere, is easy today but we are knowing now that it is not very good for the environment and we all need to try to be more eco-friendly. A final thing could be if you get sick, then you may not know what to do or where to go for help.

In my opinion I can see the good things and also the drawbacks of both options. I have also had experience of both, and I have good and some bad memories of each possibility. I think that if it is a family holiday, you should do what the majority want for the first time and then the next time you could do something completely different and then everybody would be happy.

Discussion

Teacher: Do you think that young people should have to study and do homework in their holidays?

Well it's a difficult question to answer, because on one hand I think that we all work really hard at school so that when we do have a holiday we should spend that time getting our energy back and refreshing our brains. But, on the other hand, the holidays do give us time to read more, you know maybe do more background or detailed reading on a subject. I know that I love studying early in the morning and I hate study in the afternoon, so in the holiday I get all my work done before midday, then I can enjoy the rest of the day off.

Teacher: And if you do receive homework in the holidays, do you think it is better to do it straight away or to leave it until the end of the holiday.

Well it's better to do it straight away I suppose when everything is fresh in your mind and I always say that I will do this – but I never do and am always on the last minute completing holiday assignments – but don't tell my teachers!

Teacher: Now, there is an opinion that young people can benefit from getting a job in their holidays. What do you think?

I definitely don't think this is a good idea when we are still at school because we are too young and also because there are many schools today, who organise work experience for their students and I think that is enough. When you go to university, however, I think it's a bit different. For one, the money can come in handy for most students and secondly, you are older and more mature and so you can make your work-life balance better to get the best out of each one.

Teacher: Have you had any work experience yourself yet?

Not organised by school no, we will be doing that next year, but I help out in my uncle's shop sometimes.

© HarperCollins*Publishers* 2022

Teacher: Oh really and what does your uncle sell?

He has a clothes shop on the high street of our village, which sells fashion for older children and men and women.

Teacher: Aha – now I can see why that would be interesting for you. Dare I ask if you get a discount?

Of course! [laughs]

Teacher: Many cultures have their own national holidays or celebrations. Do you think they are important?

Yes I definitely do. Here in Spain we have so many national holidays and celebrations that we love and are a vital part of our culture.

Teacher: Could you give me some examples?

Well, as you know, here in Andalucia, our Semana Santa is extremely important for people, particularly in Sevilla, our city. I think you would call it 'Easter' in English. Also we have the Spring Fair called La Feria and this is very different as it is not a religious festival but it is full of food and drink and singing and dancing and is my absolute favourite event in the whole year. Then of course there are other events like the throwing of tomatoes festival in Buñol.

Teacher: And, you said that you think that national holidays and festivals are important. Why do you think that?

Well, they allow us all to get together, to be with family and friends, to enjoy ourselves and also to not forget our country's culture and traditions. In my opinion, they give us a time when we can be proud of our nationality and our country.

Teacher: Earlier on, you expressed an interest in becoming a travel writer. Do you know of any festivals in other counties that you would like to experience in person and perhaps write about?

Oh yes – first the Lantern festival in Nagasaki, then the Sapporo snow sculpture festival, Yuki Matsuri, then Kanto, oh and of course the cherry blossom festivals as well…

Teacher: And where are those festivals celebrated?

Japan – I did say that I love Japanese culture!

Teacher: Yes you did. Thank you very much Carlos. This is the end of the test. End of recording.

Comments on the sample

Here is a teacher's comments on the student's responses above. You may find it useful to share this information with the students to help them improve their own responses.

- **Grammar:** a very wide range of simple and complex structures is used with a very high level of accuracy. Errors or slips are rare and do not impede understanding **[see highlights]**

- **Vocabulary:** a very wide range of vocabulary used precisely to discuss a variety of ideas, facts and opinions.

- **Development:** all responses are relevant and consistently very well-developed. Communication is maintained with ease throughout the whole test.

- **Pronunciation:** pronunciation is mostly clear, and intonation is frequently used effectively to convey the intended meaning.

- **Suggested mark awarded by the author: 10 marks.**

Speaking
Sample responses